A Conservative Revolutic

The Thatcher–Reagan decade

edited by Andrew Adonis and Tim Hames

The 1980s are widely seen as years in which the USA and Britain shared a political transformation under Margaret Thatcher and Ronald Reagan. This book compares and contrasts their impact across the range of public policy and upon their respective political parties. Behind it lies the question: was there a distinctive Anglo–American conservative revolution under Reagan and Thatcher? The book examines the political elites, political ideas and policy communities animating the Anglo–American right-wing during the 1980s, offering penetrating analyses of the processes and personalities shaping conservativism on both sides of the Atlantic. Successive chapters cover ideology in practice, the Republican and Conservative leaderships, the role of think tanks and the reaction of 'moderates' on the right, and key policy areas – the economy, social affairs, and the constitution. The approach of British and American conservatives to foreign policy, the core of the 'special relationship', is also assessed.

The contributors are Andrew Adonis, Richard Feasey, Tim Hames, Richard Hodder-Williams, Gillian Peele, Jack Pitney, Nicol Rae, Peter Riddell and Terry O'Shaughnessy.

This book will be of interest to university students studying British, American and comparative politics, and all those interested in the British and American scene.

Andrew Adonis is Industry Correspondent at the *Financial Times*; Tim Hames is American Studies Research Officer at Nuffield College, Oxford.

For Kathryn and Julia

A Conservative Revolution?

The Thatcher–Reagan decade in perspective

edited by Andrew Adonis and Tim Hames

Manchester University Press

Manchester and New York

Distributed exclusively in the USA and Canada by St. Martin's Press

Published by Manchester University Press
Oxford Road, Manchester M13 9PL, UK
and Room 400, 175 Fifth Avenue,
New York, NY 10010, USA

Distributed exclusively in the USA and Canada
by St. Martin's Press, Inc.,
175 Fifth Avenue, New York, NY 10010, USA

British Library Cataloguing-in-Publication Data
A catalogue record for this book is available from the British Library

Library of Congress Cataloging-in-Publication Data
A Conservative revolution?: the Thatcher–Reagan decade in perspective
edited by Andrew Adonis and Tim Hames,
    p. cm.
Includes index.
ISBN 0-7190-3668-2. — ISBN 0-7190-3669-0 (pbk.)
    1. Conservative Party (Great Britain) 2. Republican Party (U.S. 1854–)
3. Conservatism—Great Britain. 4. Conservatism—United States. 5. Great
Britain—Politics and government—1979– 6. United States—Politics and
government—1981–1989. 7. United States—Politics and government—1989–
1993. I. Adonis, Andrew, 1963– II. Hames, Tim, 1965–
JN1129.C7C586 1993
324.24104—dc20
                                                                93-13640
                                                                      CIP

ISBN 0 7190 3668 2 *hardback*
ISBN 0 7190 3669 0 *paperback*

Typeset in Hong Kong
by Graphicraft Typesetters Ltd., Hong Kong
Printed in Great Britain
by Bell & Bain Ltd., Glasgow

Contents

Contributors

Andrew Adonis: industry correspondent of the *Financial Times*; formerly Research Fellow of Nuffield College, Oxford

Richard Feasey: former student of Nuffield College, Oxford

Tim Hames: American Studies Research Officer, Nuffield College, Oxford

Richard Hodder-Williams: Professor of Politics, Bristol University

Gillian Peele: Fellow in Politics, Lady Margaret Hall, Oxford

John R. Pitney, Jr: Professor of Government, Claremont McKenna College, California

Nicol C. Rae: Professor of Political Science, Florida International University

Peter Riddell: political editor and chief political commentator of *The Times*; formerly US editor of the *Financial Times*.

Terry O'Shaughnessy: Fellow in Economics, St Anne's College, Oxford

Preface

This collection of essays grew out of a conference held at Nuffield College, Oxford, in October 1991. Billed to explore 'perspectives on Anglo-American conservatism in the Thatcher/Reagan decade', it focused in particular on elites and public policy. All but one of the chapters started life as a paper at the conference; all have since been substantially revised in the light of the discussion at Oxford and developments through 1992 and 1993.

In the 1980s, Republicans and Tories shared an unusually pronounced commonality of discourse and approach. Yet for all the claims of a symbiosis between Thatcherism and Reaganism, there is a dearth of comparative studies or even of studies geared at comparative themes. Hence these essays. None of the authors seeks to portray the Conservative and Republican parties, let alone their respective countries, in a single frame. A few of the chapters are not even directly comparative, but – notably those on elites – are intended to sit in apposition. Insights are to be had from comparing the one conservative regime with the other, not least from getting behind the copycat rhetoric and assessing the relative impact of different historical, political and constitutional restraints upon two parties and governments proclaiming a similar mission.

Inevitably the words 'conservatism' and 'conservative' are somewhat ambiguous and indeterminate. In this book 'conservatism' is generally used to refer to the philosophy of the Conservative and/ or Republican parties; and 'conservative' as an adjective to denote association with one or other of the parties. However, sometimes they clearly embrace a broader spectrum of centre-right ideas, and occasionally they denote particular radical variants of them or their supporters. Where the meaning is not clear from the context we have done our best to spell it out.

We are grateful to the Warden and Fellows of Nuffield College for providing facilities and contributing to the cost of the conference. We are also indebted to the discussants and other participants who enriched our proceedings. Special mention must be made of Vernon Bogdanor, David Butler, A. H. Halsey, Godfrey Hodgson, Graham Mather, Ferdinand Mount and Herbert Nicholas, none of whom bears any responsibility for the finished product.

A. A.
T. H.
February 1994

The election of Ronald Reagan as President of the United States in November 1980 was as much of a watershed in American affairs as my own election victory in May 1979 was in those of the United Kingdom, and, of course, a greater one in world politics ... Above all, I knew that I was talking to someone who instinctively felt and thought as I did; not just about policies but about a philosophy of government, a view of human nature, all the high ideals and values which lie – or ought to lie – beneath any politician's ambition to lead his country.

Margaret Thatcher, October 1993.
(*The Downing Street Years*, London, Harper Collins, 1993, pp. 156–7).

Introduction: history, perspectives

'More than any change of government since 1945,' writes the historian Kenneth Morgan[1] of the Conservatives' triumph at the polls in 1979, 'Margaret Thatcher's election victory was taken as marking a decisive shift in the national mood, politically, intellectually, and culturally. Commentators across the political spectrum believe the fall of James Callaghan in the summer of 1979 signalled the end of an *ancien régime*, a system of corporatism, Keynesian spending programmes, subsidised welfare and trade union power.' Move the date forwards by seventeen months, replace Thatcher by Reagan, Callaghan by Carter, and, perhaps, corporatism by appeasement, and the same could be said of the United States.

The congruence does not end there. This collection of essays explores the proposition that a fruitful comparison can be made between the Thatcher and Reagan regimes, not just in mood but in origin and action. Underpinned by closely related sets of ideas, the two addressed similar issues of decline, and were attracted to similar notions of international order, liberal economics, small government, and a mobile society. The policies and programmes deriving from them were directed at proximate goals – albeit to widely varying effect; and the two had a comparably transformative impact on their respective political classes. Both created a 'new centre', and having done so, gave way to governments of their own parties which used it as their loadstar. Rooted in the Reagan/Thatcher rhetoric and largely staffed by their lieutenants, the Bush/Major ministries distanced themselves from their predecessors, but husbanded their legacies intact. Bush has succumbed to Clinton; but for all its emphasis on executive dynamism, the former Arkansas governor, in turn, takes as given most of the Reagan paradigm.

It would be facile to portray Britain and the United States in a single frame – and no less facile to force the Republican and Tory Parties into the same mould, and to view their contexts, traditions, and philosophies as chips off matching blocks. The contributors to this volume make no such claim. Indeed, a few of the chapters are not even directly comparative but – notably those on the respective elites – are deliberately intended to sit in apposition. The studies emphasise differences as much as similarities between the two parties, cultures, and countries. Nonetheless, in the 1970s and 1980s, Republicans and Tories shared an unusually pronounced commonality of discourse and approach, more marked in the decade of Thatcher/Reagan dominance than perhaps any other in recent history, justifying serious analysis from a comparative perspective.

An understanding of the Thatcher and Reagan regimes and the structure of political debate in the 1980s must be rooted in the politics of the decade that preceded it. Decline and governability were the twin challenges facing the right – and watchwords haunting the political classes at large – on both sides of the Atlantic throughout the 1970s. For the Conservative and Republican parties, undisputed standard-bearers of the right in their respective countries, the first critical step was to extricate themselves from the failed consensus to which they not only contributed but in large measure created. Watergate in the United States, the miners' strike in Britain, were indelible blots on the credibility of the right, casting them from power and into disarray. To many of their natural and most ardent followers, decades of accommodation by successive Tory and Republican administrations following active welfare, collectivist, high-spending and unashamedly interventionist policies cast a still darker shadow, and reversing them presented a still starker challenge.

Escaping that shadow was made easier by opposition. Indeed, 'contamination', as the radical right viewed it, had always been largely a product of government: in opposition in the 1960s both Nixon and Heath spoke much the same language as Reagan and Thatcher after them; they even adopted much of the same programme, only to foresake it in government. Alfonzo Hamby[2] shrewdly notes that by the end of Nixon's term the intellectual leader of the much vaunted neo-conservatives, Irving Kristol, found himself able to muster only *Two Cheers for Capitalism*, while in Britain it was barely days after the 1970 election before Harold

Wilson was congratulating Heath for 'muting the themes of Selsdon'.[3] As Enoch Powell, an authentic 'Selsdon Man', recalled in a recent interview:[4]

The Selsdon Declaration, in a sense, was an attempt . . . to get the Conservative Party committed to the alternative-to-socialism approach to the control of the economy and relations with the unions. But, it was swept aside in the revolution or counter-revolution of 1972, and it was the disaster to which that led in 1974–76 which, I think, sickened the Conservative Party of it, and made them amenable to an alternative interpretation.

By the time the two right-wing parties were next in government, the record of their own previous failures had dimmed and paled in the face of their successors' inglorious periods of office. Moreover, as they came to regroup and rethink in opposition under the influence of new conviction leadership, the visible disintegration of the Callaghan and Carter administrations made any revisiting of the *status quo ante* not just unappealing but virtually impossible. Few even on the left favoured it. Defeat was followed by internecine strife in Britain's Labour Party on a scale unparalleled in its history, with the warring factions united only by their rejection of 'social democracy' Wilson/Callaghan style. The US Democrats retained their institutional integrity, but suffered from almost as severe a bout of collective *angst*.

Nonetheless, the challenge to turn the rhetoric of opposition into the reality of office remained formidable. The following essays are, in part, commentaries on that theme. True, the left was weaker in 1980 than it had been in 1970. But it remained as entrenched in interest groups and extra-parliamentary institutions. Furthermore, the perception of decline and sense of crisis confronting the right was altogether more serious than it had been a decade before. The trauma of decline – economic, international, political, social, even in some sense cultural and moral – had been foreshadowed in the 1960s, if not, in Britain's case, well before. Its elements came together powerfully in the 1970s, giving every appearance of becoming endemic, even institutionalised. The depth of the decline was different, of course. Britain's descent to the international second division was virtually complete by 1970; decline in this case meant dropping further behind still. The United States, a nuclear superpower, and the world's largest economy throughout this period, faced no such abyss. Even so, that nation in the 1970s was gripped by a real and abiding fear of the future, unquelled by its traditional optimism and summed up by Jimmy Carter in 1979 as a 'national malaise'.[5]

In both countries, the malaise was generally perceived to comprise three separate but distinctly related aspects: a crisis of economic standing; a crisis of international and security standing; and a crisis of executive performance and political institutions. Since, taken together, these created the political and intellectual space for Margaret Thatcher's and Ronald Reagan's brand of conservatism, an introductory word on each is merited.

Economy

Legislative reactions to the two world wars, particularly the second and the depression between them, conditioned the role of the modern state in the economy on both sides of the Atlantic. The state assumed larger and more expensive proportions in Britain, but common assumptions held sway over the elites of both countries: the necessity of policies geared to high levels of growth; low inflation and unemployment; a strong currency; a favourable trade balance; a fiscal policy emphasising direct taxation bearing progressively more heavily as income rose; and a substantial welfare state. As Terry O'Shaugnessy argues, the Phillips curve persuaded politicians that there was a straight trade-off between unemployment and inflation and 'allowed the specification of a policy menu from which they could choose an appropriate combination of policies according to how much weight they gave to the desirability of low inflation and low unemployment'.

For twenty years after 1945, this combination appeared broadly viable, albeit 'the terms of the trade-off were slowly worsening'. Relative economic performance declined in both countries from the late 1950s, while the shattered economies of continental Europe and Japan staged impressive recoveries; but as the era of Eisenhower and Macmillan drew to a close, confidence in the broad economic health of the two countries persisted, particularly among their respective leaders. As Prime Minister, Harold Macmillan spent more than half his time on foreign problems and deflected public and private criticism of his government's lack of economic vision with typically nonchalant verve. 'Of course,' he told Bob Boothby, 'if we succeeded in losing two world wars, wrote off all our debts – instead of having nearly £30,000 million in debts – got rid of all our foreign obligations, and kept no force overseas, then we might be as rich as the Germans.'[6] Subsequent deterioration could not be dismissed so flippantly. From the mid-1960s, elites in each country came to see high growth, low inflation, and sustained international competitiveness as increasingly difficult to achieve. Economic growth slowed dramatically. Between 1962 and 1972 the average annual growth rate of the US (3 per cent) and the UK (2.2 per cent) fell behind that of France, West Germany, Italy, and Japan, and that position worsened strikingly in the subsequent seven years. Britain's performance was obviously much poorer, slipping down the GDP per capita league from ninth in 1961 to fifteenth by 1971 and eighteenth in 1976, but the United States also found itself overtaken.

The slowdown in the economy did not abate demands for public spending – particularly in the field of social security. Low growth thus saw government consume a rising proportion of national income in both nations, reaching 50 per cent in Britain by 1975, a level the then Labour Home Secretary, Roy Jenkins, mused was incompatible with a free society.[7] An increasing proportion of that expenditure was met by borrowing. In the United Stated cumulative federal budget deficits increased from $63 million in the 1960s to $420 million in the 1970s. In Britain 20 per cent of all public outlays in 1975 were funded by various creditors.

Inflation, barely a factor in the halcyon 1950s, came to dominate economic and political life. By 1970 annual inflation had edged up from negligible 2 per cent or so a decade earlier to 6 per cent in the US and 8 per cent in Britain. From that already disturbing base it was to rocket further. In the US it moved into double figures by 1973 – primarily as a consequence of the OPEC oil shock – receded somewhat by the middle of the decade and then continued its steady climb reaching 14.8 per cent in the spring of 1980. In Britain the situation got worse, faster. By the close of the Arab–Israeli war inflation had increased to 13 per cent. Eighteen months later an annual rate of 27 per cent was reached with the fear of hyperinflation and deep-seated fears for the future stability of the economic order. By 1979, the worst appeared to be over – but, in Britain at least – the return of such figures seemed plausible.

The Nixon and Heath administrations abandoned their previous economic tenets and embraced state organised incomes policies as the solution to inflation. Nixon introduced his Economic Stabilisation Act of 1970 freezing prices, wages, salaries, and rents for ninety days. He followed that up with a gamut of wage and price restraints, a Price Commission, a Pay Board, Phases I, II, etc. All of which sounded very familiar in Britain where both Tory and Labour Governments first disavowed and then introduced parallel institutions and programmes, often involving a formal 'contract' with the Trades Union Congress.

Given this combination of low growth and high inflation, the international competitiveness of the two nations suffered badly. The UK's share of the value of world exports in manufactured goods slid from 16.5 per cent in 1960 (itself a decline from 25.5 per cent a decade earlier) to 9.7 per cent by 1979. The United States saw a fall from 21.6 per cent to 15.9 per cent in the same period. Record trade deficits in 1971/72 and the concurrent stress on its currency led Nixon to devalue, suspend the convertibility of the dollar into gold, and introduce a temporary import surcharge on certain goods. This set of measures ultimately ended the Bretton Woods international order. As Michael Barone notes,[8] Nixon had succeeded in expanding state power over the American economy far beyond anything that his Democratic predecessors had managed.

Having devalued in 1967 to improve its balance of payments, Britain soon found that whatever competitive advantage devaluation had yielded soon disappeared. In 1972 the Heath Government was forced to devalue again by floating the pound. Sinking might have been a more appropriate metaphor given the performance of sterling over the next five years. A further round of trade deficits, currency trauma, and continuing inflation led to the Callaghan administration's economic abdication to the International Monetary Fund in 1976 simply to guarantee the projected budget deficit for the coming year. Months later, in memorable words to the Labour Party conference, Callaghan pronounced Keynesianism as it had been practised by successive post-war governments dead. With it went the Keynesian-inspired ideal of social democracy.

Security and international standing

The post–1940 transformation in the international standing of Britain and the United States may have sent them in opposite geopolitical directions, but in each country the process of adjustment was similarly fraught, painful, and humiliating. Notions of British participation in superpower deliberations strained credibility in 1960; by 1970 they were fanciful. The United States entered the 1960s as the world's unchallenged superpower, but the decade saw a relative decline as the international system shifted to a bipolarity that was to turn to greater interdependence still ten years later.

The apparent stalemate in Vietnam raised doubts even among its allies as to America's role and made starker still the economic predicament outlined earlier. The 1970s opened with the Nixon administration disengaging in the war through a progressive withdrawal of ground forces (in favour of saturation bombing), and participating in successive peace talks while extending the conflict through the highly unpopular incursion into Cambodia. Meanwhile, the international advance of the Soviet Union, particularly in nuclear weapons, was tacitly recognised through the SALT arms control process and the deployment of *détente* as a cardinal feature of American foreign policy. Ideas of brinkmanship and the liberation of oppressed regimes under the communist yoke were forgotten. The mere continuation of containment was proving difficult enough.

In the Middle East, the United States saw its political protégé Israel taken to the edge of survival, at one stage threatening to suck in the superpowers. In the Third World, communist influence appeared to be steadily spreading: Vietnam, Cambodia, Laos, Ethiopia, Angola, and Mozambique all succumbed. Even the Americas themselves were not immune as co-existence with Cuba was enforced and the marxist Sandinistas ousted the pro-American Samoza regime in Nicaragua.

Among friends and allies, problems multiplied. American dominance of the global economy increasingly gave way to interdependence – a fact recognised and institutionalised by the meetings of the seven leading industrial nations from 1975 onwards. These gatherings saw Carter pleading unsuccessfully with the Germans over international economic growth and with the rest over energy policy. The decade ended with Carter's *détente* ripped asunder by the Soviet invasion of Afghanistan and the utter humiliation of American power by the islamic revolutionaries of Iran.

Across the Atlantic, life was only mildly less traumatic. By the mid–1960s Britain had divested itself of a vast empire, abandoned its great power illusions by withdrawing east of Suez, and retreated grudgingly to Europe. By 1974 the British were impotent even to prevent the invasion and occupation of northern Cyprus by Turkey – in defiance of a treaty of which the UK was guarantor. The 'special relationship' upon which Churchill and Macmillan had based much of their strategic thinking now appeared a rapidly depreciating asset. Although Britain finally gained entry to the European Community in 1973, it was on terms dictated by France and Germany; and it split not one but two governing parties, requiring the constitutional innovation of a referendum to finalise it in 1975.

Community membership might have been seen as the 'answer' to the 'problem' had it brought manifest economic benefits. If benefits there were, they were largely counterfactual (what might have happened had Britain stayed out). Indeed, EC membership made the comparison between Britain and its European competitors and partners more apparent. The setting of the imperial sun offered no relief. The Commonwealth looked like an unglorified talking shop, while from Iceland to Rhodesia pax Britannica became an object of ridicule.[9]

Executive performance and political institutions

Confidence in the competence of government itself came under question in the 1970s. One fairly straightforward example of this is the difficulty governments experienced in getting re-elected. In the 1950s, with the newly discovered precision engineering of Keynesian economics, commentators speculated that governments would invariably succeed in matching the economic and electoral cycles to their own benefit.

However, as growth slowed this proved untrue. Between 1959 and 1983 no British government survived through two consecutive full terms. Between 1956 and 1984 the same was true of the United States. In the twenty-year period 1960–1980 six individuals served as president (compared with three in the previous two decades) and six as prime minister (compared with four in the previous two decades). Prime ministers and presidents came and went; so did endless reshuffles of their cabinets and departments.

There were new and intense programmes of legislative action that either failed to be enacted (in the American case), or failed to be implemented fully (both nations), or just plain failed. Nor were the activist supporters of the respective administrations happy. The Wilson and Callaghan Governments found their policies savaged at successive Labour Party conferences. Gerald Ford had to endure a deeply divided Republican convention in 1976 and Carter witnessed a chilly mid-term convention two years later.

Given this record of electoral and political misfortune, it is hardly surprising that public faith in governments slumped. In the United States, James Sundquist's survey of poll evidence showed a public with deep distrust of their political institution's honesty and capability.[10] Other American data[11] showed a public generally content and hopeful about their own individual circumstances but profoundly unhappy about the progress of the nation as a whole and the performance of government in particular. Similar scepticism was recorded in Britain, perhaps deeper even. Alan Marsh's survey material[12] indicated that only 39 per cent of the public trusted the government most or all of the time and just a quarter believed politicians generally spoke the truth.

This growing sense of alienation among ordinary citizens was reinforced by severe criticism from political observers and scholarly commentators. Proposals for constitutional change in the US, virtually invisible during the 1960s, surfaced in abundance during the 1970s. Lloyd Cutler, intimate of the Carter Administration, went as far as suggesting the abandonment of the separation of powers doctrine in favour of parliamentary government. This reflected the mood of other thinkers such as Charles Hardin who argued that the United States faced in 1973 its worst political crisis since the Civil War.[13] *Mutatis mutandis*, such themes echoed in Britain, with hostile analysis of the adversary politics of the sixties and seventies prompting calls for electoral reform, constitutional innovation, and national coalition governments. Turning General de Gaulle's praise for the British Constitution in 1960 on its head, Ian Gilmour[14] wrote bluntly in 1977: 'We are no longer "sure" of ourselves. "The legitimacy and the authority" of the state have been "contested"; our political system does not now seem "well founded and stable"; the meaning of achieving "the best results from democracy" elude us; and no longer does our constitution rest on "undeniable general consent".'[15]

Had government overeached itself? James Sundquist asked if the US government could be made to function under any leadership.[16] A similar theme of system overload was at the heart of Anthony King's critique of British politics in the 1970s.[17] In Britain the language was more apocalyptic: arguments about ungovernability were a common part of the political vocabulary; the influence of pressure groups was much stronger; the retreat into corporatism much closer; the days of a post-parliamentary system much nearer. However, the differences were of degree, not kind – and the drama of Watergate was in a class of its own. Given this, it was little shock that disillusion in Government spread to a wider crisis for political institutions.

There is plenty of evidence that dissatisfaction extended beyond discontent over particular events and leaders in both countries. The same opinion surveys that recorded increasing dismay at the performance of governments also outlined a wider crisis of confidence in the political system. Material collected by the US National Elections Studies Centre revealed that the proportion of voters who could, on a barrage of questions, be defined as politically cynical increased from 16.4 per cent in 1964 to 50 per cent by 1978. The proportion that could be described as trusting had fallen from 57.1 per cent to 15.1 per cent in the same period. Other data displayed cynicism towards the federal executive branch, government officials, Congress, big business, organised labour, the press. Even the professions of medicine and higher education were touched by this wave of malcontent. Although Britain lacked the volume of polling evidence that the United States had accumulated, what evidence there was pointed strongly in the same direction.

Public discontent focused on political parties more than any other institution. Opinion polls in the United States showed striking apathy towards them. According to information gathered by CBS news and the *New York Times*, the proportion of the public with highly favourable ratings of the parties fell by a third for the Democrats between 1967 and 1980, and by half for the Republicans. Combined with the loss of the presidential nomination to the primary system this fall in public esteem left the parties dangerously exposed. A not dissimilar process occurred in Britain. The share of the vote won by the two main parties fell from 96.8 per cent in 1951 to 76.8 per cent in 1974 as Scottish and Welsh nationalists, Irish sectionalists, and a revived Liberal Party gained strength. Public support for a coalition arrangement soared. By April 1977 only 32 per cent of the public expressed backing for the traditional majoritarian government system. Despite the heated political rhetoric of the 1974 elections only 35 per cent of major party identifiers perceived significant differences between the parties.[18]

Such public discontent spilt over into the electoral arena. It did so in two ways. The first was a decline in electoral participation. In the United States – where turnout has always been notoriously low – participation in presidential contests fell from 62.6 per cent in 1960 to 54.4 per cent in 1976. There was an equally marked fall for mid-term elections. These were levels of non-voting unknown since the 1920s. In Britain, turnout in the 1970 and October 1974 polls fell below 72 per cent far lower than the 1950s and among the lowest levels in Western Europe. The second signal was voter volatility. The United States saw a large increase in the number of voters willing to split ticket, this being especially true of highly educated voters. Great Britain saw voters swing from Labour to Tory and back again with significant numbers of ballots going to smaller parties.

Alongside this was the rise of a 'negative pluralism' and protest politics. The US experienced an upsurge in various forms of direct democracy initiatives, California's radical anti-tax Proposition 13 of 1978 being only the most famous. Single-issue groups proliferated and the number of pressure groups, lobbying bodies, and political action committees exploded. Similar patterns could be found in Britain with an increase in trade-union activity, a massive rise in the numbers and functions of pressure groups, and the mushrooming of local community action groups campaigning on political questions. In one sense all this activity did broaden and even enhance the nature of democracy in the two countries. It also undermined traditional concepts of representative government and, occasionally, the rule of law. In Britain's case it seemed that various nationalist groupings would succeed in altering its whole nature as a unitary state.

Towards Thatcher and Reagan

That, as they saw it, was the inheritance of Thatcher and Reagan. These essays compare and assess their respective attempts at refashioning it, and how the parties they led changed under them. The first section addresses ideology and public policy, the second elites.

Historically, both Tories and Republicans have professed to carry their ideological baggage lightly. Not so in the 1980s. Peter Riddell looks at how Reagan and Thatcher adapted bold blueprints to the constraints and realities of office. The constraints, he argues, were more substantial in the US, with its divided government and separation of powers. But the collectivist status quo was more deeply entrenched in Britain, and its defenders retained a strong hold on the public mind despite repeated Tory general election triumphs. Ultimately, the greater freedom accorded to government in Britain's parliamentary system allowed Thatcher to implement more legislation than Reagan, even though at her peak she enjoyed a lower level of popular support than the president, and had to confront a more uniformly hostile public opinion. But if taxes and public spending – in other words, the reach of government in the social sphere – are the yardstick, Reagan's legacy is likely to prove the more enduring.

Apart from limiting the power of the trade unions, Thatcher's greatest domestic achievements were in areas – notably privatisation – which had barely featured on the 'new right' agenda in the 1970s, and within which entrenched interests were weak. Top of that agenda, of course, was the economy, where the approach of the two leaders was close and its success, both sides of the Atlantic, partial at best. As Peter Riddell and Terry O'Shaughnessy show, faith in the efficacy of 'neo-monetarist' cures waned rapidly in both countries, and by the later 1980s both were victims of domestic crises which, apart from the October 1987 collapse in equity values, had little in common, and for which the nostrums of the late 1970s and early 1980s had little to offer.

Even in the depths of depression, in both London and Washington the economy had to vie with foreign policy and defence for the attention of the thinkers and leaders of the New Right. In his study of the special relationship, Tim Hames charts Thatcher's remarkable success in recreating part of the illusion, and at least a little of the substance, of Pax Britannica; and the importance of interaction with the Reagan administration in enabling her to do so. Of course, in Washington the relationship was just one of many necessary to sustain America's world role, and only intermittently of real importance. But the impact of Thatcher in fortifying and adding credibility to the Reagan worldview is not to be gainsaid, and the reverse is also true.

Richard Hodder-Williams examines constitutional politics in the two countries during the 1980s. No chapter highlights better the importance of historical and cultural forces in shaping the respective principles and priorities of the Conservative and Republican parties, however similar their ideological mainsprings. To Reagan's Republicans, courts were as important as Congress, and the language of rights and constitutional guarantees as dominant as the discourse on markets. By contrast, Thatcher's Conservatives, secure in the sovereignty of a Parliament at their beck and call, sought only to preserve and strengthen its prerogatives, greeting with suspicion, increasingly with bitter hostility, infringements of it by local government and the European Community. In the 1980s, Conservatives resorted to arguing that old-style Tory notions of property and individual autonomy were the best defences against an overmighty state, while unalloyed electoral success, of the kind never experienced by Reagan's Republicans, led them to believe that the Thatcherite settlement could be upheld and sustained without the aid of constitutional protection. Nothing was further from the Reaganite conception, in theory or practice.

Less straightforward are the contrasts between the programmes and practice of the two right-wing governments in the spheres of religion and social policy, as Gillian Peele shows. In discourse, the two leaders had much in common. Thatcher's celebrated May 1988 address to the General Assembly of the Church of Scotland ('if a man will not work, he shall not eat'; 'any set of social and economic arrangements which is not founded on the acceptance of individual responsibility will do nothing but harm', etc)[19] could easily have been delivered by Reagan; and her notion of their being 'no such thing as society', just 'individuals and families' sustaining their local communities was straight from Robert Nozick's book. But not even at her zenith was Thatcher the British Government. In policy terms, the social programmes of the two right-wing governments had little in common. Again, this was partly a function of institutional constraints: Robert Runcie was no Jerry Falwell, and the Church of England, a pillar of both the liberal and social democratic orders in Britain, was the antithesis of the sects campaigning for the 'moral majority' in the Bible Belt. But the absence of such sects spoke for the weakness of respectable moral fundamentalism in Britain, particularly at elite level, circumscribing Thatcher's capacity to give 'Victorian values' anything but rhetorical expression.

In the 1980s, the elites of the Republican and Conservative parties came to reflect their electorates to an unprecedented degree. That, as much as anything else, accounts for the populist strand in the politics of the two parties (it was, emphatically, not just a question of the personal style of their leaders), and the self-confidence with which they attacked opposing interests and ideologies. Jack Pitney and Andrew Adonis assess the nature of change in the two elites, Pitney stressing the importance of generational shifts within the higher echelons of the Republican Party, Adonis pointing to the significance of social shifts within the Conservative Parliamentary Party. In both cases, however, it is a mistake to regard new elites as the harbingers of new ideologies. On the contrary, Adonis emphasises the extent to which 'new Tories' were new mainly in the self-confidence with which they preached, and sought to implement, an essentially reactionary message. As Nigel Lawson puts it in the essay on 'the new Conservatism' in his memoirs, the single most important guide to British right-wing politics in the Thatcher decade:

Old lessons have had to be painfully relearned. The old consensus is in the process of being re-established. To the extent that new Conservatives turn to new sages – such as Hayek and Friedman – that is partly because what those writers are doing is avowedly reinterpreting the traditional political wisdom of Hume, Burke and Adam Smith in terms of the conditions of today . . . the essential point is that what we are witnessing is the reversion to an older tradition in the light of the failure of what might be called the new enlightenment. This is important, politically, not in the sense of some kind of appeal to ancestor-worship or to the legitimacy of scriptural authority: it is important because these traditions are, even today, more deeply rooted in the hearts and minds of ordinary people than is the conventional wisdom of the recent past.[20]

On the American right, 'ancestor worship' was more vocal, and the legitamacy of the founding fathers' scriptural authority more earnestly invoked and hotly disputed. But the same held true. Prone both of them to pithy platitudes, either Reagan and Thatcher could have uttered Lawson's concluding words: monetarism, nationalism and a healthy distrust of government are old truths:

All that is new is that the new Conservatism has embarked on the task – it is not an easy one: nothing worthwhile in politics is; but at least it runs with, rather than against, the grain of human nature – of re-educating people in some old truths. They are they are no less true for being old.[21]

Notes

1 Kenneth Morgan, *The People's Peace: British History 1945–90* (Oxford, Oxford University Press, 1992) p. 437.

2 Alfonzo Hamby, *Liberalism and its Challengers*, 2nd edn (Oxford, Oxford University Press, 1992).

3 House of Commons debates, *Hansard*, 2 July 1970. A meeting of the Conservative shadow cabinet at the Selsdon Park Hotel in January 1970 had decided on a sharp move rightwards on economic policy, a shift that Heath abandoned in office.

4 Enoch Powell in John Ranelagh, *Thatcher's People* (London, Fontana, 1991) p. 167.

5 President Carter, 15 July 1979.

6 A. Horne, *Macmillan 1957–1986* (London, Macmillan, 1989) p. 239.

7 Quoted in Peter Riddell, *Mrs Thatcher's Government* (Oxford, Martin Robertson, 1983).

8 Michael Barone, *Our Country* (New York, Free Press, 1990).

9 For narrative accounts see Lord Blake, *The Decline of Power 1915–64* (London, Grenada, 1985) and Stephen Ambrose, *Rise to Globalism: American Foreign Policy since 1939*, 6th edn (New York, Penguin, 1991).

10 James Sunquist, 'The Crisis of Competence in Our National Government', *Political Science Quarterly*, 95, p. 184.

11 W. Watt & L. Free, *State of the Nation* (New York, Universal Books, 1973).

12 Alan Marsh, *Protest and Political Consciousness* (London, Sage Books, 1977).

13 Charles Hardin, *Presidential Power and Accountability* (Chicago, University of Chicago Press, 1974).

14 Ian Gilmour, *Inside Right* (London, Hutchinson, 1977) p. 195.

15 *Ibid.*, p. 195.

16 Sundquist, 'The Crisis of Competence', p. 188.

17 Anthony King in King (ed.), *Why Is Britain Becoming Harder to Govern?* (London, BBC Books, 1976).

18 All polls from Samuel Finer, *The Changing British Party System 1945–1979* (Washington, DC, AEI, 1980).

19 *Guardian*, 23 May 1988.

20 Nigel Lawson, *The View from No. 11* (London, Bantam Press, 1992) p. 1041.

21 *Ibid.*, p. 1054.

Part I
Ideology in government

Ideology in practice

The conservative counter-revolutions in Britain and the USA had parallel inspirations in the failures of the 1970s; similar, though not identical, objectives; but very different outcomes and legacies. The differences primarily reflected contrasts in the institutions of the two countries, but they were also the result of the dissimilar personalities of Margaret Thatcher and Ronald Reagan. This affected the way their successors – George Bush in the USA from January 1989 and John Major in Britain from November 1990 – handled their inheritances. After the heroic, crusading years, a more difficult, managerial phase began.

In retrospect, Reagan's achievements were more in foreign policy, laying the foundations for the end of the Cold War in 1989–91, while Thatcher's were more at home. In part, that was because Britain's underlying economic and industrial difficulties at the end of the 1970s were worse than the USA's but also because her party's strong position in parliament enabled her to implement more.

The central questions in this chapter are how far Mrs Thatcher and Mr Reagan themselves made a difference to what happened in their countries and how much the changes of the 1980s were common to all industrialised countries, whether ruled by nominally left-or right-wing governments. The extent to which the fiscal and monetary policies they pursued were the product of cirmcumstance rather than deep-seated ideological change also points to whether they would survive in the different conditions of the 1990s.

The shared starting point for the counter-revolutions was a reaction against the failures of right-of-centre governments in the early 1970s. Both the Nixon/Ford administrations in the USA and the Heath administration in Britain were seen by many members of their own parties as having taken a wrong direction. Both embraced prices and incomes controls and large-scale intervention in their economies; they did little to limit the power of the State. Conservative opposition to these policies began to grow, initially on a small scale, but then more substantially as inflation rose and expansion slowed in the mid-1970s. That fuelled the challenges to the existing leaders. In February 1975, Margaret Thatcher successfully ousted Edward Heath a year after the Tories had lost power, while in 1976 Ronald Reagan came near to defeating the incumbent President Ford for the Republican nomination.

The conservative diagnoses of what had gone wrong were reinforced by the failures of the subsequent left-of-centre administrations – headed by Jimmy Carter in the USA for four years from January 1977 and the Wilson and Callaghan governments in Britain from March 1974 until May 1979. There were common themes on both sides of the Atlantic. These included a belief that, at home, government had expanded too far, was pushing up taxes on ordinary working people and was sapping personal initiative and, that overseas, the west had failed to counter the growing military power of the Soviet Union. Underpinning both Thatcher's and Reagan's approaches was a strong commitment to individual freedom and private enterprise and a rejection of the consensus welfare capitalism of the post-war era.

The new British approach was summed up in a policy statement produced by the Conservatives in October 1977 and signed by the eclectic group of Sir Geoffrey Howe, Sir Keith Joseph, James Prior, David Howell and Angus Maude. In *The Right Approach to the Economy* (1977), they highlighted strict control of the growth of the money supply, firm management of government expenditure, lower taxation on earnings and savings and the removal of unnecessary restrictions on business. The main inspiration of Conservative policies in the late 1970s was economic. It was broadly monetarist, at least in the eyes of Thatcher and her close allies. In the USA, Reagan offered similar economic goals. In his first major statement in February 1981, 'America's new beginning: a program for economic recovery', he argued that 'only by reducing the growth of government can we increase the growth of the economy'. The programme stressed a reduction in the growth of federal spending, in individual and corporate tax rates, in federal regulation and in inflation, via monetary restraint. In neither case were the proposals as novel as they were made to appear; both the Callaghan and Carter administrations moved during the late 1970s to a formal recognition of the importance of monetary targets, to accepting that marginal tax rates had become too high and to recognising the need for deregulation (implemented in the USA with dramatic effects in relation to the airline industry).

Nevertheless, the roots of Ronald Reagan's successful capture of the Republican nomination in 1980 and his later victory over Carter were more widely based than Thatcher's. Whereas Thatcher developed her approach mainly out of discussion with senior parliamentary colleagues, Reagan drew on much more widely spread sources of support, outside both Congress and Washington. In the late 1970s, and in the election year of 1980, he was backed by groups as diverse as strong anti-communist and pro-defence advocates, the then rapidly expanding Religious Right/Moral Majority of 'born again' Christians, anti-public sector supporters of tax cuts (especially after the passage of proposition 13 in California in 1978 which capped property taxes), anti-abortion campaigners, enthusiasts for school prayer in schools, and libertarians.

By contrast, in Britain, the Conservative Party drew support from some 'family values' groups but carefully avoided taking sides on issues such as abortion. That was in line with the British parliamentary tradition that such matters should be decided not on party lines but according to individual MPs' own views. While Thatcher herself strongly backed the return of capital punishment, she was regularly opposed by a half, and at times more, of her own Cabinet, as well as by a substantial minority of Tory backbenchers. Moreover, for all her advocacy of Victorian values, Thatcher was more interested in proclaiming the virtues of hardwork, thrift and personal responsibility than reversing the liberalising laws of the 1960s in areas of personal morality. She supported the right to an abortion subject to certain widely accepted limits. She was personally sympathetic to friends and associates who got in any personal or sexual problems. In Britain the campaign to ban abortions crossed party lines and, while it may have had some impact in Catholic constituencies in Scotland and north-western England, the issue was never at the centre of the party battle.

Yet if Thatcherism was more specifically economic than Reaganism, there was a similar sense of seeking to change national destiny, of reversing decline. That was distinctive about the appeal of both leaders. In a lecture delivered two months after she came to office in May 1979, Thatcher said:

The mission of this Government is much more than the promotion of economic progress. It is to renew the spirit and solidarity of the nation. To ensure that these assertions lead to action, we need to inspire a new national mood, as much as to carry through legislation. At the heart of a new mood in the nation must be a recovery of our self-confidence and our self respect. Nothing is beyond us. Decline is not inevitable. But nor is progress a law of nature. The ground gained by one generation may be lost by the next. The foundation of this new confidence has to be individual responsibility. . . . It will not be given to this generation of our countrymen to create a great Empire. But it is given to us to demand an end to decline and to make a stand against what Churchill described as the long dismal drawling tides of drift and surrender, of wrong measurements and feeble impulses.

The implementation of Thatcherism and Reaganism differed for both institutional and personal reasons. Thatcher had one key advantage over Reagan – possession of a large working majority in the House of Commons throughout her period as prime minister. This ensured that what she decided would be enacted, no matter how widespread the doubts of her own Cabinet colleagues, let alone those that Tory MPs and others might have. The legislation introducing the community charge or poll tax was the extreme example of her ability to push her ideas through carefully chosen Cabinet committees and then through Parliament, in spite of widespread doubts at the top of her party, thanks to tight whipping of Tory MPs. In the USA, an idea such as the poll tax would never have survived the first leak in the Washington press; it would, like the later Reagan budgets, have been dead on arrival on Capitol Hill.

By contrast, the Republicans never controlled the House of Representatives during Reagan's term and only had a majority in the Senate for six years up to the end of 1986. In practice, the Reagan White House had the legislative initiative solely from January 1981 until the summer of 1982, that is while the Democrats were on the defensive after their sweeping defeats in November 1980. Reagan could mobilise a majority for his tax and spending programme from a combination of his Senate majority and an alliance in the House of the minority Republicans and southern Democrats (the boll weevils, including the formidable Democrat later turned Republican Phil Gramm). But Reagan lost that initiative after the Democrats made big gains in the House in the November 1982 mid-term elections. Afterwards he had to govern in coalition with the Democrats and Speaker Tip O'Neill. After the Republicans lost control of the Senate in November 1986, and with the simultaneous emergence of the Iran/Contra scandal, the Reagan presidency became paralysed, at least on the home front, and much of the initiative was in the hands of the Democrats, notably House Speaker Jim Wright. Similarly, George Bush had to work in coalition with a Democrat controlled Congress – though he successfully used his veto to prevent the passage of legislation to which he objected.

The other institutional contrast worked to Reagan's advantage compared with Thatcher. His administration was much more ideologically conservative than Thatcher's, at least at first. That was because he could choose whom he wanted, and various conservative groups lobbied successfully to ensure that their people occupied many of the thousands of executive branch posts filled by political appointees. The Heritage Foundation, which was at the height of its influence during the early 1980s, sent large numbers of résumés over to the White House.

In Britain, Thatcher had to work with what she was given – that is the membership of the House of Commons, over whose selection and election she had practically no influence. Many of her initial Cabinet were sceptics about her economic approach – monetarism as it came to be known, even though it was imperfectly monetarist in practice. In a ruthless exercise of prime ministerial power, Thatcher removed critics and sceptics in a series of Cabinet reshuffles during the first half of the 1980s. The replacements were at first her enthusiastic supporters like Nigel Lawson (however much he later parted from her), Norman Tebbit and Cecil Parkinson. But over time she was forced to promote many mainstream Tories like Kenneth Clarke, Malcolm Rifkind and Chris Patten because that was where the talent lay. They would later become the leaders of the Cabinet coup against her. Thatcher often ran roughshod over notions of collective Cabinet discussion, notably over the disastrous decision to introduce the poll tax, but she was, nonetheless, to some extent constrained by the need to take colleagues into account over the most significant issues like public spending.

The Reagan administration was throughout much more ideological than the Conservative Party in Britain. There is a marvellously evocative passage about the influx of young 'movement' believers into Washington in the early 1980s in the memoirs of Peggy Noonan (*What I saw at the revolution*, Random House, New York, 1990), the best known White House speechwriter of the Reagan years.

Everyone wore Adam Smith ties that were slightly stained from the mayonnaise that came from the sandwich that was wolfed down at the working lunch on judicial reform. The ties of the Reagan era bore symbols – eagles, flags, busts of Jefferson – and the symbols had meaning. I had a dream: the ties talked; they turned to me as I walked into the symposium. 'Hi I'm a free market purist!' said the tie with the little gold curve. 'Hullo there, I believe in judicial restraint!' said the tie with the liberty bell. 'Forget politics, come fly with me!' said the tie with the American eagle. . . . There were words. You had a notion instead of a thought and a dustup instead of a fight, you had a can-do attitude and you were in touch with the zeitgeist. No one had intentions, they had an agenda and no one was wrong, they were fundamentally wrong and you didn't work on something you broke your pick on it and it wasn't an agreement, it was a done deal. All politics is local but more to the point all economics is micro. There were phrases: Personnel is policy and ideas have consequences and ideas drive politics and it's a war of ideas – ideas were certainly busy! – and to do nothing is to endorse the status quo and roll back the Brezhnev Doctrine and there's no such thing as a free lunch, especially if you're dining with the press.

There were many fewer 'movement' conservatives in Britain. Some entered the Commons in the 1983 and 1987 general elections. But for all the high profile enthusiasm for privatisation and free markets of the No Turning Back group of MPs in the Commons (many of whom became ministers in the late 1980s and early 1990s), most Conservative backbenchers were in no sense ideological. They may have been pro-business but they were not necessarily therefore monetarists or advocates of a vigorous competition policy or limiting the role of government in social provision. They had adapted their views to those of party leaders and to the fashion of the time – for example, against incomes policy and in favour of a greater emphasis on monetary policy – but not in any deep-seated ideological way. The same can be said of many Republican senators and congressmen, as opposed to members of the administration. In Britain, the 'movement' conservatives were limited to a small number of devotees of a handful of think tanks and policy groups like the long-established Institute of Economic Affairs, the Centre for Policy Studies (at least in the late 1970s), and the Adam Smith Institute (particularly in the second and third Thatcher terms). These bodies had an influence on, and maintained close contacts with, Mrs Thatcher and her close advisers, as well as some sympathetic ministers.

The various free market think tanks co-operated in exchanging ideas and personnel. For instance, the Heritage Foundation had links with the Adam Smith Institute, among others, while the Institute of Economic Affairs kept in contact with the American Enterprise Institute. There was a regular two-way traffic of scholars and researchers across the Atlantic and a number of joint conferences were organised. This developed also into visits by Conservative ministers to America and, to a lesser extent, visits by members of the administration to Britain. The British side were most interested in American experiments in social policy, notably in training, workfare and magnet schools, while Americans looked at the British experience in developing privatisation and enterprise zones. The New Paradigm ideas of James Pinkerton, a senior White House aide in the Bush administration, about empowerment and extending choice to the poor were echoed by members of the No Turning Back of MPs in Britain and by advisers in free market think tanks.

These free market groups can claim some influence in Britain on adding a cutting edge to the privatisation programme, the poll tax and deregulation, Thatcher came to rely as much on energetic civil servants in the development of policy. Moreover, as I discuss in my own books on the Thatcher governments, Mrs Thatcher never had a consistent free market ideology. She had clearly defined values, but these were sometimes – notably in the case of her defence of mortgage interest tax relief – disputed by most free market economists.

Her own familiar question, 'is he one of us?' shows how Thatcher regarded herself and her supporters as a minority within her own government. She often talked of the government in the third person as if she had little to do with it. That sense of a guerilla band fighting against the establishment was underlined by the

changes in tone and direction initiated by John Major's administration.

There were also important personal contrasts. Reagan was at
heart an inspirational figure. He believed in a few key objectives,
cutting back government, reducing taxes, fighting communism and
ending the nuclear arms race. As Lou Cannon details in his masterly
biography, *Ronald Reagan* (Simon & Schuster, New York/Lon-
don, 1991), the president was often not involved in detailed decisions and the arguments between subordinates within his own
administration. His 1984 re-election campaign was remarkably
free of content. Although he played an important role in helping
to push the important tax reform legislation of 1986, the details
were determined more by senior Treasury officials like James Baker
and Richard Darman and by leading members of the Senate Finance
and the House Ways and Means committees. His lack of involvement in domestic policy was even more pronounced in the last
two years of his second term. By contrast, Thatcher remained
involved in the detailed implementation of policy right up to her
forced departure in November 1990. Her fingerprints were on
many government policies, to the frequent irritation of her ministers. She was very resilient and had an ability to pick herself up
when faced with reverses, as after the sharp rise in unemployment
and inner city riots of 1981 and in the summer of 1986 after the
Westland crisis and the rows over the sale of Land Rover and the
US bombing of Libya. Her administrations managed to renew
themselves and to maintain their radicalism, until they had tested
the patience of voters and Tory MPs once too often. The 'revolutionary' phase of challenge and change therefore lasted far longer
in Britain than in the USA.

Yet, contrasting though they were in their styles, Reagan and
Thatcher both made a big personal difference to the development
of policy during the 1980s. Reagan may have been uninvolved and
uninterested in the detail of many measures, but his ability to
mobilise a national constituency, almost above the heads of Congress, did play a crucial role in putting together the coalition of
conservative Democrats and Republicans which carried his most
ambitious economic legislation in 1981–82. Without him, the tax
and spending proposals might not have been approved. Similarly,
Thatcher's determination and single-mindedness played a key role
not only in foreign crises such as the Falklands War but also in

defeating the miners' strike in 1984–85, in pressing on with the phased laws to curb trade union powers and in the shift in industrial and economic policy. She was willing to challenge vested interests in the way that her predecessors, and many of her colleagues, were wary of doing; sometimes with disastrous results, as in the case of the poll tax. Nonetheless, the USA and Britain were not unique in the industrialised world in seeking to rein back the growth of the public sector, to cut direct taxes and to reduce regulations. They may have been the pioneers and have taken the process further but by the second half of the 1980s these ideas were the conventional wisdom of finance ministries, both in Europe and in many Third World countries. Privatisation and lower marginal tax rates became the watchword of the new governments in the former communist regimes in central and eastern Europe.

Differences between Reagan and Thatcher in their ability to implement decisions and in their ideological commitments had a profound affect on how the conservative counter-revolutions developed in the USA and Britain. On both sides of the Atlantic it is striking how important were early decisions on levels of expenditure and taxation. In Britain the priority was fiscal probity. Even though expenditure on defence and law and order was raised and marginal rates of income tax were cut across the board (in two main stages in 1979 and 1988, with smaller cuts in between), the need to contain public sector borrowing meant that indirect taxes were raised sharply. In the USA, Mr Reagan had similar spending priorities and a strong desire to cut taxes. The dramatic budget package of summer 1981 achieved these aims, but at the cost of a soaring deficit. He neither wanted to raise other taxes, as happened in Britain, nor would Congress even in 1981 have agreed to a measure like a Value Added Tax. This approach also reflected the supply-side theories of Art Laffer and others who argued that deep cuts in tax rates would be self-financing by stimulating economic growth and hence more revenue. This view was specifically rejected by Thatcher's economic ministers. While they accepted that cuts in marginal tax rates would stimulate enterprise and boost revenue over the longer term, they believed that such benefits should not be assumed in the short term. On the British view, the priority remained cutting public sector borrowing and if spending was pushed up by, for example, a recession, that should be at least partly offset by an increase in the tax burden.

That occurred most dramatically in March 1981 when Sir Geoffrey Howe as Chancellor raised the tax burden in face of sharply increasing unemployment, in a clear rejection of Keynesian economics. The Howe doctrine was dropped ten years later when John Major and Norman Lamont accepted a big rise in public borrowing in the early 1990s in response to the sharp increase in spending and lower tax receipts produced by another deep recession.

During the mid-1980s British ministers had argued that the leap in the budget deficit in the USA and the move towards a public sector surplus in Britain justified their view. In the Mais lecture in June 1984, Nigel Lawson, then Chancellor, disputed the American argument that the 1981 tax cuts and the increased budget deficit had contributed to a period of strong growth and rising employment (which continued until 1989). He argued that it was more efficient and competitive markets that led to the rise in employment rather than the budget deficit. Anyway, Lawson said the American option was not open to any other country since the USA had the unique position of having the dollar as the world's reserve currency.

There was the paradox in the first half of the 1980s that the high deficit and the Federal Reserve's vigorous anti-inflation policy and consequent high interest rates pushed up the dollar, boosted the American current account deficit and imposed strains on the world's financial system. The dollar later dropped and the current account deficit fell as America moved into recession. But the budget deficit continued to rise in spite of occasional tax and spending packages, as in 1987 and 1990, which attempted to reverse the trend. This was partly because of political inertia as the Democrat run Congress sought to defend prized social programmes from cuts. But many conservative Republicans were also not too worried about the budget deficit, in sharp contrast to their counterparts across the Atlantic. This was partly because there were few obvious adverse consequences as the economy continued to expand until 1989. Many conservative Republicans and supply-siders blamed the 1990–91 recession on Bush's attempts to check the rise in the deficit by very modest increases in taxes. Such conservatives also saw the deficit as the only way to discipline a free spending Congress, a further contrast to Britain where the executive and not the legislature controls both the level and the distribution of spending. These supply-siders feared that cuts in borrowing, especially if financed by higher taxes, would merely encourage

Congress to spend more. Therefore it is better to have a big deficit as a means of holding down spending, a strategy which depends on the infinite capacity of investors, notably overseas, to buy US Treasury bills and other public sector debt.

Within these broad fiscal trends, there were similarities in the distribution of spending. Both the Reagan and Thatcher administrations increased defence expenditure up to the mid-1980s, before budgets levelled off and then fell from the late 1980s onwards. Discretionary domestic spending was cut on both sides of the Atlantic; in Britain spending on public housing and subsidies and in support for industry fell sharply – by 74 and 57 per cent respectively in real, inflation adjusted, terms during the 1980s. By contrast, defence spending rose by 18 per cent. Total public spending fell as a proportion of total national income during the 1980s, from a peak of $47\frac{1}{4}$ per cent in 1981–82 to $39\frac{1}{2}$ per cent in 1988–89, before rising again to 45 per cent during the 1990s' recession. It is more difficult to make precise comparisons in the USA because so much spending is decided at a state and local, rather than a federal, level. While the Reagan administration was initially able to shift some of the burden of social provision onto the states, Congress resisted larger-scale cuts. The scope of government in the USA hardly altered; central government expenditure as a percentage of Gross Domestic Product began and ended the 1980s in the 23 to 24 per cent range.

About the most that can be said is that in both countries the rise in the share of public expenditure in national income was halted (after taking account of sharp cyclical variations), though the growth of spending was also checked in other industrialised countries without such a self-consciously conservative approach. There were common financial pressures after the build-up in deficits and inflation of the 1970s. The rise in spending was reversed to a small extent in Britain thanks to the political initiative commanded by the Thatcher government for most of the decade, as well as, of course, the Tories' majority in the House of Commons. The main obstacle to further cuts was the public attachment to the post-war welfare state, both in Britain and the USA. It was as early as 1982 that Thatcher first had to offer reassurance that the National Health Service was safe in her hands; all subsequent changes to improve efficiency and cost control have been based on the premise of continued free provision at the point of delivery. During the first three Tory terms health spending rose by more than 50 per cent in real terms. In social security, a series of changes trimmed away at the edges of universal provision – child benefit being frozen for a while until uprated by the Major government – but the basic principles of benefits for those in need were retained. In the USA, even any suggestion of trimming back social security benefits for the retired roused instant public opposition and a veto by Congress. While many welfare benefits were cut substantially during the 1980s, the cost of Medicare and Medicaid health payments continued to rise rapidly.

On the tax side, the overall burden of direct and indirect taxation changed little, but marginal rates of tax on individuals and businesses were reduced substantially in the hope of stimulating enterprise. The British tax changes, cutting the top rate on earned income from 83 to 40 per cent, came in two stages, in 1979 and 1988, while US actions, reducing federal top rates from around 50 per cent to 28 per cent for the wealthiest, came in legislation in 1981 and 1986. These changes not only simplified both countries' tax codes – while apparently not affecting the employment of accountants – but also substantially diluted the previous progressive bias of the tax system. In the late 1980s marginal tax rates were also reduced in a number of European countries not ruled by right-wing or avowedly free market parties.

Both Thatcher and Reagan were committed to reducing government regulations and freeing private enterprise. Price, pay, dividend and exchange controls were lifted in Britain and there were a series of far-reaching measures to limit the power of trade unions and to shift the balance of power in the labour market. That was less necessary in the USA where union membership was anyway much lower and unions were already subject to tighter legal controls. Many government regulations on business were eased in the USA. There was a substantial deregulation of financial markets with mixed results, especially in the USA where taxpayers in the 1990s were having to pay the costs of the lax and lop-sided supervision of savings and loans and banks in the 1980s.

In Britain, the most important change was the privatisation of many previously state-owned enterprises. Between 1979 and 1993, two-thirds of state-owned industries had been sold to the private sector, in the process substantially increasing the number of shareholders, from 7 to over 21 per cent of the adult population.

In the USA there was less scope for privatisation since almost all the industries sold off in Britain, such as British Telecom, British Gas, British Steel and the electricity and water companies were already in private sector hands across the Atlantic. However, some state and local authorities in the USA joined in privatisation of services and contracted-out the provision of some operations which they continued to finance. In Britain, the central government was also able to order local councils to sell rented houses and flats to their tenants. This contributed to a big rise in owner occupation over the decade, from 53 to 66 per cent. In the USA, the federal government could not tell state or local governments what to do with their housing, though it could, and did, reduce housing subsidies.

Overall, neither the Reagan nor the Thatcher governments had as much impact as the Roosevelt administration of the mid-1930s in the USA or the Attlee government of the late 1940s in Britain. Both the Reagan and Thatcher governments helped to reverse some of the economic ossification of the 1970s by challenging previous assumptions and encouraging private sector entrepreneurs to flourish, in some cases to excess. But there was not a marked or sustained transformation of the economic performance of either country. In spite of a rapid growth of employment, the USA still had the problem of a high budget deficit in the early 1990s. In Britain, productivity growth and corporate performance did improve during the mid-1980s, trade-union power was curbed, many markets were liberalised and employment also rose sharply. But by the end of the decade a second recession had taken much of the gloss off the earlier successes. In terms of social policy, neither leader succeeded in undermining popular and political support for the welfare state – and to large extent they never tried.

The most lasting domestic impact of the Reagan administration – continued by Bush – may have been in judicial appointments, both to the Supreme Court (where a clear conservative majority was established) and in the federal courts. The significance of these appointments is often underestimated in Britain where it would be difficult to discern any change in the pattern of judicial appointments under governments of either party. They are mainly recruited from a small group of barristers, most of whom have the same social and educational background.

William Niskanen, a member of the Reagan council of economic advisers in the first term and now chairman of the free market and libertarian Cato Institute, concluded that:

In the end there was no Reagan revolution. Although the growth of federal spending was reduced, the federal budget share of Gross National Product, until recently, continued to increase. Although individual and corporate tax rates were reduced by more than anyone anticipated, some of the reduction in tax rates was financed by shifting taxes to the future (via the deficit) or by increasing the taxes on new investment. Some deregulation was offset by a net increase in trade restraints. Moreover, the failure to reform the remaining governmental role in several industries left a legacy of a high rate of bank failures, a large future bill to close those banks that are insolvent but still operating, increasing air traffic congestion, and the prospect of some reregulation.

Mr Niskanen argued that the primary reason why Reaganomics did not prove to be a revolution was that there had not been a fundamental change in the perceptions about what the federal government should be doing, at least among elected officials. On his view, Reagan offered a vision but was reluctant to face hard choices. As in Britain, the main feature of the 1980s was popular resistance to tax increases, and a desire for reductions in marginal tax rates, but no comparable change in attitudes to what should be provided by the state. There was a continuing search for savings from the elimination of waste, improved efficiency and cuts in grants to subordinate authorities at a local level, but resistance to any reduction in basic entitlements such as inflation-proofed retirement pensions and similar services. The ambiguities of popular resistance to higher taxes continued into the early 1990s. Even at the 1992 presidential election, after the Democrats had campaigned for improved health-care and on the theme of more active government, the polls showed that voters favoured, by a three to two margin, smaller government which provided fewer services and cost less in taxes over a government which provided more services but cost more in taxes.

As the heroic age of the conservative revolution ended in the late 1980s and a managerial phase began under George Bush and John Major, there was a shift of emphasis. This was a reflection both of circumstance and of temperament. The long expansion of the second half of the 1980s could not be sustained. Consumers, companies and, particularly in the USA, government built up debt. This reflected both lax macro-economic policies, especially in the USA with the rise in the Budget deficit, and a lop-sided liberalisation of financial and other markets. Thus controls were removed on the operations of banks and savings and loans in the USA to encourage competition, but at the same time supervision to ensure prudence and safety in lending was also relaxed. The result was not only an over-expansion in the amount of debt well beyond safe levels but also many unsound, and even fraudulent, loans. In Britain, tight prudential supervision was, with few exceptions retained, but the deregulation of the banks did lead to a sharp rise in lending to both households and companies. Much of this borrowing was used to finance consumption and purchases of assets like housing. So that when the boom ended, a lengthy period of readjustment was needed as debt was reduced to more sustainable levels. In the USA, the direct legacy of the mistakes of the Reagan administration was seen in the collapse of the commercial property market, the need to rescue the savings and loans industry and the weakness of many banks. The bursting of the Reagan bubble and the permissive regulatory policies of his administration directly contributed to the difficulties which his successor had to tackle. In Britain, the mistakes of the Thatcher regime were less dramatic, but a failure to rein in the late 1980s' expansion earlier and regulatory errors also led to a build-up in debt which took time to reduce under Major.

Moreover, neither of the two new leaders was a crusader. Both were reconcilers, problem-solvers. While adopting a more conciliatory, non-confrontational style, they both sought to entrench the legacies of their predecessors rather than to take dramatic new steps. They lacked the political strength to push through unpopular reforms, as Reagan and Thatcher had been willing to do in the early 1980s. Bush largely accepted the political constraints of a Democrat-controlled Congress and a shift of control and financing of many programmes to a state and local level. His strategy of vetoing controversial legislation approved by the Democratic controlled Congress – with only one successful challenge just before the 1992 election – amounted to a surrender of the political initiative. Any significant legislative measures, such as the clean air, child – care and rights of disabled acts of 1990, were the result of lengthily crafted compromises with Congress. In both the USA and Britain, the economic achievements of the previous decade, such as reducing marginal tax rates, were not challenged, but equally there was little attempt to push them further. The enormous political unpopularity which Bush incurred in the Republican Party for agreeing to a small overall increase in taxes as part of the deficit reduction agreement in autumn 1990, thus appearing to reverse his 'no new taxes pledge', showed how ingrained had become the opposition to higher taxes, even when the budget deficit was still rising.

Bush also showed little interest in domestic policy, as opposed to foreign affairs. He was absorbed by relations with the Soviet Union and, then, its collapse, with the results of the end of the Cold War, with the invasion of Panama and, above all, by the Gulf crisis and war of August 1990 to March 1991, when his popularity was at its height. The USA could mobilise an international coalition to recapture Kuwait, and finance the operation largely through contributions from Arab allies, Japan and Germany. But that was an exception. The political benefits of his initial success proved to be relatively short-lived. Bush largely wasted the political capital he built up as a result of the end of the Cold War and the allies' swift victory in the Gulf War. He never fully realised that the American public wanted the drive and energy which he showed in foreign affairs to be applied to urgent domestic problems.

The financial constraints of a high deficit and public opposition to raising taxes inherited from his predecessor severely limited what he could do. In a survey of the Bush presidency in the *New York Times* in June 1992, Ronald Steel, the historian, argued that, 'the huge deficit made it impossible for the administration to fund an activist foreign policy. When all of these opportunities to develop free markets and democracies were out there in Eastern Europe and Russia, we could not afford to nurture them'. Stanley Hoffman, who runs the European studies centre at Harvard, has put the point more bluntly. American foreign policy seemed to be reduced to two conflicting statements: 'We are the only superpower left, and we are broke so we cannot do anything.'

During the first few years I think the Bush people thought they saw the future almost the way it looked in 1945 – we would clearly be the number one superpower, but the Soviet Union would follow our lead. The two great powers and a few lesser ones would do things together. That is not going to happen. Now we have to 'shut up or put up, and, since we don't want to put up, we may have to shut up.'

These restrictions – and an inward looking attitude in Congress after the end of the Cold War – have affected not only what the USA can contribute to the economic changes in eastern Europe and the former Soviet Union but also its financial and political relations with the Third World, as was shown in the clumsy isolation of Bush at the Earth summit in Brazil in June 1992.

At home, Bush's room for manoeuvre was even more restricted by lack of funds. He could fairly point to the budget agreement as preventing spending and the deficit from growing even higher. And one of his first initiatives on becoming president was to push through legislation rescuing depositors in the savings and loan industry, even if the initial funds were inadequate and had to be substantially increased later. His administration also announced much-needed, and far-reaching, plans for overhauling banking laws which had contributed to the problems of banks and were weakening America's competitive position. But Bush never sought to employ his political muscle to push through a comprehensive reform package against the powerful vested interests of parts of the banking and insurance industries which were well represented in Congress. In the end, as so often, the forces of inertia won and only a minimal measure shoring up the fund to protect bank depositors was approved by Congress. Despite the urgency of wider reform repeatedly emphasised by Nicholas Brady, his Treasury Secretary, Bush was unwilling to take the risks needed for passage, as Reagan had over tax reform in 1986. The same combination of lack of interest, unwillingness to follow through and push proposals and fiscal constraints also limited what the administration was able to do in relation to the inner cities and education. The weaknesses in the former policy were exposed in the debates in the aftermath of the Los Angeles riots of spring 1992.

Bush had from the start proclaimed himself the education president and had put forward a number of proposals, very similar to those in Britain, for improving standards, via a series of goals from eliminating illiteracy to raising the high school graduation rate from 75 to 90 per cent. He emphasised parental responsibility, increased choice, community action and curriculum standards. This was to be achieved by local initiatives since there was little Federal government money available. Washington anyway financed only 6 per cent of public education costs, a drop of 40 per cent since the late 1970s. But many of the proposals made little progress because of opposition from Congress, where the majority Democrats argued that schemes such as operating more than 500 new showcase schools would not help the 110,000 existing public sector schools. Conservative supporters of Bush's ideas criticised the White House for failing to mobilise support. Stuart Butler, the British-born director of domestic policy studies at the Heritage Foundation, argued that, 'the stuff on paper is great. But there is absolutely no follow-through politically with any of these items. It's a deficiency of the White House in general in the domestic area.'

Major handled the transition more successfully than Bush. This was, in part, of course, because he had a working majority in the House of the Commons which he managed to preserve at a reduced level after the April 1992 general election. In that respect, he retained the initiative in face of an uncertain opposition. Like Bush, Major was much more a managerial than an ideological politician. But, with his stronger domestic political position and with the advantage of the cohesiveness of British government, he had a more coherent programme – even if much of it was a piecemeal series of proposals rather than the frontal assault of the Thatcher era. Like Bush, Major also had to deal with the difficulties bequeathed by his predecessor – a long recession and a slow unwinding of a big build-up of personal and corporate debt.

His main challenge was over Europe, a source of growing tension during the later Thatcher years of and directly responsible for the resignations of two of her previously closest ministers, Nigel Lawson and Sir Geoffrey Howe. The latter's departure, and his unexpectedly dramatic resignation speech, triggered the crisis which brought about her downfall in November 1990. Major promised to put Britain 'at the very heart of Europe' and secured a number of concessions for Britain at the Maastricht summit in December 1991. But this compromise was attacked by Thatcher, both before and after her departure from the Commons, and a significant minority of Tory MPs remained dubious – sceptical in the phrase of the day – about the trend towards closer political union. They favoured a looser free-trade grouping of nation states. For all Major's efforts at conciliation, Europe had become the main fault line within the Conservative Party, especially in parliament. The opponents of the Maastricht treaty were prepared to push the Major government to the brink of defeat, as in November 1992.

Major recognised the need to show that there had been a change of gear. The impression was given that after the Thatcher years there was a new government, continuing the substance of macro-economic policy but with a different style. While seeking to carry forward the fight against inflation and privatisation, he shifted the priority to improving public services. He recognised that the Tories had been seen by many voters as not caring about the welfare state even though Mrs Thatcher's governments had substantially increased spending on health and education. Not only did the Major government further increase spending, to the alarm of the Thatcherites, but the prime minister personally put greater emphasis on ensuring that services which had to remain in the public sector or remain monopolies were more responsive. This was primarily via the Citizen's Charter, an initially much derided exercise to lay down specific commitments for the performance of various services by central government, the health service, and the remaining publicly owned utilities. Strengthened regulators were supposed to produce the same results in the still largely monopoly utilities which had been privatised like British Telecom, British Gas and electricity distribution.

In both Britain and America the experiences of the 1980s and the continuing constraints on public spending led to a re-examination of the role of government. In the 1980s the emphasis had been on cutting back expenditure and on privatisation. But by the early 1990s there was a greater concern about how to manage those services which would continue to be funded by taxpayers. The creed of the public sector reformers was a book *Reinventing Government* by David Osborne and Ted Gaebler (Addison-Wesley, Reading, Mass and Wokingham, UK, 1992.) They argued that 'the kind of governments that developed during the industrial era, with their sluggish, centralised bureaucracies and their heirarchical chains of command, no longer work very well'. Instead, the authors urged changes based on the principles of treating the consumers of public services as customers, encouraging competition between providers of services, decentralising decisions and focusing on outcomes rather than inputs, results rather than expenditure. Governments should 'steer not row'. These ideas were praised both by Democratic centrists such as Bill Clinton, when he was

governor of Arkansas and before he became the Democratic Party's presidential candidate in 1992, and by Republican advisers
such as James Pinkerton, one of the most original members of the
domestic policy staff at the Bush White House. Many of these
proposals have been echoed among the various free-market think
tanks in Britain. This approach is at the heart of the Citizen's
Charter and the division between purchasers and providers which
has underpinned the changes in the structure of the health service.
The theory is that the government should plan levels of provision,
raise the necessary finance and act as a regulator of standards.
Services should be run and delivered by wholly or partly independent providers working under contract. The public should have
enforceable rights under various charters. Insofar as there was a
working philosophy behind the Bush, and certainly the Major,
approaches to government it lay in such ideas.

For all the similarities of personality and political style of George
Bush and John Major, especially in contrast to their predecessors,
the key difference was in their attitude to domestic policy. Bush's
lack of interest doomed his re-election campaign, even more than
the sluggish state of the American economy. An ironical paradox
of 1992 is that Major and the Tories won in April 1992 when the
British economy was still in deep recession, while Bush lost in
November 1992 when the American economy had been recover-
ing for some time, even though the full extent of the pick-up was
not clear by election day. That underlines the point that Bush lost
because he failed to offer voters a reason to re-elect him. David
Broder of the *Washington Post* concluded that Bush was:

a victim of his times, his temperament; and his administration team. Bush
had prepped, consciously or not, to be the perfect Cold War president. . . . But his mindset worked against his success in the domestic
field. Ronald Reagan was propelled by an ideological hostility to big
government. Bush had no passion to dismantle the bureaucracy or reform
the programmes it ran. He was comfortable with the status quo to the
point of complacency. As long as the debt-financed prosperity of the
Reagan years continued, Bush's hands-off attitude brought little public
protest. But when the economy soured – and the recovery stalled – Bush's
inaction was viewed as indifference to people's needs.

By contrast, Major appeared as the fresh head of a new government, still with plenty of ideas and a sense of direction. Major also
had the benefit of a main opposition party which voters still did

not trust because of its divisions and swing to the left of the early 1980s. In the USA, Clinton distanced himself from earlier more left-wing Democrats and presented himself as a mainstream candidate, especially on issues of taxes and spending. Both Major and Clinton offered the prospect of achieving change and improvement.

Looking back after a few years of the mixed fortunes of their successors, it is possible to put the contributions of Reagan and Thatcher into some perspective. The personal interventions of both made a difference, especially in their early years in power when they pushed through changes which would not otherwise have occurred. After the doubts and divisions of the 1970s Reagan defied the sceptics and helped restore the presidency as an institution. He used the 'bully pulpit' of the White House to go over the heads of Congress and to mobilise popular support for far-reaching economic changes, however mixed their longer-term results were. The extent of Reagan's achievement in his first term was shown by the drift over domestic policy towards the end of his presidency and after Bush took over. He managed to override the inherent stalemate produced by the longstanding division of political control at the heart of the American government. Under the very different conditions of Britain, Thatcher also overrode the forces of inertia in Whitehall and used the powers of the executive to the full in Westminster to push through changes which would have been dismissed as wholly unrealistic a few years earlier.

If the solid achievements of Thatcherism and, in particular, Reaganism turned out to be less that their supporters claimed, they did help to change the political agenda. Both leaders responded to, and stimulated, a suspicion of government and made it impossible for any politician or party seriously interested in office to advocate a general increase in taxation. Voters may have retained their attachment to welfare state social provision, but they were reluctant to pay more for it. Politicians were willing to take the chance on repeated polling findings in Britain that voters would pay more for better public services and preferred improved services to income tax cuts. The parties believed that this general altruism was subordinate in the ballot box to a more specific concern about personal well-being and tax deductions. That was underlined in the April 1992 general election in Britain when the Tories made the centrepiece of their strategy an attack on

Labour's tax and spending plans. Labour had carefully constructed a scheme showing that only 15 per cent of the better-off would pay more in tax, substantially more in some cases. But the Tories played on fears that Labour intentions would mean higher taxes for almost all, including those aspiring to higher incomes. A widespread conclusion from the election was that even hinting at higher taxes for some was a serious electoral liability. In the USA, Clinton was careful to say that only the very well-off, those earning more than $200,000 a year, would have to pay more in taxes, even though that begged questions about how the deficit would be reduced.

The other main legacy of the 1980s has been the spread of a commitment to free markets and deregulation, not only through the industrialised world but in Third World countries like Mexico and, most recently, in eastern Europe and the former Soviet Union. Reagan and Thatcher may be best remembered as joint stand-ard bearers of capitalism and democracy in the final days of the Cold War, as the inspirers of a shift in thinking. In some respects their names are more revered in the former communist states than in the west. The attitudes of both leaders to the Soviet Union changed considerably. Reagan's strong line against the 'evil empire' and the big build-up in defence spending (in fact inaugurated by Carter) not only risked confrontation with Moscow but also ex-posed the weaknesses of the communist regime. It would be a gross exaggeration to say that either he or Thatcher were responsible for the changes in the former Soviet bloc. But they were not bystanders either. Both Reagan and Thatcher responded with flair and imagination to the economic and political reforms in Moscow inaugurated by Mikhail Gorbachev from 1985 onwards. Their initial strength and later willingness to talk and negotiate stimu-lated, and later supported, the upheavals which swept eastern Eu-rope from 1989 onwards and contributed to the end of the Cold War. In his turn Bush's biggest achievement may have been his constructive handling of the break-up of the former Soviet bloc and his opining up of a new, more cooperative relationship with Moscow.

Reagan and Thatcher made a difference to the course of politics in their own and other countries. Their rise coincided with a broader change in the direction of policy which they encouraged and stimulated. As always happens in democratic politics, their crusades ran out of momentum. And not everyone was converted, far from it. And, as the 1990s began, there was a shift of emphasis and direction. Voters demanded action to deal with some of the areas neglected during the earlier 1980s – notably in education, health care and infrastructure spending. These demands took different forms on either side of the Atlantic in view of the differing scopes of the public sector. But both Major's Citizen's Charter, and the associated changes in public services, and Clinton's backing for more active government represented a shift compared with the 1980s.

Many of the achievements of Ronald Reagan and Margaret Thatcher – and the difficulties they bequeathed – will have a lasting impact. They helped change the way voters think about the role of the state, taxation and markets much more than they changed percentage shares of national income. They may not have buried socialism and collectivism entirely, but they did make it much more difficult even for social democratic, let alone more avowedly socialist, parties to get elected. By their example, Reagan and Thatcher also helped to change other countries, possibly more than their own. They altered the political landscape.

Constitutional and judicial politics

I

Where constitutional and judicial politics are concerned, there is a basic asymmetry between the United States and the United Kingdom. In the United States, constitutional politics are primarily focused on courts; in the United Kingdom they are primarily dominated by party concerns. In the United States, judicial politics are primarily open and highly politicized; in the United Kingdom, they are primarily arcane and depoliticized. These differences are very real and rooted in institutional and cultural factors. But political societies do not remain unchanging and this asymmetry, while still the most obvious feature of any comparison, has for a generation begun to blur.[1]

Differences in conceptual understandings are found both between and within the countries. Judicial independence, for example, has different connotations on different sides of the Atlantic, while the very notion of conservatism is an essentially contested concept both in the United States and in the United Kingdom. Clearly there is a temptation, which must be avoided, of equating the policies of politicians claiming to be conservative with conservatism itself. Although it is clear that the danger of tautology should be avoided, there is unfortunately no reference guide which provides a universally accepted definition of this slippery concept. And there is clearly no space here to argue out the niceties of different interpretations. However, if any insights are to be gained from comparison, then a working definition of conservatism to be applied to both systems is a prerequisite. So I shall set down the assumptions upon which this chapter is based.

Conservatism, it seems to me, has three distinct strands: economic, social and institutional. On the first, the differences between the two countries are negligible, on the second slight, but on the third they are considerable. Economic conservatism I take to encompass a commitment to private property, a belief in the market and a concomitant suspicion of state involvement in economic (and social) management. Social conservatism presumes the existence of some superior values, often mythic reformulations of past practice (e.g. so-called 'Victorian values'),[2] extolls popular preferences over elite and minority views in a populist tradition and is strongly nationalistic. Institutional conservatism presents greater problems, since it is composed of several distinct, and potentially conflicting, strands. One is essentially pragmatic, protective of existing practices and institutions, and imbued with a philosophy that approves change only when manifestly necessary.[3] I shall call this procedural conservatism, most closely associated in the legal field with a belief in *stare decisis* and a caution in developing the law. Another has a much clearer ideological agenda involving the proper role of the state and holds that a weak state and dispersed power best protects liberties and citizens' interests. Another, by contrast, favours a strong and centralized state (but not necessarily an economically or socially intrusive government) to uphold order and enhance homogeneity. Both of these I call substantive conservatism because of their direct links to public policy itself. As we shall see, neither the Reagan nor the Thatcher years were unequivocally conservative in these terms.

Finally, I take this collection of essays to be concerned with two distinct questions. The first relates to the impact of President Reagan and Prime Minister Thatcher as proactive leaders *increasing* the degree of conservatism in their respective countries while the second, and more problematic, question relates to the extent to which these leaders were the expressions of an underlying conservatism already gaining ground. Did they, on the one hand, act on a favourable tide as catalysts which assisted an enduring change in their nations' expectations and perceptions, or were their terms of office of ephemeral significance in the face of an unchanging basic distribution of ideological beliefs? That the Conservative Party's proportion of votes cast declined in each election and the Democrats' hold of Congress in 1989 was virtually identical to that in 1979 suggests that this latter perspective needs to be taken very seriously.

Consequently my chapter is structured in three further parts. One will focus on institutional changes (or constitutional politics); the second will examine conscious proactive attempts to affect judicial branches; and the third will consider whether judicial behaviour in fact shifted during the 1980s as a result of the actions of the Thatcher governments and the Reagan administrations.

II

Constitutional politics in the United States is essentially judical politics. The formal, codified Constitution has only twenty-six amendments. Only sixteen have been passed in the last two hundred years, the last virtually a generation ago in 1971. Yet proposals for constitutional amendments proliferate literally in their thousands. Forty per cent of all proposals during the first 200 years (4,074 in number) were offered in the twenty years 1965–1985.[4] Few are taken seriously by legislators; fewer even generate hearings in the Congress. Nevertheless, they are not to be ignored entirely, for they do reflect genuine concerns as well as offering opportunities for individual congressmen to play symbolic politics.

Disaggregating the gross number of proferred amendments (and ignoring their differential saliency), it is noticeable that they fall into essentially three categories. The most numerous are basically populist attempts to limit further the period of office for president, to make judges electorally accountable, or otherwise to increase the direct links of accountability between citizens and rulers. A second set concern the formal structure of government, by giving the District of Columbia full congressional representation or strengthening the autonomy of the states withing the federal system, for example. Finally many, but by no means a very large category, focus on specific policy issues or themes. Some of these are liberal, such as the recurring proposals for an Equal Rights Amendment, while some are conservative, such as proposals to reverse decisions like *Roe* v. *Wade* (which first established a constitutional right to an abortion)[5] or *Abington School District* v. *Schempp* (which asserted that prayers in elementary schools violated the Constitution's prohibition against an establishment of a church)[6] or give explicit support for capital punishment.

The multitude of amendments offered do not translate into proposals from Congress. The handful which generate Hearings rarely reach the stage of a vote. Nevertheless, in the early 1980s there were deliberate (and, in comparative terms, successful) attempts to use the amendment process to advance a conservative social agenda. President Reagan gave his explicit public support to an amendment designed to permit the saying of prayers in the nation's public schools;[7] he lent his implicit support to another group of amendments aimed at reversing *Roe* v. *Wade*.[8] Each made some progress, but neither emerged from Congress with the appropriate majorities.

One reason usually given for the paucity of constitutional amendments is the difficulty of the process itself. Of course, this is partly true. An Amendment needs two-thirds of the House of Representatives and the Senate to propose it and the legislatures of three-quarters of the states to ratify it. Only those with very broad support, such as the 26th Amendment for which the whole process took less than a single year, can survive this challenging course. But there is another reason. That is the status of the Constitution itself. This has both a pragmatic and a metaphysical aspect. The experience of the Prohibition amendment, perhaps the only issue-specific amendment since the Bill of Rights which did not clearly enhance democracy, has persuaded most serious legislators that Constitutional amendments are inappropriate vehicles for the making of public policy. Metaphysically, the Constitution is too revered a document ('totem and fetish' as one academic described it during the crisis of the 1930s)[9] and too charged with the personification of the American virtue of constitutionalism, to be dragged down into the sordid and shifting arena of contested public policy issues.

The truth of the matter, of course, is that the Constitution is being perpetually amended. The central player in this enduring saga is the Supreme Court, which explains why constitutional politics are essentially judicial politics. Indeed, it is doubtful whether the Union could have survived had the Court not regularly brought the Constitution's meaning into line with the dominant ideas of an age and the needs of the nation.[10] But there is more to be said about this commonplace, so artlessly summarized in Charles Evans Hughes's famous aphorism 'the Constitution is what the judges say it is'.

In fact, the meaning of the Constitution is contested and its application worked out in places far from the confines of the Marble Palace. Let me take two recent examples. The constitutional injunction that the Senate should 'advise [on] and consent to' presidential nominations to the Supreme Court was widely discussed during the saga of Robert Bork's failed nomination in the summer of 1987; its meaning is unclear and the Supreme Court has never (and probably never would) resolve disputes over its meaning. Practical politics defined the Constitution's meaning here.[11] In *Goldman* v. *Weinberger*, the Court dismissed a First Amendment claim that military regulations unconstitutionally denied a Rabbi's free exercise of religion by prohibiting the wearing of all headgear (in this case, his yarmulka) indoors on the grounds that executive power gave the military full discretion to decide what regulations enhanced discipline within the army.[12] The Congress then used its legislative powers derived from Article I and rewrote military regulations specifically to permit the wearing of yarmulkas, thus effectively overturning the Supreme Court's pronouncement on the meaning of the Constitution.[13]

If I left the discussion of constitutional politics there, a whole dimension of interest and importance would have been omitted. The *federal* Constitution may enjoy a mystique which insulates it from regular attempts to alter it (which the Indian Constitution does not enjoy); but the *state* constitutions lack that advantage. There has been a dramatic increase in the last two decades in popular attempts to amend constitutions, normally through the device of the initiative which permits ordinary people (if sufficiently spread across a state in the required numbers) to propose amendments to constitutions. Most popular in the western half of the country, where parties have traditionally been weakest, these attempts to bypass the intermediaries (Gaullist democracy turned entirely upon its head) have met with increasing success in the 1980s.[14]

The conventional wisdom at the beginning of the decade was that initiatives were relatively unimportant. American electorates were instinctively suspicious of such attempts to change state policies or constitutional rules and, on principle, voted them down unless they genuinely reflected a widespread support for change. But the 1980s have altered this wisdom. Better advertising and financing together with a greater animus against government have combined to make the initiative a genuinely proactive institution in the political process. But it has been used, both successfully and unsuccessfully, by both conservatives and their opponents.

There have been clear conservative successes. Limiting the level of taxes (like Proposition 13 in California) enhances economic conservatism; limiting the length of time representatives are to serve (as in California and Washington state) is redolent of the old populism and a conservative suspicion of government; freeing a state to limit support for abortions advances a conservative social agenda. On the other hand, several attempts to constrain states' powers to tax or to restrict access to abortions have failed, and constitutional amendments which are environmentally friendly or favourable to unloved minorities (such as homosexuals) have been passed. There has certainly been no one way traffic on this front.

How different are constitutional politics in Britain. Initiatives do not exist and the status of a referendum (prima facie the quintessence of democratic practice) remains low. Without a codified Constitution, of course, there is no formal process to employ to improve it or use it to make political capital. The development of the Constitution to meet new needs or changing ideals has essentially been due to parliamentary action, not judical involvement. Here, however, there is a need to pause for a moment.

An initial difficulty with the British Constitution is its very definition. I have taken a parsimonious view, or Americo-centred bias. A good deal that is written on the Constitution is devoted to descriptions and analyses of how the political institutions function; that seems too broad a conception.[15] My notion of the British Constitution, therefore, is the basic rules governing the distribution of authoritative power and the principles upon which the rights of citizens and the powers of the state are built. In other words, I conceptualize the existence of a codified Constitution.

Britain may have no entrenched Bill of Rights; but the courts recognize certain rights. Indeed, some of the judges are proud of the way they believe citizens' rights are protected by them.[16] The common law tradition is constantly discovering rights and defining them, balancing one against another, and generally monitoring them. These rights may not be entrenched; for Parliament can always legislate where it believes the judges have incorrectly extended the reach of the common law. Just as courts concern themselves with individual citizens' rights, they also watch over

governmental actions to ensure that they do not exceed the powers granted ministers (although such cases are mostly ones of
statutory construction) and comport with natural justice (very much
an instance of 'making law'). In the fair fares case, for example,
when the Judicial Committee of the House of Lords struck down
the Greater London Council's deliberate policy of subsidizing fares,
the concept of a fiduciary duty laid upon local government was
conjured from virtually nowhere and was used to find unlawful a
policy supported by a majority of duly elected councillors on the
Greater London Council.[17]

The 1970s and 1980s saw a flowering of public law in Britain.
Of course, the courts had for long been enmeshed in disputes
which were not of the classic private law kind such as contract or
tort. The extension of government, through the proliferation of
agencies and other quasi-governmental organizations, into an ever-
widening sphere of citizens' lives inevitably gave rise to more disputes between a citizen or corporation, on the one hand, and a
governmental institution on the other. The increase in such disputes, encouraged by a new generation of lawyers not very different from their better resourced public interest equivalents in
the United States, had begun to be felt more acutely in the 1970s;
the 1966 practice statement legitimating the Judicial Committee to
overturn precedents gave an added incentive to lawyers to turn to
litigation in order to alter public policy.[18] These lawyers were
overwhelmingly unconservative, if not entirely anti-Conservative,
and, to the extent that they prevailed, they held back conservative
policies.

In fact the recourse to judicial review (a request to the courts to
consider a challenge to some discretionary act of a public authority)
has not been as great numerically as is often thought. Stripped of
the immigration cases, the number seeking judicial review declined
in the first half of the 1980s.[19] They then increased in the second
half, but not to a level very different from that at the beginning
of the decade. But a developing judicial journalism gave cases a
greater publicity and altered the climate in which issues of
maladministration were conceived. This change – and it *was* a
change in legal culture – has altered the relationship between citizen and state, but in a curious way. Theoretically, by providing an
opportunity (however small) for the citizen to challenge the state,
it advances the populist strand of institutional conservatism; in

its practice, however, it has favoured those who oppose specific conservative social policies.

Most constitutional politics take place in precisely that arena where it is almost wholly absent in the United States: the party competition for electors' votes. Clearly two items were widely contested in the 1980s. First chronologically was the debate over the Bill of Rights. It had been Conservative politicians who, faced with Labour governments prepared to use state power to nationalize industries and constrain economic freedom, were first interested in this theme.[20] Once the Conservatives were themselves in office, their enthusiasm for limitations of government waned and others, notably Liberals and Social Democrats, began to take up the issue. It developed into discussions about the electoral system, where the Liberal Party (and its subsequent manifestations) argued cogently for a form of proportional representation. But power, and the lure of power, held the two major parties back from embarking along a route that would, in its Bill of Rights guise, have constrained the sovereign power of a parliament presumed to be at the service of the majority party's leadership, or, its electoral reform guise, would have destroyed the likelihood of ever providing a majority to exercise that sovereign power.

Second in time, the debate over Britain's relationships with the European Communities, which was partly responsible for the downfall of Mrs Thatcher, has come more and more to dominate the constitutional agenda. It is a strange debate in much the same way that the debate over the Kilbrandon Report was strange. The level of sophistication of the public debate in Britain when dealing with concepts like federalism or devolution has been strikingly low. Crude appeals to simplistic notions of sovereignty have been matched by bland statements of support for a higher degree of integration, with little argument over what realistically an enhancement of authority in Brussels or Strasbourg might actually mean.

The debate illustrates well the confusion in British conservatism. Enlargement of scale essentially enhances governmental power and thus is antagonistic to the conservative view of a minimalist state; it also derogates from that other conservative belief in the nation state. On the other hand, it assists economic conservatism by increasing the potentialities of the market. As far as social, or populist, conservatism is concerned, its relevance depends upon a person's conception of 'We, the People'; the more nationalistically

English the conception, the less conducive to social conservatism is a closer Europe, in which public policy is likely to veer away from the narrower nationalist values (prejudices) of the English. For the Welsh or, more significantly, the Scots, who already carry two identities comfortably enough, the fear of a more integrated Europe with genuine subsidiarity is much reduced. It is little wonder that an issue that cuts through conservative beliefs in different ways has cut through the Conservative Party.

The asymmetry in constitutional politics should by now be clearer. There are areas in which similar processes are at work; the American Constitution can be amended as stealthily as the British through the working out of conventions and the British courts can exercise a degree of judicial power in protecting individuals against the state or demarcating the proper boundaries of state authority. What is strikingly similar on both sides of the Atlantic is the contrast between the concerns of intellectuals and the concerns of politicians. Constitutional issues have excited academics and other thinkers in the United States and the United Kingdom; great has been the production of books. The bicentennial of the American Constitution produced both a hageography to two hundred years of American exceptionalism and frustration with a political structure that seemed to obviate good government. Politicians who are losers have also sought to ameliorate some of their frustration by espousing constitutional change (Hailsham in opposition, the Liberals perpetually, Reagan on social issues). In Britain, electoral winners have had little reason to diminish the enjoyment of their victories by changing the rules and insufficient agreement to embark upon a proactive revision of the fundamental rules under which the country is governed.

III

The Reagan Administration had a clear judicial agenda. Spelled out in the 1980 Republican Party Platform, it was far more explicit even than Richard Nixon in its determination to nominate to the federal courts judges who espoused 'a jurisprudence of self-restraint' rather than judges who 'legislated'.[21] This crude dichotomy, much favoured by politicians and journalists, posits two polar positions. One presumes the constitutionality of legislation and regulations passed by duly elected or appointed political authorities, unless the claimed violation of the Constitution is egregious. The other is more suspicious of majoritarian governments, sees the Constitution as designed to limit governmental power and protect unpopular minorities against the passions of prejudiced majorities and believes that judges should exercise their undoubted power to protect such rights. In reality, judicial philosophies are located along that continuum between self-abnegation and active involvement.[22]

The main point to make, however, is that jurisprudence conceived in this way is neither conservative nor liberal. In the 1930s, liberal politicians espoused the philosophy of judicial self-restraint because they favoured the legislation passed by elected politicians, while conservative politicians saw the courts as a bulwark against what they deemed to be the excesses of overzealous governments. In the 1970s, it was the conservative politicians who favoured a philosophy of judicial self-restraint in defence of the policies of elected officials, while liberal politicians saw the courts as a necessary protection for the legitimate interests of minorities against the tyranny of majorities.

One problem is the failure to distinguish between substantive and procedural activism and self-restraint. Substantive activism depends ultimately on the law-makers, since activism in this sense is discovered simply whenever courts find the actions of elected officials unconstitutional. Quite simply, liberal laws challenged, as in the 1930s, give rise to accusations of a conservative court; conservative laws challenged in the 1960s characterized the Court as liberal. That is the substantive side. But procedurally, Justices may come to decisions according to quite different jurisprudences; an activist jurisprudence accepts the court's role as an interpreter of an evolving Constitution and as the bulwark of minorities, while a self-restrained jurisprudence would remain deliberately fixed to past precedents and unkeen to extend rights or lines of interpretation into new fields. Most commentators are dominated by the end product (striking down the New Deal or establishing a right to an abortion) and not to the routes by which conclusions have been reached.[23] The philosophical arguments are too often *post hoc* rationalizations of public policy preferences. In short, one's position depends very much upon whose ox is gored.

This caricature of judicial philosophies presumes erroneously

that the only significant constitutional questions revolve around
the definition and application of individual rights. But there are
fundamental problems also in drawing clear lines between the
legitimate authority of the branches of the federal government and
between the central government and the states. Here, too, self-
styled liberals and conservatives have found themselves on opposite sides of the divide in the last thirty years. The vision of the
strong presidency modelled on an idealized vision of the Kennedy
and early Johnson presidencies had, in liberal circles, given way by
the 1980s to a fear of an overweening, imperial presidency as
epitomized by Richard Nixon.[24] For liberals, the Congress, and
especially the House of Representatives with its intimate links to
popular influence, seemed to epitomize the heart of the country's
democratic system. For conservatives, more concerned with order
in the economy and in the wider world, the primacy of the
presidency had, by the 1980s, become fashionable and they donned
the mantle of 1960s liberals in their presidential focus. The populist
impulses of some conservatives were sorely tested as they perceived
a popular president of one party facing a popularly elected House
of another party. Where, then, lay the voice of 'We, the People'?

Different attitudes towards federalism have again not always
coincided with different ideological dispositions. Especially among
those who call themselves conservative, there is a conflict between
the romantics seeing states as the primary centre of a citizen's
political loyalty and as laboratories for the diversity inherent in a
continental and pluralist nation and the pragmatists seeing the
national government (and especially the presidency) as the only
authority capable of imposing coherent and rational policies on an
incoherent and selfish polity. While liberals have tended to favour
the centre over the states, partly as a reaction to the segregatory
practices protected by old-style federalism, partly as an ideal to
ensure a degree of equity and social progress for all Americans,
they have increasingly been drawn back into the populist politics
which uphold local and state autonomy against the confluence of
economic power reflected in Washington's rulers.

It is, therefore, not immediately apparent that Reagan's conception of the judicial realm was intrinsically conservative. Certainly
he and his allies knew what they liked and what they did not like.
They favoured untrammelled executive power in foreign relations,
a dominant executive power in intra-branch disputes, political space

for the states *vis-à-vis* the federal government, and a raft of social policies (on abortion, the separation of church and state, suspects' rights, affirmative action) opposed to the liberal positions staked out by the Supreme Court. This composite agenda reflects a mixed ideology, but it was an ideology that was something very much more than a metaphysical belief; it provided a call to action.

This can be illustrated in a number of ways. It can be seen in the Justice Department's careful personnel policy,[25] in its ordering of priorities,[26] in its public criticism of the liberal jurisprudence it despised,[27] and in its own litigating practice.[28]

The reaction against the Great Society policies of Lyndon Johnson and the perceived preferences enjoyed by minority groups in the years thereafter had spawned by the late 1970s a community of conservatives. Many were lawyers, often trained at the University of Chicago, largely gathered together through the Federalist Society; many had joined the conservative think tanks which had grown up on the model of the their more famous, essentially liberal establishments like the Brookings Institution.[29] This group, outsiders in the Washington even of Nixon, developed a camraderie and missionary zeal which was immediately exploited when the Reagan presidency needed manpower. The Justice Department was their chief home.

Once there, they settled in to challenge and turn back the liberal trends which judicial decisions had hastened on and protected. The emphasis on civil rights was reduced; the claims of affirmative action were challenged; the rights of suspects, most notably those incorporated as the Miranda guidelines, were opposed; the cases in which the Administration participated were chosen to assist this agenda and the Solicitors-General more openly and more regularly than their predecessors argued the Administration's line in a conscious attempt to alter the jurisprudence of the Supreme Court.

More important in the long run than the sharp ideological shift in the Justice Department was the conscious policy of nominating to the federal courts men (and some women) who would exercise their judicial power in line with the newly confident jurisprudence of judicial self-restraint. No Administration is entirely cavalier about the selection of judges, of course, but none had set in place so carefully constructed a system of selection as the Reagan Administration did. Centred within the White House and staffed with enthusiasts for the cause, the selection panel scrutinized possible candidates with a care and attention that did two things: it ensured, as near as was humanly possible, that nominees did share the Administration's conception of their role and it reduced the power of Senators to place upon the federal bench their own personal nominees. The new focus certainly added a fresh gloss to the idea of judicial independence. While it was true that judges could still retain office on good behaviour (although a number of federal judges were actually impeached during these years), those judges obtained their positions through a real dependence upon the officials in the Justice Department.

Contrast this with the United Kingdom. At one obvious level, the difference is immense. The appointment process lacks virtually all the acknowledged political content and visibility of the American system. The ease with which statistics can be compiled to generate figures showing the party preferment practised by presidents would shock the British legal fraternity. The secrecy of the ballot, developed somewhat late in Britain's democratic development, now extends virtually into a presumption that it is improper to seek out a person's party affiliation. In any case, the pool from which judges are chosen is entirely different. District judges in the United States are drawn from a range of occupations, among which politician is common, and a range of experiences, among which political connections and activity is virtually obligatory. Appeals Court judges are not necessarily drawn, by promotion, from the ranks of district judges. Nor are Supreme Court Justices inevitably drawn from the Appeals Courts (although more are nowadays, as presidents seek more objective evidence of what a Justice might do).

In Britain there is a hierarchy up which aspiring candidates for judgeships must normally go. The pool of candidates is known and the Lord Chancellor's office keeps notes upon likely possibilities for preferment. The kind of information sought is essentially, but not entirely, limited to legal matters and the number of individuals suitable for each opening is relatively few. The opportunity for the executive to 'pack the courts' is less. Although the formal process involves the Lord Chancellor and the Prime Minister, the procedure through which names emerge is certainly consistent with an apolitical and independent search. To hear Lord Hailsham on the rational, meritocratic selection and promotion of judges or to read the most recent description of the process printed by the

Lord Chancellor's Office, with Lord Mackay's introduction, to counter suspicions of political infection in the judicial body, certainly strengthens the claims of this logical possibility.[30]

Once again there is a distinct political culture dimension. Americans, although they extol the ideal of a 'government of laws, not men', know well enough the intensely political nature of the judicial appointment process. In Britain, the independence of the judiciary and its apolitical connotations still dominate discourse and thinking on the subject. It was striking, for example, how much space the quality newspapers in Britain devoted to the nomination of Clarence Thomas to an Associate Justiceship of the Supreme Court, but how little space or comment was given to the appointment of three new Law Lords to the Judicial Committee of the House of Lords.

Much depends, of course, on the definition of political. Party affiliation or political activity are now rare as criteria for preferment. Lord Chancellor Jowett tried hard to establish the primacy of legal considerations after the end of the Second World War; Lord Kilmour deviated occasionally from this developing convention; despite his public protestations to the contrary, it is said that Lord Hailsham wanted more politicians on the bench particularly because the number of administrative law questions had increased.[34] The simple fact is that politicians *do* get appointed, such as Sir Thomas Williams in 1981; and Lord McCluskey, the 1986 Reith lecturer, had not only sought a parliamentary seat but had been Solicitor-General for Scotland under both Harold Wilson and James Callaghan and a government spokesman in the House of Lords before his appointment as a Senator.

Politicians becoming judges is one thing; political considerations in the promotion of judges to the Judicial Committee of the House of Lords or to the other senior judicial posts is another. The three major judicial officers in the United Kingdom are, arguably, the Lord Chancellor, the Lord Chief Justice (who is the senior appeals judge on the criminal side) and the Master of the Rolls (who is his equivalent on the civil side). All three became vacant during Mrs Thatcher's premiership; all three reflected her priorities and none was an automatic elevation.

Lord Lane's reputation as a judge fitted neatly with Mrs Thatcher's concern for judicial leadership in her determination to fight increasing crime rates and to protect law and order. The appointment of Sir George Donaldson to follow Lord Denning as Master of the Rolls owed a great deal to the feeling that he had been scandalously treated by the Labour party in the 1970s as a result of his being President of the National Industrial Relations Court. He had a political track record, first with the young con-servatives and then as a member of the Croydon Council. And when Lord Hailsham retired and Lord Havers shortly thereafter was forced to step down from the Lord Chancellorship, Mrs Thatcher turned to a Scottish judge as the hinge between the executive and the judicial branch. Lord Mackay of Clashfern had two obvious virtues; first, his public life had indicated that he was a pragmatic and instrumental lawyer prepared to embrace notions of efficiency in policy-making; second, his experience in Scotland, where lawyers are not divided into Barristers and Solicitors, gave him the right kind of background to take on the English legal profession in the Thatcherite era of challenges to established and vested interests. There was thus a policy dimension as well as a quality dimension to the choice.

It would indeed be odd if the Prime Minister and the Lord Chancellor did not have policy considerations (that is to say, political motives) when selecting the senior members of the judicial branch. The privacy of the selection process, however, which is still so integral a part of much of British public life, inevitably encourages speculation about motives and influence. In 1984 it was suggested by one writer that aspiring judges should become Freemasons, since he alleged that those who made the crucial decisions were themselves freemasons.[32] This was, of course, denied. But there remains the suspicion that it is not merit alone which decides who shall be promoted to the Appeals Courts. Merit, in any case, is subjective. Mr Major's recent appointments indicate that a variety of calculations come into play when choosing between able candidates and that these have clear policy components.[33]

The contrast between the United States and the United Kingdom is real. The one is public and overtly political; the other is arcane and depoliticized. The powers of the Judicial Committee and other Appeal Court judges are certainly not as great as those exercised by Justices of the Supreme Court, where the supremacy of the Constitution established a very different context for judging from the principle of parliamentary sovereignty underpinning the Brit-ish Constitution. Nevertheless, judges inevitably 'legislate' to some extent; Lord Denning certainly did, although he was in his later years frequently reversed on appeal,[34] and his successor has crafted new legal rights and obligations in the regular process of adapting the common law. Mrs Thatcher capitalized on the room for manoeuvre in making appointments within the civil service, small though the leeway might have been, to reward those of whom she approved;[35] there seems every likelihood that she did the same thing with judicial appointments.

IV

The impact of President Reagan's appointment policy could not be felt until the last years of the decade. His first appointment, in 1981, placed Sandra Day O'Connor on the bench in place of Potter Stewart; it was five years before another vacancy arose. Then, in 1986, he elevated William Rehnquist to the chief justiceship and brought Antonin Scalia onto the bench as an Associate Justice. After his failure to get Robert Bork confirmed in 1987, he successfully nominated Anthony Kennedy early in 1988. Thus, it was not until his successor George Bush had entered the White House that his legacy could begin to be measured. This inevitable lag, however, means that it is possible to judge whether there was a conservative trend already developing and which new appointments might hasten on.

Procedural conservatism would be realized if the balance between state power and central power shifted towards the states, if the federal courts became less hospitable to litigants' claims, and if the principle of *stare decisis* generally prevailed. Substantive conservatism would be recognized if certain specific Supreme Court decisions (such as those establishing a right to an abortion or a wall between church and state, and approving of affirmative action) were reversed. There is, of course, a contradiction between these two brands of conservatism. Reversing precedents because they are felt to have been wrongly decided is procedurally activist. And conservatism is also confused when issues of central government power is concerned; the populist tradition would weaken the authority of the executive while the nationalist tradition would strengthen it.

Supreme Court opinions are the most obvious manifestations of judicial ideology. But the Reagan Administration's policy had focused on the lower courts (virtually half the judges on the Circuit Courts of Appeal and the District Courts had been nominated by him when he left office) and the impact of the appointments was beginning to be felt by the end of the decade. Early research indicated a mixed impact, which is what should be expected. Some fulfilled the expectations of the agenda-minded conservatives; some did not because their procedural conservatism led them to confirm relatively liberal decisions handed down by earlier courts through their attachment to the principle of *stare decisis*; yet others, although relatively few, found that being a judge gave them a new perspective on social and legal matters and encouraged a more rights-based jurisprudence than had been expected.[36]

One of the most striking changes of the early 1990s has been the diminution in the number of cases actually accepted by the Supreme Court for oral argument and disposal by written opinion. From a regular 150 or so in the early 1980s, the 1991 Term dealt with only 107. There are several reasons for this. Undoubtedly the most important is that the Reagan judges in the lower courts are now handing down judgements which an increasingly conservative Supreme Court does not wish to disturb. Since *certiorari* is granted normally in order to reverse the lower court, an increased consonance between the levels results in fewer writs being granted. Additionally, a procedurally conservative Supreme Court will, at the margin, tend not to take cases rather than otherwise and to defer to state courts rather than challenge them. It looks, therefore, as though there has been a clear Reagan legacy.

There is little doubt that the Court's jurisprudence has shifted since the 1970s, although the 'rootless activism' which characterized those years has certainly not given way to a new principled self-restraint.[37] By extending the focus into the Bush presidency, two points may be made. The first draws attention to the development of a centrist bloc of three Justices whose conservatism is essentially procedural and whose impact is therefore reinforcing rather than reforming. In every case in which Justices O'Connor, Kennedy and Souter voted together in the 1991 Term, they were in the majority. Their jurisprudence was procedurally conservative in essence as they consciously tried to limit themselves to the narrowest of questions and seek to adapt past precedents to current debates. This is most obviously seen in the 1992 abortion case when the three explicitly drew attention to the importance of assuming that *Roe* v. *Wade* was the controlling precedent. Although the right to an abortion may have been cut back, its theoretical existence was reaffirmed.[38]

The second point is that power in Washington, especially in the latter half of the 1980s, was divided between a Republican executive and a Democratic controlled legislature. One consequence of this was the failure to nominate Robert Bork to the Supreme Court. There were special factors at work here, most obviously the peculiarly high profile nature of the candidate himself and the shift of political authority following the Iran–Contra affair and the Democrats regaining the Senate.[39]

But of greater significance was the action of Congress over civil rights bills. The examples of increased substantive conservatism outlined above have to be seen in the context of the 1991 Civil Rights Act. This major bill reversed parts of no less than eight Supreme Court decisions and fundamentally degutted the new conservatism of the late 1980s.

The evidence in the United States, therefore, must be read two ways. On the one hand, the ability of President Reagan to nominate so many individuals to the federal courts has indeed produced a jurisprudence which is not entirely consistent but which is unquestionably conservative in some senses of that adjective. On the other hand, the American people elected to the Congress representatives who, in 1987, rejected the most articulate and well-known conservative lawyer as a Justice and, in 1991, passed a Civil Rights Act which undid what the conservative supporters of the new Court thought it had wrought.

In the United Kingdom, attention must be given both to the rulings of the courts and to the political process itself which, through the sovereignty of parliament, in fact controls the basic contours of constitutional change. The Judicial Committee of the House of Lords had increased its profile in the 1970s and its activism had begun to generate a new interest in its judgements from political scientists as well as from lawyers.[40] In the 1980s, however, this surge of judicial power seemed to abate. A cynic might argue that John Griffith's contention that Law Lords are certainly conservative and probably Conservative was supported by the differential degree of activism occurring during the years of Labour Governments (1974–79) and Conservative Governments (1979–).[41]

While the Judicial Committee is indeed the nearest equivalent to a Supreme Court in the United Kingdom, it was the supranational European Courts which made the greatest impact on British rights in the 1980s. Of the first fourteen cases dealt with by the Court of Human Rights twelve went against the United Kingdom, many on important issues. Their decisions are not strictly relevant for my concerns, because I am interested in specifically British institutions, but they draw attention not only to the obvious fact that the final resolution of many constitutional questions involving the proper relations between state and individual has now shifted from London to Luxembourg and Strasbourg but also to the critical impact on the British Constitution caused by membership of the European Communities.

Constitutional change in the 1980s was considerable in two areas. The Single European Act and the subsequent argumentations over Britain's place in the Europe of the 1990s was an ongoing saga and one which unquestionably had profound effects on the Constitution itself. The second area of change was the relationship between the central government and the local authorities. A series of government policies laid additional statutory obligations upon the local authorities while at the same time establishing ceilings upon expenditure and taxing levels. The result was to reduce markedly the area of autonomy left to local government and to increase both centralization and homogenization of local services. The dominant strain of conservatism here was clearly nationalist rather than populist, even though the rhetoric of the Thatcher government in many other areas stressed an extension of choice, of private ownership and the market. In many areas, the authority of the state, especially when represented by nationalized industries, was reduced, but the privatized alternatives did not appear to be any more subject to popular pressure than their state-centred predecessors.

One issue which had been much publicized in the 1970s, a Bill of Rights, rumbled on and the House of Lords addressed itself to the question on more than one occasion.[43] But there was little passion or commitment from the government, without which there was little chance of progress, and back-benchers, too, had other priorities. By the end of the decade, the question of Britain's future relationship with Europe advanced onto the centre of the agenda, dividing the Conservative party and ultimately becoming one factor in the defeat of Mrs Thatcher. The dispute epitomized the conflict within conservatism. On the one hand, the economic conservatives and the procedural conservatives saw a necessity in greater integration and Britain playing a major role at the centre of Europe. The social conservatives and the nationalists, however, saw closer union as likely to weaken the autonomy of the United Kingdom and as a trojan horse for liberal, state interfering policies like the Social Charter.

It is thus difficult to evaluate the extent to which constitutional change in the United Kingdom reacted to conservative pressures. Without the separation of powers, there were no institutional arrangements which pitted conservative views against liberal views, as to some extent there had been in the United States; but, at the same time, the parties – more especially the Conservative Party – struggled to contain essentially irreconcilable visions of the country's future and, on occasions, very different conceptions of the state's role in the domestic sphere. This is hardly unexpected because, as I pointed out initially, conservatism is a broad concept under which several approaches, some of which are mutually contradictory, coexist.

That does not make the United Kingdom different from the United States, where the same ideological differences existed, although perhaps not in the same proportions. What *is* different is the institutional structure in which the forces play out. The independent court system in the United States, despite the British courts' increased politicization, are major players in the game of constitutional politics and become the primary focus of groups wishing to alter the Constitution. In the United Kingdom, by contrast, the parties, trying to remain united as far as possible, are the vehicles for the projection of new ideas about the Constitution. The Conservative Party expressed part of its conservatism by a studied lack of concern for constitutional matters *per se*, except when the European Communities became involved, although the consequences of policy decisions certainly adjusted the distribution of power and resources within the country in a fundamental way. The emasculation of local government autonomy and the privatization of many services traditionally thought of as the prerogative of the state, represent a major change, perhaps a greater change

in terms of the distribution of power than occurred in the United
States in the same period.

V

This overview of judicial and constitutional politics has of necessity been broad brushed. The advantage of this approach is that
it sharpens the differentiating lines; the disadvantage is that the
focus becomes sharper than the fuzziness of reality should allow.
What is striking ultimately is the significance of institutions. This
can be seen in two ways. First, and most obviously, the structure
of government grants the courts in the two countries quite different powers and roles on constitutional matters, just as it also es-
tablishes different powers for the legislatures and executives. Not
surprisingly, therefore, the locus in which disputes about constitutional arrangements and constitutional rights took place differed.
Since Constitutions are not neutral in respect of apportioning power,
political actors naturally seek to adapt or alter constitutions to
advance their own interests, whether the long-term ones of con-
solidating political advantage or the shorter-term ones of influencing specific public policy issues. Hence, one central variable must
be the power holders themselves. In the United Kingdom, the
Conservative Party was not restrained by the division of powers,
the separation of powers, or a supreme Constitution interpreted by
an independent Supreme Court.

A parliamentary system centralizes the locus of decision-making
and the dynamics of constitutional development therefore reflect
the partisan battles of the parliamentrary process. Throughout the
1980s, the Conservative Party held assured, and sometimes, large
parliamentary majorities and so much of the debate about constitutional reform which had been predicated in the 1970s on the
need to constrain governments died away in the face of a Conservative Party unconcern for weakening government authority.
Being in power increased the use of powers. Indeed, many of the
changes (most notably those involving relations with local government) enhanced the authority of the central government; but the
driving force was policy interests not constitutional philosophy. In
a federal system practising a genuine separation of powers, by
contrast, there were always places which could, and did, challenge
the policies and preferences of the conservative coalition that backed

President Reagan. This can be seen in the states themselves, in the Congress and, to some extent, in the Supreme Court, at least in the early 1980s.

Such a conclusion is unexceptionable, indeed to be expected. Perhaps more interesting is the different mix of ideas and emphases that went together to produce the blends of conservatism in the two countries. It is essential to see conservatism as a coalition or a blend; in neither country was it a single coherent philosophy. In the United States the conflict between the substantive and procedural strands of conservatism were manifestly evident. The populist tradition was a strong force behind President Reagan's concern to rewrite the Constitution in order to authorize specific policy positions which he held. But he was only marginally successful, because the philosophical support for a Constitution which stands above the political fray and provides a defence against the winds of popular passion were strong. In the United Kingdom, this particular strand of populism was weak, for it ran aground on the conservative belief that conscious constitutional change is retrograde. However, since the workings of the political system depend so much upon parliamentary forces, some constitutional changes did take place (as a result of membership of the European Communities and as a result of institutional changes designed for very instrumental purposes), but they did not take place in a context of philosophical discussion about the Constitution. While the leaders of the two countries claimed to be conservative, their understanding and application of that description differed. Nowhere, perhaps, is this difference of perception more obvious than in the realm of constitutional and judicial politics.

Notes

1   See Richard Hodder-Williams, 'Courts of last resort', in Richard Hodder-Williams & James Ceaser (eds), *Politics in Britain and the United States: Comparative Perspectives* (Durham, NC, Duke University Press, 1986), pp. 142–72.

2   A view much beloved of Margaret Thatcher in her public prouncements of the early 1980s.

3   Michael Oakeshott, 'On being a conservative', in his *Rationalism in Politics, and Other Essays* (London, Methuen, 1962), pp. 168–96.

4   See Richard A. Davis, *Proposed Amendments to the Constitution* ... (Congressional Research Service, Report No. 85–36 Gov, 1985).

5   *Roe v. Wade*, 410 US 113 (1973).

6 *Abington School District* v. *Schempp*, 374 US 203 (1963).

7 *Voluntary School Prayer Constitutional Amendment: Hearings* (Serial No. J–98–34, 1983), pp. 5–7.

8 A variety of public occasions offered President Reagan the chance to add to the formal words of welcome or congratulation an observation about the sanctity of life and an implicit criticism of the abortion decisions. See *The Public Papers of the President of the United States* (Washington, Government Printer, various), *passim*.

9 Max Lerner, 'Constitutions and Court as symbol', *Yale Law Journal*, 46 (1945–46), 1294. See also Larry R. Baas, 'The Constitution as symbol: patterns of meaning', *American Politics Quarterly*, 8 (1980), 237–56.

10 Richard Hodder-Williams, 'Making the Constitution's meaning fit for the 1980s', in Joseph Smith (ed.), *The American Constitution: the First 200 Years 1787–1987* (Exeter, Exeter University Publications, 1987), pp. 97–110.

11 William G. Ross, 'The functions, roles and duties of the Senate in the Supreme Court appointment process', *William and Mary Law Review*, 28 (1986–87), 633–82; Charles L. Black jnr., 'A note on senatorial consideration of Supreme Court nominees', *Yale Law Journal*, 79 (1969–70), 657–64.

12 *Goldman* v. *Weinberger*, 475 US 503 (1986).

13 National Defense Authorization Act, Public Law No. 99–435, 100 Stat. 2467 (1988).

14 David B. Magleby, *Direct legislation: voting on ballot propositions in the United States* (Baltimore, John Hopkins University Press, 1984); Thomas E. Cronin, *Direct democracy: the politics of initiative, referendum and recall* (Cambridge, Mass., Harvard University Press, 1989).

15 See, for example, the annual articles by Donald Shell in *Parliamentary Affairs* entitled 'The Constitution in 19. . '.

16 See, for example, John Herbert McCluskey, 'Importing American rights', in R. C. Simmons (ed.), *The United States Constitution: the First 200 Years* (Manchester, Manchester University Press, 1989), pp. 1–15.

17 *Bromley* v. *GLC* (1983) 1 AC 768; (1982) All ER 129.

18 See Carol Harlow and Richard Rawlings, *Pressure Through Law* (London, Routledge, 1992).

19 Maurice Sunkin, 'What is happening to applications for judicial review', *Modern Law Review*, 50 (1987), 432–67.

20 Lord Hailsham, *Elective Dictatorship* (London, BBC Publications, 1976).

21 See the Republican Platform, reprinted in *Congressional Quarterly Weekly*, 30 (1986), 2034 *et seq.*

22 Stephen C. Halpern & Charles Lamb (eds), *Supreme Court Activism and Restraint* (Lexington, Mass., Lexington Books, 1982).

23 Norman Reddich, 'A Black–Harlan dialogue on due process and equal protection: heard in Heaven and dedicated to Robert B. McKay', *New York University Law Review*, L. 1975, pp. 20–46.

24 Arthur M. Schlesinger jnr, *The Imperial Presidency*, new edn (Boston, Mass., Houghton Mifflin, 1989).

25 David O'Brien, *Judicial Roulette: Report of the Twentieth Century Fund Task Force on Judicial Selection* (New York, Priority Press, 1988); Herman Schwartz, *Packing the Courts: the Conservative Campaign to Rewrite the Constitution* (New York, Scribner's, 1988).

26 Joel L. Selog, 'The Reagan Justice Department and civil rights: what went wrong', *University of Illinois Law Review* (1985), pp. 785–835.

27 Edwin Meese III, 'The Attorney-General's view of the Supreme Court: towards a jurisprudence of original intention', *Public Administration Review*, 45 (1985), 701–704.

28 Lincoln Caplan, *The Tenth Justice: the Solicitor-General and the rule of law* (New York, Knopf, 1987).

29 Sidney Blumenthal, *The Rise of the Counter-Establishment: from Conservative Ideology to Political Power* (New York, Random House, 1986).

30 *Judicial Appointments: the Lord Chancellor's Policies and Procedures* (Lord Chancellor's Department, November 1990).

31 Hugo Young, 'The man who did not become a judge', *Sunday Times*, 28 June 1981.

32 Stephen Knight, *The Brotherhood: the Secret World of Freemasons* (Panther Books, 1985).

33 Louis Blom-Cooper, 'Major reshuffle on the bench', *Financial Times*, 30 September 1991.

34 Jeffrey L. Jowell & J. P. B. W. McAuslan (eds), *Lord Denning: the Judge and the Law* (London, Sweet & Maxwell, 1984).

35 Peter Hennessy, *Whitehall* (London, Fontana, 1990).

36 See, for example, 'All the President's men: a study of Ronald Reagan's appointments to the US Courts of Appeals', *Columbia Law review*, 87 (1986–87), 766–93.

37 Vincent Blasi (ed.), *The Burger Court: the Counter-revolution that Wasn't* (New Haven, Conn., Yale University Press, 1983).

38 *Planned Parenthood of Southeastern Pennsylvania* v. *Casey* (1992).

39 See Ethan Bronner, *Battle for Justice: how the Bork Nomination Shook America* (New York, Norton, 1989); Stephen M. Griffin, 'Politics and the Supreme Court: the case of the Bork nomination', *Journal of Law and Politics*, 5 (1988–89), 551–604; Richard Hodder-Williams, 'The strange story of Judge Bork and a vacancy on the Supreme Court', *Political Studies*, 36 (1988), 613–37.

40 Alan Paterson, *The Law Lords* (London, Macmillan, 1982); Michael J. Elliott, 'The role of law', in Henry Drucker *et al.*, *Developments in British Politics* (London, Macmillan, 1987), 266–78.

41 J. A. G. Griffith, *The Politics of the Judiciary*, 3rd edn (London, Fontana, 1985).

42 See Malcolm Grant, 'The role of the courts in central-local relations', in M. Goldsmith (ed.), *New Research in Central-Local Relations* (Gower, 1986), pp. 191–204.

43 The House of Lords debated a Human Rights and Fundamental Freedoms Bill for five days during the 1985–86 session and returned again to this issue in March 1988 (especially Lord Jenkins of Hillhead) and May 1990 (Lord Irvine of Lairg). The Commons held their first full day debate on the Constitution for forty years on 17 May 1991; it was, of course, a Friday.

Culture, religion and public morality

The 1970s and 1980s saw the emergence in the United States and the United Kingdom of a new style of right-wing politics under Reagan and Thatcher.[1] Although there clearly were continuities with the politics of the preceding decade, conservatism in both countries exhibited some sharp discontinuities with the immediate past at the level of ideology, of organization and support. One feature of the new conservatism which attracted much attention in both the United Kingdom and the United States was the extent to which its agenda was broader than the traditional right-wing concerns of foreign policy and the economy. Although anti-communism and the promotion of free market policies were central themes of the resurgent conservatism, there was also an attempt to alter the underlying cultural values of the two societies. It is the purpose of this chapter to explore this dimension of the new conservativism in the two countries and to show that, while there were some parallels, there were also significant differences.

In the United States the emphasis on the moral content of conservativism was extremely strong at the beginning of the Reagan presidency as political conservatives sought to weld conservative religious groups into a new alliance of the right.[2] Political entrepreneurs such as Paul Weyrich (of the Committee for the Survival of a Free Congress) and Howard Phillips (of Conservative Caucus) saw social and moral issues as the key to bringing religious Americans who shared their values into a coalition. Such a coalition, they hoped, could tap new sources of electoral support, especially the increasingly self-confident evangelical community.

The effort to broaden the traditional sources of support for political conservativism would not have been possible had there not already been a degree of mobilization among American evangelicals and fundamentalists.[3] This mobilization had been occurring since 1945 as individuals such as Carl McIntire and Billy James Hargis formed organizations to draw attention to the dangers of communism. In the 1960s theologically conservative Christians became increasingly concerned about the clash of values between their own biblically based morality and the secular liberalism which they saw inspiring a range of governmental policies and legal decisions. In particular they objected to Supreme Court judgements restricting religious observance in schools.[4]

The new Christian right which emerged in the 1970s drew on the strong religious sub-culture of Protestant fundamentalism which had been concentrated in the south and west but which was not entirely confined to those regions.[5] Fundamentalism, it should be noted, had become more assertive in the post-war period as a result both of rising numbers of adherents and a new determination to maintain its distinctive position in theological debates. It had become less oriented towards denominational exclusiveness and more interested in broad appeals across denominations. It had also become interested in what one authority has called special purpose groups focused on cultural and lifestyle issues as well as on defending such special concerns of fundamentalists as the burgeoning Christians' schools.[6] The result by the 1970s was a network of overlapping and complementary (but not identical) pressure groups with an agenda which focused on such issues as abortion, homosexuality, sex education, prayer in schools, creation science and obscenity; and there emerged a movement which challenged many of the existing assumptions about the separation of church and state.

Some of the groups in this network – most notably Rev. Jerry Falwell's and Tim LaHaye's Moral Majority Inc which became prominent in the 1980 election – attracted a good deal of publicity. But there were many others including the National Federation for Decency, Christian Voice (founded by Robert Grant and organized for a time by Gary Jarmin) and Religious Roundtable. Although the Moral Majority ceased to exist in 1989 and was replaced by the Liberty Foundation, the political mobilization of conservative Christians has continued. In the same year as the Moral Majority closed its operations, Rev. Pat Robertson, a televangelist with strong links to the charismatic community, founded the Christian

Coalition. This group – which claimed 250,000 members in 49 states – had a distinctive agenda that was to be promoted by electing 'pro-family Christians to Congress and transforming the ideology of the Republican Party'.[7]

The demise of the Moral Majority and the advent of Robertson's group underlines the fact that the new Christian right is not itself monolithic and that its organizations have exhibited a variety of tactics and styles. As with the more secular right there has been some discontinuity as groups have changed their names and priorities. Some of the discontinuity has been the result of changing financial strength. For example, direct-mail entrepreneur Richard Viguerie experienced financial difficulties over the 1980s which caused a restriction of his political and publishing activities. Nevertheless the mobilization of the new Christian right has continued to be politically significant. Most dramatically it appears – at least temporarily – to have succeeded in giving the Republican Party a morally conservative platform and associating it with a range of causes on which the GOP might hitherto have been neutral. In 1992 at its Houston Texas Convention the Republican Party made the support of 'family values' one of the principal features of its appeal to the electorate – a move which showed not merely the power of the religious right within the Republican Party but also how important cultural divisions had become in American politics. Not surprisingly the Democrats attacked the Republican emphasis on family values as a hypocritical attempt to divert electoral attention from the 'real' issues of the campaign which revolved around the economy. Democrats were also able to exploit President Bush's 1992 veto of the Family Leave Act as further evidence of the hollow nature of his commitment to family values. Many observers attributed the Republican defeat in the presidential election of 1992 precisely to the willingness of George Bush to allow his party to be captured by the religious right.

It is worth emphasizing that the continuing strength of the moral right was not entirely predictable. In the 1980s there was much scepticism about the extent to which religious and quasi-religious movements would remain an important force in American politics. However, the power of these groups was acknowledged by the Republican Party which felt obliged to accommodate them as a distinct force within its ranks and pay attention to their demands in its platform.[8] And in the period after the 1992 elections it seems highly likely that the Republicans will experience great internal disharmony as 'moderates' and religious right activists struggle for control of the party.

Yet the religious and moral conservative vote in many ways remains unpredictable. In the 1988 presidential election campaign, there was much speculation about what would be the impact of a well-financed campaign by Pat Robertson. As it turned out his support was limited to the charismatic groups and did not unite the whole conservative Christian community.[9] In the 1992 presidential election, by contrast, there was some speculation on whether the Democratic nominee Bill Clinton (a Baptist from a southern state) could make inroads into the evangelical vote, despite the Republican Party's heavy emphasis on family issues.[10] The Clinton–Gore ticket proved extremely effective in weakening the Republican hold on the south in 1992 – a hold which had owed a good deal to the influence of religion. The Democrats took Arkansas, Georgia, Louisiana, Kentucky, Tennessee and West Virginia. Even though Bush appears to have retained the support of a small majority of white Protestants and an overwhelming majority of white born-again Christians in the South, his support among all whites in the south stopped short of 50 per cent.[11]

In the United Kingdom the new conservativism which evolved in the mid-1970s was also anxious to change the country's cultural values. But the Conservative Party after 1975 concentrated much more heavily on encouraging enterprise and entrepreneurialism and on discouraging dependency on the state than on calling for a return to biblical standards of morality. It is true that Mrs Thatcher tried on occasion to signal her own distaste for permissiveness and her support for traditional morality. She even preached a sermon to the General Assembly of the Church of Scotland on these themes, a sermon which was largely written by Professor Brian Griffiths who at one stage headed her policy unit and was an evangelical.[12] But the rhetorical invocation of religious morality and 'Victorian values' did not easily translate into public policy, although clearly it may have made the handling of some issues (such as the Aids campaign) more sensitive under her premiership.[13] Although government policy on Aids was not substantially affected by Mrs Thatcher's personal opinions on the subject, it was clear in 1991 that a minority group within the Conservative Party – the Conservative Family Campaign – was willing to challenge liberal opinion on attitudes to Aids victims. Thus when a UK Declaration of Rights of People with HIV and Aids was drawn up with cross-party and religious support, the Conservative Family Campaign responded with its own HIV – infected citizens charter of responsibilities – a move which caused the resignation from the group of Jerry Hayes, one of the CFC's thirty MPs.[14]

The issue of how to deal with the problem of Aids underlines the fact that there were important moral issues on the British public agenda as in the United States. The British laws on abortion and homosexuality, which had both been liberalized in the 1960's, generated opposition; and there was a certain amount of organized opposition to 'unnecessary' sex and violence in the media. Some of the campaigns were essentially single issue groups; others engaged in a more general campaign to restore moral decency. The major contrast with the United States, however, is that these groups never aligned with the Conservative Party which for its part kept a healthy distance from such causes, largely because there was no substantial middle-class elite support for highlighting these issues. Of course individual MPs (of all parties) were sympathetic to some of the campaigns and in some cases the Conservative Government was happy to allow them to make the running on moral issues. This was certainly true of the abortion issue where a Liberal MP David Alton took up the issue of abortion law reform thus allowing Conservative MPs to vote whichever way they chose without danger of damaging the government. In the United States the new conservatism saw such moral and social issues as the political glue which would bind conservative Christians in a new alignment with the Republican Party.

Before looking in more detail at the moral and cultural dimension on contemporary conservatism on both sides of the Atlantic, it is important to note two important general differences between the political systems of the United States and the United Kingdom. The first relates to the position of religion in the two societies; the second to the role of pressure groups in the policy process.

The position of religion in the United Kingdom and the United States

England has an established national church – the Church of England. Twenty-six bishops of the Church of England, appointed by the monarch, sit in the House of Lords representing the theoretical religious unity of the country. In fact the United Kingdom of Great Britain and Northern Ireland exhibits much more denominational pluralism than this formal picture suggests. In Scotland the established church is Presbyterian; and in Wales and Northern Ireland the Anglican Church (known as the Church in Wales and the Church of Ireland respectively) is the denomination of a minority. In addition to substantial numbers of non-conformists and Roman Catholics, immigration has brought to the United Kingdom adherents of quite different religious traditions from the Judaeo-Christian – Moslems, Buddhists, Sikhs and Hindus. Indeed by 1987 the number of practising Anglicans (1.6 million) was only slightly larger than the number of practising Muslims, Sikhs and Hindus (1.3 million).

Internal debates have recently threatened the position of the Church of England in British society. The decision to admit women as priests was taken in 1992 after a long period of debate; but opposition to the move remained strong and there is the possibility that the Church will lose a large number of adherents on the issue, or even suffer a schism. The problems of the Church of England raised the issue of disestablishment and the extent to which a Church which had divided could claim to be a national church. The separation of the Prince and Princess of Wales at the end of 1992 further focused attention on the established Church. For, if the monarch were not formally head of a church which did not believe in divorce, the heir to the throne could legally end an unhappy marriage.

The heightened attention given to the Church of England in 1992 should not, however, be interpreted as evidence that religion plays a major role in British society. The United Kingdom is a highly secular society with a declining level of church attendance, at least among trinitarian churches, over the period of the 1970s and 1980s.[15] If the public pronouncements of the Church of England in particular inevitably receive publicity, there is little evidence that they carry much weight with the general public. According to the Social Trends survey of 1990, in 1970 the Church of England had 2.2 million active members; by 1987 it was down to 1.6 million, only slightly ahead of the Presbyterians (1.3 million), and easily outnumbered by practising Roman Catholics (2.1 million). The number of active members of non-Trinitarian religions, half a million in 1970, had risen to 1.6 million by 1987.

Politically, the Conservative Party and the established Church have grown progressively further apart since the war. In the 1980s there was a near divorce. The churches were increasingly opposed to the policies of Mrs Thatcher's governments which emphasized the virtues of capitalism and pursued policies of public expenditure cuts which in the view of the church leaders fell most heavily on the weakest sections of British society. Certainly the bishops, although not great participants in House of Lords debates, voiced strong opposition to government policy over the 1980s.[16] Hostility between the Church of England and the Conservative Party was particularly evident when the Church of England published its report *Faith in the City* in 1985 which blamed the government for an approach to social policy which ignored injustice and inequality in Britain's deprived inner-city areas.[17] The Church of England also found itself at odds with the Thatcher government on the 1984/5 miners' strike and educational changes; and it particularly antagonized Mrs Thatcher by resisting attempts to celebrate victory in the 1982 Falklands War in unambiguously patriotic terms.

Thus the relationship between religious opinion and the Conservative Party under Mrs Thatcher's leadership was more one of conflict than of co-operation. This is not to say that the leaders of Britain's churches were united in their political support for any party or ideology; rather that they revealed an increasingly solid opposition to the new conservatism's conjunction of free market economic and social policies and a robust nationalism.

Religion occupies a much more significant place in American than in British social and political life. The First Amendment to the Constitution prohibits the establishment of any church at the federal level and, although the population of the United States was originally overwhelmingly Protestant, the American religious scene is now one of tremendous diversity. This diversity is partly the result of immigration which brought large number of Roman Catholics, Orthodox Christians and Jews to the United States and which more recently has brought a substantial Asian population whose religious affiliations include Buddhism and Shintoism. It is partly also a result of America's generation of new sects – such as the Church of Jesus Christ of Latter Day Saints or Mormons – and

Table 4.1 *Membership of US Religious bodies, 1985*

	Membership (000s)	Churches
Roman Catholic	52,655	24,251
Southern Baptist Convention	14,477	36,898
United Methodist Church	9,267	37,990
Jews	5,835	3,416
National Baptist Convention USA Inc	5,500	n.a.
Mormons	3,860	8,396
Church of God in Christ	3,710	9,982
Presbyterian Church (USA)	3,048	11,554
Lutheran Church in America	2,898	5,817
Episcopal Church	2,739	7,274
National Baptist Convention of America	2,669	n.a.
Lutheran Church–Missouri Synod	2,638	5,876
American Lutheran Church	2,332	4,940
African Methodist Episcopal Church	2,210	6,200
Assemblies of God	2,083	10,761
Greek Orthodox Archdiocese of North and South America	1,950	n.a.
United Church of Christ	1,684	6,408
American Baptist Churches in the USA	1,660	5,814
Churches of Christ	1,604	13,150
African Methodist Episcopal Zion Church	1,202	6,057
Baptist Bible Fellowships International	1,406	3,449
Christian Church (Disciples of Christ)	1,116	4,214
Christian Churches and Churches of Christ	1,051	5,487
Jehovah's Witnesses	730	8,220
Christian Methodist Episcopal Church	719	2,340

partly the result of splits and fissures within denominations. Table 1 shows the breakdown of Christian and Jewish religious groups within the United States in 1985 and the number of churches affiliated to each denomination.

While these figures show the formal strength of the evangelical community in 1985, a figure revealed by the Gallup organization at the time of Jimmy Carter's election to the presidency in 1976 (which was itself an indication of the increasing respectability of evangelicals) underlined its significance: Gallup found one in three

Americans claiming to be 'born again' – an experience which is one of the defining characteristics of an evangelical.

In the United Kingdom, the political stance of the churches has become solidly liberal and reformist in ideological terms, although this does not necessarily translate directly into party politics. The British Conservative Party is therefore highly unlikely to want to expand the influence of religion in British politics since it would be an influence that would almost certainly be directed against its own policies. Of course there might still be a constituency, as Martin Durham has noted, for a populist campaign on moral and cultural issues; but any attempt by the Conservative Party to tap this constituency risks engaging church leaders whose intervention might be damaging politically among the population at large.[18]

In the United States, by contrast, there is a much greater diversity of theological opinions about politics. The social gospel is not preached by all denominations and for some sects the experience of wealth is itself a sign of blessing. For some churches the primary issue is the extent to which social and other policies of a party conform to their own fundamentalist morality. Thus although some American church leaders might have disapproved of Ronald Reagan and Republican policies, there was a great deal of disagreement among the churches and within them on policy issues. (Indeed there were severe conflicts within the Southern Baptist Convention over the 1980s as a result of the fundamentalist 'capture' of that organization and the marginalization of its moderates.[19]) Individual pastors are free to preach their own messages, and to respond to their own congregations in a way which is quite different from the more institutionalized religious structure in the United Kingdom.

Pressure groups, parties and single issues

The second important structural point to note about the difference between Britain and the United States relates to the role of pressure groups. In Britain the new conservatism gained its successes in the mid-1970s primarily by influencing the Conservative Party, although as is noted in the essay by Tim Hames in this book (Chapter 10) the United Kingdom also experienced a surge of think tank activity, albeit on a minor scale by comparison with that of the United States.

In the United States, the new conservative movement emerged primarily through pressure groups and political action committees (PACs), think-tanks and policy institutes. Moreover, the conservative movement maintained a sense of separate identity from the Republican party even though it came to influence it dramatically.

Pressure groups in the United States obviously exhibit considerable organizational diversity. They may be small and poorly resourced; or they may be well-funded and large. Since 1971 pressure groups through their PACs have been able to exert a good deal of muscle in the political process through their ability to make direct donations to political campaigns. The influence of PACs has been enhanced by changes in the relationship between candidates for office and political parties. The highly decentralized nature of American campaigns has made the resources of pressure groups – in terms of money, volunteers and facilities – more important to political candidates who essentially need to be able to organize their own campaigns.[20] Groups backing religious, moral or cultural causes were therefore able to employ a range of strategies to promote their ideas. They could become directly associated with a candidate or they could enter the campaign as an independent PAC. Apart from direct political involvement, they could through their charitable tax exempt wings provide 'educational' material to make their views known.[21] Not merely therefore was the American political system a highly receptive environment for group activity – with multiple points of access; it was also an environment in which politicians and pressure groups developed mutual interests.

Thus far this essay has highlighted some of the differences between the moral and cultural dimension of the new conservatism on the two sides of the Atlantic in part to offset the danger of seeing the evolution of British conservatism after 1975 as a reflection of American developments. Nevertheless there were important parallels and points of contact on moral and cultural issues. In order to draw these parallels out it is necessary to look at the evolution of the conservative movement in both countries a little more closely.

The components of American conservatism

If one had taken a snapshot of the American conservative movement in 1980 one would have seen an entity with a number of distinct strands. Three will be highlighted here. First there were the 'neo-conservatives' – themselves a disparate group of individual academics, journalists and social critics – operating primarily at the level of intellectual argument.

Secondly there were the more practical operatives of the new right. They were the people who helped found or expand policy institutes and think tanks such as the Heritage Foundation and the American Enterprise Institute, political consultants specializing in political polling and the newer techniques of money raising through direct mail (such as Richard Viguerie) and conservative activists such as Paul Weyrich who were skilled at putting together coalitions of like-minded groups and individuals through such groups as the Library Court Group and his own Committee for the Survival of a Free Congress.

Thirdly there were the moral and religious groups such as Moral Majority and the Right to Life Movement. Mention should also be made here of the power of the 'televangelists' whose television ministries had produced personal power for such individuals as Jerry Falwell, Pat Robertson and James Robison as well as multifaceted business enterprises. These religious television networks were especially significant in the south of the United States but their influence was not confined to that region.[22]

In addition mention must be made of the Republican Party itself which in the 1976–80 period experienced a major revival of political and organizational strength under the party chairmanship of Bill Brock as well as benefiting from the conservative resurgence. However, because the conservative movement and the GOP were not identical, Republican officials were necessarily aware of the tensions generated by the operation of new forces within Republican Party ranks.

Although these strands in the conservative movement were all concerned with moral and cultural issues to some extent, their approach to these issues varied significantly.

The 'neo-conservatives', although they did not have a common viewpoint, did share a critical concern with the trends exhibited by American society and culture during the 1960s and early 1970s. In particular they were concerned that an unrepresentative liberal elite had captured key institutions, especially the media and the universities, and were promulgating values which would ultimately undermine the fabric of the nation. The neo-conservatives were particularly concerned about the breakdown of family values, of the work ethic and morality in a society which many of them saw as increasingly individualistic and hedonistic. It should be noted that the defence of religious values and indeed of the institution of the family was thus to a large extent functional, although individual neo-conservatives of course might also be committed religious believers.[23]

Perhaps the most important point about the 'neo-conservative' critique of liberalism was the extent to which it allowed the conservatives to seize the intellectual initiative. Although the positions of individual neo-conservatives such as Irving Kristol, Jeane Kirkpatrick, Nathan Glazer and Norman Podhoretz differed on some issues, they created the impression of an onslaught on both the 'adversary culture' of the 1960s with its hostility to American values in foreign policy and to the free economy. They produced a coherent critique of the federal government's ambitious anti-poverty measures of the 1960s. In addition to their general scepticism about the efficacy of welfare policies they were also sceptical about such domestic policies as affirmatives action and busing and some were opposed to new social movements such as feminism.

From the point of view of the broader American right the neo-conservatives were important on a number of levels. They provided a useful bridge between the world of academe and the world of practical politics since, although at home in the university environment, they could also turn their hands to political polemic. They were able to construct highly readable defences of the capitalist system and of the American style of democracy as well as debate the specifics of complex social issues. The arguments put forward both in such books as Irving Kristol's *Two Cheers for Capitalism* and in journals such as *Commentary* and *Public Interest* provided a new legitimacy for conservatives and meshed well with other intellectual developments which were working against the left in the course of the 1970s.

The 'neo-conservatives' were not entirely divorced from practical politics, partly because their own academic disciplines involved the analysis of public policy issues and partly because of their associations with think tanks (such as the American Enterprise Institute) and policy institutes which helped to spread the conservative message through the 1970s and 1980s.

The second strand in the conservative movement – the political operatives of the new conservatism – were much more organizational men and practical politicians than men of ideas. Men like Paul Weyrich of the Committee for the Survival of a Free Congress and Howard Phillips of Conservative Caucus were good examples of this element in the conservative movement. They were distinct from the neo-conservatives and the regular Republicans in two ways. First, they tended to be ideological purists unsympathetic to open-ended debate and political compromise. Secondly their mission was to get *conservative* politicians elected and *conservative* policies enacted. This agenda took precedence over partisan loyalty to the Republican Party which some conservatives such as Richard Viguerie openly despised. Although most of these new right conservatives regarded Ronald Reagan as a hero and admired some other Republicans such as Jack Kemp, there was little regard in these quarters for George Bush. Social or family issues were central to the agenda of this group. Their insistence on such themes as school prayer and hostility to abortion was the result of their belief that not merely were these issues important in their own right; they were also issues which could be used to fragment the Democratic coalition which had been formed in the 1930s. In particular they believed that the Democratic party in the 1960s, in adopting policies geared towards minority politics, had neglected the interests of second or third generation white ethnics who were upwardly mobile and whose moral values were conservative. By highlighting these issues the new conservatism hoped to be able to break down the New Deal majority even further and to make a much more popularly based Republican Party.

It is not possible here to describe each and every one of the 'social issues' in detail. Mention has already been made of the key issues of abortion, school prayer, busing, gay rights, textbook censorship and obscene publications. These issues spawned their own pressure groups such as the Rev. Donald Wildmon's American Family Coalition and the various right-to-life groups as well as generating opposition groups. However, in a publication which emphasized the crucial nature of cultural values to contemporary American politics, the Institute for Cultural Conservatism (an offshoot of Weyrich's Free Congress Research and Education Foundation) explored a new national agenda which in addition to themes of the family, education and welfare addressed economics, institutional design, crime and punishment and the environment.

Of the issues which helped mobilize the religious groups into politics and allowed them to make common cause with secular conservatives, abortion was probably the most controversial. Initially this was seen as a Roman Catholic Church issue because of that Church's strong doctrinal opposition to abortion.[24] However the opposition of many fundamentalist churches to abortion strengthened after the *Roe* v *Wade* decision of 1973 and this opposition was reinforced by the religious right's tendency to associate supporters of choice with a range of liberal 'anti-family' values.[25]

On educational issues the new religious right had several causes of concern: the preservation of their own schools, the right to school prayer, opposition to relativistic sex education and a desire to use textbooks which were not in conflict with fundamentalist beliefs especially on the issue of creation.

Several vigorous campaigns were waged around the key issues of the religious right. The impact of these campaigns was, however, patchy. On abortion, of course, an increasingly conservative judiciary narrowed the scope of *Roe* v *Wade* by allowing greater discretion to the states. By 1992 the issue had become highly explosive for the Republican party which found it difficult to retreat from a hardline position even though it seemed likely to lose them votes. Indeed one author has spoken about a Republican 'pro-choice insurgency' after the 1989 *Webster* decision had presented a real threat to abortion rights in the United States.[26] Several constitutional amendments were introduced into Congress to make prayer in school constitutional, although none of these passed. And a case which some thought might validate a moment's silence in schools in fact was overruled by the Supreme Court.[27] A major bill on a range of family related issues launched under Senator Paul Laxalt's name in the 1980s also failed to make headway.

Nevertheless it would be mistake to write off these campaigns. A 1992 survey by People for the American Way (a group which was formed to fight the influence of religion in American political life) showed that censorship in American schools had increased by 50 per cent in the previous year and that the religious right was increasingly fighting the use of school material it deemed objectionable. The group documented 348 incidents in which a parent, a school official or a church group had demanded that classroom or library books be removed and in 41 per cent of the cases the challenge was successful. This process of censorship involved such books as Steinbeck's *Of Mice and Men* and Mark Twain's *Huckleberry Finn*, as well as photographs of Madonna.[28] (The United Kingdom has experienced efforts to restrict the use of teaching materials including the passage of legislation to prevent the sympathetic discussion of homosexual lifestyles in schools.)[29]

This process suggests that even if few concrete legislative changes had been recorded at the federal level over the 1980s and early 1990s, at the state level attitudes had been shifting and turning the intellectual climate in a direction more consonant with the values of the religious right. (It is however worth noting that the Bush administration secured passage of a bill to limit pornography.)

The Republican Party and the new conservatism

The reaction of the regular Republican Party to these developments was complex. On some social issues the party moved to the right quite easily. This seems to have been the case with affirmative action where the 1980 platform came out explicitly against quotas. (The problem returned to haunt President Bush in his 1989–92 administration, however, as the President had to decide whether to veto or sign successive civil rights bills designed to reverse some 1989 Supreme Court decisions on the subject of employment discrimination.[30])

The Republicans had much more difficulty with the Equal Rights Amendment. Both the Republicans and the Democrats had supported the Equal Rights Amendment which had been passed by Congress in 1972. However it then needed to be ratified by a majority of the states. This process stalled in the late 1970s and time ran out in 1982. In the period between 1978 and 1982 there was extensive opposition to ratification both from conservative men and from women (of whom the most notable was Phyllis Schlafly) mobilized around hostility to feminism.[31] However the issue divided the Republican Party deeply at both the national and the state level.

The abortion issue remained an extremely complex one for the Republicans.[32] For the conservative movement this was a litmus-test issue since the constitutional right to an abortion identified in

Roe v *Wade* symbolized an attack on the right's family values and
a perfect example of a style of jurisprudence which was anathema
to them. Key figures in the Republican Party including George
Bush moved to a position of staunch opposition to abortion over
the 1980s; but the results of the 1990 elections suggested to
Republican strategists that the party's earlier embrace of this issue
was not altogether wise.

The 1980s saw new groups becoming active in Republican politics
and the result was not always harmonious. Clashes between new
right and new religious right activists and the regular party organizations became commonplace and affected the Republican
parties in a number of states including Alaska, Georgia, Louisiana
and Alabama. Thus in 1992 John Treen, the Republican Party
Chairman in Jefferson Parish, Louisiana noted the extent to which
Christian Coalition activists (who controlled more than half of the
Louisiana central party committee) were antagonizing 'mainstream'
Republicans.[33] Both the tactics and the message of the Christian
Coalition were bound to be disruptive of party unity. The message
– with its emphasis on the need for America to return to its
Christian roots – would inevitably embarrass large sections of the
Republican Party while the tactics of carefully targeting the GOP's
electoral processes seemed bound to fuel resentment.

The poor Republican showing in the 1992 elections, and especially the loss of the presidency, was directly attributed by many
to the visible influence of the religious right at the 1992 Republican convention. Yet it was not entirely clear how easy it would
be to shift the Republicans back towards the centre ground especially since many of the potential Republican leaders who might
be future presidential candidates would need the right's support
for any bid for the presidency in 1996. By the end of the Bush
presidency the Republicans seemed destined for a period of internal discord and conflict which would make the routine management of the aprty difficult.

The evolution of British conservatism

The path taken by the new conservatism in Britain from the mid-
1970s was very different. The loss of the general election of
February 1974 under Edward Heath's leadership unleashed an
extensive re-examination of the whole direction of post-1945 social

and economic policy. There was initially only a limited cultural and moral content to this new debate. Nevertheless there was some, though it was very different in tone from the American debate. Sir Keith Joseph, in his series of lectures delivered between 1974 and 1975, addressed the issue of national decline and the family. However, his remarks about the relationship between socio-economic class and the birth rate were viewed as sufficiently ill-judged to remove him as a leadership contender. Mrs Thatcher, who in a sense picked up Sir Keith's mantle, was less interested initially in moral and cultural issues than in economic and foreign policy. However, her leadership of the Conservative Party was seen as an opportunity for new groups to exert influence and reverse the trends of the post-war period.

The election of any leader carries with it a certain symbolism. In Mrs Thatcher's case the symbolism was ambiguous. On the one hand there was the evident symbolism of becoming Britain's first woman prime minister. Mrs Thatcher herself liked to claim that this had been achieved without recourse to affirmative action or the women's movement and was the result of individual effort. Feminist critics, apart from regretting Mrs Thatcher's unwilling-ness to promote the cause of women more directly, noted that her life had been made considerably easier by a wealthy husband.

Mrs Thatcher's approach to political and ideological debate on becoming leader in 1975 had been to encourage right-wing think-tanks to move in advance of official Conservative Party policy. Free market and monetarist enquiries flourished as did interest in reconstituting the more traditional base of Conservative theory. Thus in addition to the wealth of material coming from groups such as the Centre for Policy Studies and the Institute of Economic Affairs one finds some individual conservative thinkers such as Roger Scruton putting greater emphasis on notions of race and culture. This paradox, some authors such as Andrew Gamble have argued, is not in fact a parodox at all: a stronger more authori-tarian state is needed for Britain to free up markets and allow greater rein to capitalism.[34]

The stronger emphasis on capitalism than on religion or moral-ity was nicely brought out in the debate about Sunday trading. Here the government in 1986 attempted to impose a revision of the Sunday trading laws to allow shops to open on Sundays. This move was opposed by a coalition of traditionalists who wanted to 'keep Sunday special', the churches and the Labour Party which wanted both to defend the rights of shop-workers and to inflict a defeat on the government. Although the government had imposed a three-line whip, the bill to change the Sunday trading laws was defeated. Yet when pre-existing legal restrictions on Sunday trading broke down in the face of widespread non-observance, and as ambiguous signals came from the European Court of Justice in 1991–92, the government did not lift a finger to defend the law.

One area of policy where the Conservatives have attempted to reintroduce a traditional moral dimension has been education. It is not perhaps surprising that education should be seen as a key area of policy, since as Michael Apple has written:

Education . . . is an arena in which . . . ideological conflicts work themselves out. It is one of the major sites in which different groups with distinct political, economic and cultural visions attempt to define what the socially legitimate means and what the end of a society are to be.[35]

Education in both the United Kingdom and the United States has thus seen debates about such issues as vouchers, educational standards and the content of the curriculum. The organization of British education has undergone major changes in the last decade – most notably those brought about by the Education Act of 1988. Yet education policy has also revealed the conflict in Conservative thought between reliance on market principles and consumer principles and ideas of a return to notions of authority and basics. The thrust of policy since the late 1980s has been to combine both by allowing greater freedom of choice and competition between schools but imposing a national curriculum on schools, emphasizing the basic skills of numeracy and literacy.

Within the context of educational debate there has also been a degree of controversy over the control of sex education and intermittent concern with grounding education in the cultural values of Christianity.

Although a small number of activist groups argued in the 1980s against any kind of sex education in the schools, the major concern within the Conservative Party involved the approach taken to homosexuality.[36] The efforts of some left-leaning local councils (such as the London boroughs of Haringey and Ealing) to present homosexuality in a sympathetic manner in the classroom and to devote council funds to combatting discrimination against homosexuals appeared to many critics on the right as another manifestation of the 'loony left'. The Conservative government had originally granted little to critics who wanted parents to be able to withdraw their children from sex education and had simply emphasized the need for teaching sex education in a 'moral framework'. However, as the debate about family values hit the popular press, the Conservative government made concessions to the right – most notably by accepting a backbench amendment to the 1988 Local Government Act to prevent the promotion of homosexuality or the teaching of its acceptability as a 'pretended family relationship'.[37]

The relationship between religion and education was highlighted in the early 1980s when a Bradford headmaster – Ray Honeyford – appeared to denigrate Islamic values in an article in the *Salisbury Review*.[38] Support for the idea of locating education firmly in Christian values continued to find favour with Conservative ministers and John Patten, appointed Secretary of State for Education in 1992, emphasized it in a white paper published in July 1992. The religious content of education was further highlighted in a discussion document published shortly afterwards. It is not however clear what this will mean in practice. Nor have the churches been particularly supportive of the government's plans.

Conclusions

During the 1970s conservatism and right-wing politics on both sides of the Atlantic were transformed as a result of radical criticism of the trends inherent in British and American society. The questioning of many of the assumptions of existing economic and social policies together with the infusion of new ideas, new elites and new sources of electoral support could be said to constitute a 'new conservatism', despite the many continuities with the past. However, although the right in both countries embraced a broader agenda than previously, significant differences marked the pattern of politics in the United States and United Kingdom. In the United States cultural issues came to play a leading role as Republicans sought to take up the causes of traditional morality and family values and as the style of campaigning pushed symbolic politics to the fore. Although Reagan's successor George Bush had not himself been sympathetic to the causes of the moral right he moved in that direction during the 1980s. In the United Kingdom the emphasis was on much more on reducing the role of the state and turning power back to individuals and families. Although the Conservative Party as a whole did not swing towards a new ideology, expressions of personal religious commitment and appeals to moral conservatism became more frequent from individual MPs and Mrs Thatcher during her period as leader seemed on occasion to exhibit sympathy with the causes of the moral right. However, the fact that her successor as leader – John Major – appeared much less in sympathy with the moral right meant that its causes could expect only limited support from the Conservative Party. Thus, while it would clearly be a mistake to ignore the fact that there are some parallels between British and American conservatism which may yet become more pronounced, it would equally be a mistake to exaggerate the similarities. Ultimately the American Republican Party has embraced much of the moral right's agenda; the British Conservative Party has only occasionally flirted with it.

Notes

1 On Reagan and Thatcher see Geoffrey Smith, *Reagan and Thatcher* (London, The Bodley Head, 1990).

2 An early assessment of this process can be found in G. R. Peele, *Revival and Reaction: the Right in Contemporary America* (Oxford, Oxford University Press, 1984). Later overviews include Steve Bruce, *The Rise and Fall of the New Christian Right* (Oxford, Oxford University Press, 1988) and Clyde Wilcox, *God's Warriors: the New Christian Right in America* (Baltimore, Johns Hopkins University Press, 1992).

3 The terms 'evangelical' and 'fundamentalist' can be controversial. Here I am using as a working definition of fundamentalism David Martin's notion of a package of dogma, scriptural inerrancy and moral conservatism ('Fundamentalism: some definitions', *Political Quarterly*, April–June 1990, p. 160.). For a useful discussion of the phenomenon of fundamentalism see James Barr, *Fundamentalism*, 2nd edn (London, SCM Press, 1981).

4 The key cases of the 1960s were *Engel v Vitale* (1962) 370 US 421 and *Abington School District v Schempp* (1963) 374 US 203.

5 For an overview of the religious beliefs of George Gallup Jr. and Jim Castelli, *The People's Religion: American Faith in the 90's.* (New York, Macmillan, 1989).

6 See R. Wuthnow, *The* Restructuring of American Religion (Princeton, Princeton University Press, 1988).

7 Michael Isikoff, Christian coalition steps boldly into politics, *Washington Post*, 10 September 1992.

8 See Wilcox, *God's Warriors*.

9 See Wilcox, *God's Warriors* and Steve Bruce, *Pray TV: Tele-vangelism in America* (London, Routledge, 1990).

10 See *Washington Post,* 1 September 1992.

11 For an early analysis of the 1992 election results based on exit polls see Pippa Norris, 'The 1992 elections: trust or change?', *Government and Opposition* (Spring 1993).

12 For an overview of the relationship between politics and moral issues in Britain see Martin Durham, *Moral Crusades: Family and Morality in the Thatcher Years* (New York, New York University Press, 1991).

13 For an overview see Martin Durham, *Moral Crusades.* For a discussion of British government policy on Aids see John Street, British government policy on aids, *Parliamentary Affairs*, vol. 41, 4 (1988).

14 See Vivek Chaudhary, Tories fall out as declaration pushes rights, *Guardian*, 28 August 1991.

15 Source: *Social Trends*, 1990.

16 See Donald Shell, *The House of Lords*, 2nd edn (London, Wheatsheaf, 1992).

17 *Faith in the City* (1985). See also *Living Faith in the Cities* (1990).

18 Martin Durham, *Moral Crusades.*

19 On this see Ammerman, Nancy T., *Baptist Battles: Social Change and Religious Conflict in the Southern Baptist Convention* (New Brunswick, Rutgers University Press, 1990).

20 There is a massive literature on the role of PACs; of special relevance to this study is Larry Sabato, *PAC Power*, 2nd edn (New York, Norton, 1990).

21 The exploitation of charitable status for political purposes itself became a frequent cause of complaint against many of the groups on the right.

22 On religious television see Charles E. Swann and J. Hadden, *Prime Time Preachers* (Reading, Mass., Addison-Wesley, 1981). Also Steve Bruce, *Pray TV* For a discussion of the role of religion in the south see Charles Reagan Wilson, *Perspectives on the American South, Vol 5: Religion* (New York, Gordon and Breach, 1991).

23 For an early overview of the neo-conservatives see Peter Steinfels, *The Neo-Conservatives: the Men Who Are Changing America* (New York, Simon and Schuster, 1980) Also Jerone Himmelstein, *To the Right: the Transformation of American Conservatism* (University of California Press, 1990).

24 There is a vast literature on abortion but a good overview is provided by Kristin Luker, *Abortion and the Politics of Motherhood* (1984).

25 *Roe* v *Wade* 1973 410 US 113. See also the companion case of *Does* v *Bolton* 410 US 179.

26 See Michele McKeegan *Abortion Politics: Mutiny in the Ranks of the Right* (New York, The Free Press, 1992).

27 *Wallace* v *Jaffree*.

28 Mary Jordan, Reports of school censorship increase, *Washington Post*, 2 September 1992.

29 For a discussion of Clause 28 see Martin Durham, *Sex and Politics*.

30 On this see G. R. Peele, Civil rights in G. Peele, C. Bailey and B. Cain (eds), *Developments in American Politics* (Basingstoke, Macmillan and New York, St Martins Press, 1992). Also *Yale Policy and Law Review*, 8: 2, 1990 for an interesting overview of civil rights in relation to employment discrimination.

31 For a discussion of the failure of ERA see Mary Frances Berry, Why ERA failed, *Politics, Womens rights and the Amending Process* (Indiana University Press, 1986). Also Conover, *Feminism and the New Right* (Praeger, 1983).

32 For a recent illuminating discussion of this issue in the Republican Party see Michele McKeegan, *Abortion Politics*.

33 John Isikoff, 'Christian coalition steps into politics', *Washington Post*, 10 September 1992.

34 A. Gamble, *The Free Economy and the Strong State* (London, Macmillan, 1988).

35 Michael W Apple, 'The politics of common sense: schooling, populism, and the New Right', in Henry Giroux and Peter McLare, *Critical Pedagogy: the State and Cultural Struggle* (State University of New York Press, 1989).

36 Valerie Riches and the Responsible Society, for example, argued consistently against teaching about contraception and attacked the work of the Family Planning Association. See Martin Durham, op. cit.

37 For a full discussion see Martin Durham, *Moral Crusades*.

38 See Ray Honeyford, 'Education and race: an alternative view', *Salisbury Review*, 6 (1984).

5 *Terry O'Shaughnessy*

Economic policy

...the ideas of economists and political philosophers, both when they right and when they are wrong, are more powerful than is commonly understood. Indeed the world is ruled by very little else. Practical men, who believe themselves to be quite exempt from any intellectual influences, are usually the slaves to some defunct economist.[1]

1 Introduction

The Reagan and Thatcher Governments came to office expressing similarly strong commitments to market-oriented economic policies. Policy at the macroeconomic level was to be explicitly monetarist. At the microeconomic level the emphasis was to be on reducing the role of government and especially the burden of regulation and taxation on individuals and companies, with a view to improving the performance of the 'supply side' of the economy. In practice, however, trans-Atlantic differences were evident. Economic policies under Reagan and Thatcher were subject to different constraints, were implemented in different circumstances, and had different outcomes. There were also important differences in the versions of monetarism and supply-side economics that found favour in Washington and London. This chapter examines the similarities of and differences between economic policy-making under Reagan and Thatcher in order to learn something about the role of economic ideas in the world of practical men – and women.

The chapter is divided into six sections. After this introduction there is a short account of the economic performance of the United States and the United Kingdom prior to the elections of Mr Reagan and Mrs Thatcher. Section 3 deals with the ideas about macroeconomics that influenced policy-making in the 1980s while sec-

Table 5.1   *US and UK economic performance, 1948–73*

	Growth rate (% p.a)	Unemployment (%)	Inflation (% p.a)
US	3.86	4.77	2.83
UK	3.33	1.82	4.58

Source: OECD, *Economic Outlook*, various years.

Table 5.2   *US and UK economic performance, 1974–80*

	Growth rate (% p.a)	Unemployment (%)	Inflation (% p.a)
US	2.20	6.81	8.17
UK	0.93	4.34	16.60
OECD	2.57	5.04	9.40

Source: OECD, *Economic Outlook*, various years.

tion 4 examines the policy impact of concepts derived from microeconomics. Section 5 outlines the macroeconomic and microeconomic outcomes for both economies while section 6 concludes.

2   The economic background

Macroeconomic performance

By the end of the 1970s it was clear that both the US and UK economies were performing badly when measured in comparison with their own past performances (see Tables 5.1 and 5.2). There was a view current that they were performing less well than other advanced market economies, although the evidence here is less clear.

Until the 1970s it had seemed that unemployment and inflation were more or less inversely related. This inverse relationship – the Phillips curve[2] – played an important role in the way in which macroeconomics was taught. The reason for this was that it seemed to fulfil two important functions. First, it made endogenous a variable – the level of money wages or the price level – taken as exogenous in Keynes's formulation of the principle of effective demand. Second, it allowed the specification of a policy menu that could be presented to policy-makers and from which they could choose an appropriate combination of policies according to how much weight they gave to the desirability of low inflation and low unemployment. Macroeconomic policy-making could then be specified in the standard way economists prefer: as a problem involving the maximisation of an objective function (the policy-maker's social welfare function) subject to a constraint (the Phillips curve).

There is still dispute about whether policy-makers really saw themselves as choosing from such a Phillips curve trade-off. For a start, the Phillips curve relationship was viewed sceptically by some Keynesian economists, especially in the UK.[3] Others, including those most closely associated with Keynesian-inspired policy-making in the US during the 1960s have since argued[4] that they never advocated higher inflation as part of policy for reducing unemployment. Nevertheless, the Phillips curve was widely accepted as a way of thinking about unemployment and inflation data. Moreover, it was recognised that most policies designed to deal with one of these economic problems would have a potentially unfavourable effect on the other.

Two new features of the data used to construct the traditional Phillips curve emerged in the late 1960s and the 1970s. First, it became apparent that the terms of the trade-off between unemployment and inflation were slowly worsening. Thus more unemployment had to be tolerated in order to keep inflation below some target level or, looked at another way, more inflation was the consequence of achieving a given unemployment goal; in other words, the Phillips curve was shifting outwards, away from the origin. The second blow to the Phillips curve occurred when simultaneous rises in inflation and unemployment were observed; these can be interpreted as resulting from a much more sudden shift outwards in the curve.

One influential explanation that was put forward at the time[5] gave a key role to expectations. According to this view, the position of the Phillips curve depends on the prior expectations of inflation that agents in the economy hold. There is not just one Phillips curve, but a whole array, as sketched in Fig. 5.1. The original Phillips curve is drawn on the assumption that agents expect inflation to be zero: this is the lowest of the three Phillips curves shown in Fig. 5.1. However if agents have learnt to expect, say, 5 per cent inflation, they will incorporate this expectation into

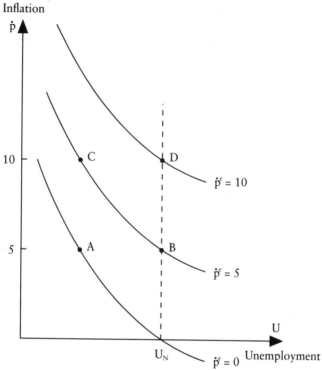

Figure 5.1 The expectations – augmented Phillips curve.

their wage- and price-setting behaviour and the outcome will be
a new Phillips curve located above the original curve. It follows
that attempts to reduce unemployment below U_N, the point at which
the original Phillips curve cut the horizontal axis, will prove futile
in the long run. It is true that, in the short run it is possible to
move up along the original curve, say to point A, but this will
result in inflation of, in this example, 5 per cent. As agents learn
to expect 5 per cent inflation they will find themselves on a new
Phillips curve. Moreover, the only point on this new curve where
the inflation they *observe* corresponds to the inflation they *expect*
is point B, where unemployment is again at U_N. Moving from U_N
to A to B has achieved nothing, except to raise the underlying rate
of inflation in this economy from zero to 5 per cent. Further
attempts to reduce unemployment below U_N by moving from B to
C will be frustrated in a similar way, with the economy ending up

Table 5.3 *Annual average labour productivity growth for the largest OECD countries, 1963–73 and 1974–81*

	1963–73	1974–81
US	1.9	0.0
UK	3.0	0.8
France	4.6	2.3
Canada	2.4	0.1
Japan	8.7	3.3
Italy	5.4	0.9
West Germany	4.6	2.5

Source: J. Cornwall, *The Conditions for Economic Recovery* (Oxford, Martin Robertson, 1983), table 1.2.

at D, where inflation is even higher and unemployment is no lower.

Microeconomic performance

In addition to these concerns about macroeconomic performance, there was a widespread perception in both the US and the UK that other countries were achieving faster growth because they had developed a more favourable microeconomic environment. Various indicators were used in cross country comparisons, including labour productivity as shown in Table 5.3.

Debates about relative economic performance were, of course, not new; in fact, in the UK's case this debate has been carried on in a more or less vigorous form for a century or more. Many familiar themes were rehearsed, especially by those who stood to gain from changes in policy. Some participants in this debate called for more state intervention in, say, education or research and development in order to match the perceived outcomes in more successful economies, especially in Japan and Germany. Others called for less intervention, arguing that lower taxation, less regulation and more reliance on markets would transform microeconomic performance. There was rather more agreement about the desirability to increase investment and it was argued that this would require saving a larger proportion of national income. Again, international comparisons were deployed, but the evidence was not always clear cut. Tables 5.4 and 5.5 list indicators often taken as relevant in assessing supply-side performance:

Table 5.4   *Total outlays of government as a percentage of GDP, 1979 and 1989*

	1979	1989
US	31.7	36.1
UK	42.6	41.2
Japan	31.6	31.5
Germany	47.7	45.5
France	45.0	49.4
Italy	45.5	51.5
Canada	39.0	44.6

Source: OECD, *Economic Outlook*, June 1992, table R 15.

Table 5.5   *National saving as a percentage of GDP, 1979 and 1990 (net household saving is shown in brackets)*

	1979	1990
US	20.7 (7.2)	14.3 (5.2)
UK	18.9 (12.0)	15.6 (9.0)
Japan	31.5 (18.2)	34.4 (13.6)
Germany	22.7 (12.7)	25.0 (13.9)
France	24.5 (18.8)	21.1 (12.2)
Italy	26.2 (24.7)	19.5 (16.1)
Canada	23.8 (13.2)	18.0 (10.4)

Source: OECD, *Economic Outlook*, June 1992, tables R 12 and R 13.

government outlays as a percentage of GDP and national saving as a percentage of GDP. (Data from the end of the decade is included for future reference.)

From Table 5.4 it is clear that a number of successful economies showed evidence of a higher level of government intervention in the economy than occurs in the US or even in the UK. Clearly, these raw figures are not very useful and disaggregation is called for: what matters, from the point of view of microeconomic performance, is precisely where and to what end governments intervene. Nevertheless, the data presented in Table 5.4 should be enough to caution against a simple association of less intervention with better performance.

The evidence from Table 5.5 seems less ambiguous since, in almost every case, more saving is associated with faster growth.

The problem here, however, involves the direction of causality. Keynesian and neoclassical economists share the view that faster growth will generate more savings, though they differ about mechanisms. Keynesians argue that the causal link runs from investment to saving. Higher levels of investment push up the prices of capital goods and this bids resources away from the consumer goods sector of the economy, which in turn raises the price of consumption goods relative to wages. This reduces the share of national income going to wage-earners and raises the share going to profit-receivers. Since the latter have a higher propensity to save, savings rise which helps to fund the higher level of investment. It follows from this analysis that attempts to raise the level of saving without increasing investment first will be counterproductive. The effect will be to reduce the demand for consumer goods and thus the price of consumer goods relative to wages. Firms in the consumption goods sector will respond by cutting back on output and employment and probably on investment as well. Incomes will fall, especially those of profit-receivers. The net effect will probably be to reduce rather than raise aggregate saving.

Neoclassical economists do not see a cause for concern in the relationship between saving and investment since they believe that higher household saving will flow through into investment without causing output to deviate from its full employment level. However they, too, posit a link running from faster growth in income to higher saving, based on the life-cycle analysis of household saving. Thus it may be the case that saving is higher in, say, Japan and the various continental economies because they have been growing faster than the UK and the US, rather than vice versa.[6]

3   Thinking about macroeconomics

The monetarist counter-revolution

Johnson, in an early account of the shift away from Keynesian economics and towards monetarism, spoke of 'The Keynesian revolution and the monetarist counter-revolution'.[7] In doing so, he emphasised the continuities that exist between pre-Keynesian theory and monetarism, continuities that are further invoked when advocates of the later, rational expectations version of monetarism describe themselves as 'New Classical' economists.[8] Like pre-Keynesian economists, monetarists believe that economies, left to themselves, will produce some 'natural' level of output that is, in some sense, optimal and that attempts to raise output above this level will be futile. Corresponding to this level of output there is a 'natural' rate of unemployment which monetarist economists identified with U_N in Fig. 5.1. There is also a shared belief that observed unemployment is largely or wholly voluntary, despite whatever claims to the contrary are made by the unemployed themselves.[9] And both agreed that the only macroeconomic variable the authorities can permanently influence and with which they should be concerned is the price level.

In putting forward these claims, monetarists felt they had to confront certain stylised facts about the Phillips curve relationship. It is important to emphasise that they took this relationship as being empirically well-established. Far from arguing that the Phillips curve had completely broken down, they were concerned to show that such an inverse relationship between inflation and unemployment could arise even in a well-behaved equilibrium model in which there was no exploitable policy trade-off between these two variables.

Two influential analyses along these lines were developed by Edmund Phelps and Robert Lucas.[10] Phelps asks us to think about a world in which firms employ workers with firm-specific skills. Firms face hiring and training costs which make life very costly for them if labour turnover is high. Workers in Phelps's world seek to maximise their real incomes but they suffer from a lack of information: they know their current nominal wage and the current prices of the goods they plan to consume, but they do not know what wages other firms are offering. Moreover, they can only find out by quitting their current job and visiting other firms to enquire about vacancies and wage rates. Let us suppose they can visit one firm in each time period. If they feel their current wage is rather low, they will quit and search until they find a wage high enough to discourage further search; in this, they act perfectly rationally, given their limited information. Firms also act optimally: they observe the quit rate, the rate at which unemployed workers turn up at the factory gate to enquire about vacancies and wage rates and the proportion of enquiries that result in the acceptance of a job; they also (obviously) know the price of their product. Each firm sets a wage which maximises profits, taking into account the fact that a low wage secures high profits on each unit of output, but leads to high turnover while a high wage reduces turnover costs but also the profit margin on each unit of output.

If both workers and firms are acting optimally there will be an equilibrium level of output and an optimal number of workers searching; that is, an optimal amount of unemployment. This can be altered, however, if someone – let us say the government – introduces some inflation into the model. Suppose prices and wages to go up by some fraction between, say, periods 10 and 11 but, as before, workers observe their own wage and not other wages and prices. Workers who are searching will find the wage they are offered in period 11 looks good in comparison with those they sampled in, say, periods 8, 9 and 10 while those in employment will see their current wage rise relative to what they expect prices to be: the former are very likely to accept a job in period 11 while the latter are less likely to quit. Thus unemployment falls and output rises. However as soon as prices stabilise at the new, higher level the quit rate will rise again as workers realise their real wage has not increased and they could do better by searching.

Two features of this model are worth stressing. The first is an often noted characteristic of monetarist models: increased output and lower unemployment can be secured if inflation occurs, but these gains are temporary. Nevertheless, the fact that a gain is temporary is not a reason for rejecting it. A more powerful argument against using inflationary policy in a model like this derives from a second, less emphasised characteristic of the model: the increased output that results from a burst of inflation is not enough to compensate rational, searching workers for the leisure they give up and for the lost opportunity of finding a more suitable job if they continue searching. In other words, they are tricked into taking the next job they are offered, even though this is not in their interest. It is in this sense that a policy of increasing employment in Phelps' model is actually *welfare-reducing*.[11]

A key feature of Phelps's model is that agents form their expectations *adaptively*: they adapt their expectations as they collect more data and, in the meantime, they can make mistakes. An alternative and, it has been argued,[12] preferable assumption to make about expectations is that they are formed *rationally*: in other words, agents form their expectations by making the best possible use of all the available information, so that the outcomes they expect are the same as the outcomes that are predicted by the relevant economic model. Rational expectations can be imposed on any model in which expectations play a important role: this includes Keynesian as well as monetarist models. It is well-established that, when applied to the latter, the rational expectations assumption tends to make the models 'better behaved' and to make policy even less effective: what role, then, for Phillips curve type phenomena?

An answer was given by Lucas.[13] In a world that seems even further removed from the concerns of macroeconomic policy-making than that proposed by Phelps, Lucas examines a model in which agents form their expectations rationally but in which there is some irreducible uncertainty. The structure of his model involves a series of overlapping generations. When they are 'young' agents work and save so that when they are 'old' they can consume in their retirement. Physical commodities cannot be stored so savings must be in the form of a financial asset: 'money'. How much work you do now when you are young depends, in part, on what prices are expected to be in the next period when you are old, so that expectations play a crucial role in determining current output and employment. Lucas next introduces a key assumption: his world is made up of two physically distinct regions between which there is no communication. The old are allocated equally to these two regions[14] but the fraction of the young allocated to each ($\theta/2$, $1 - \theta/2$) is a random variable: suppose that, instead of half the young ending up in each region in each period, the outcome is (0.4, 0.6) in the first period, (0.7, 0.3) in the second, and so on. Price in each region in each period will depend on the proportion of young to old: if there are only a few of the former, the latter will bid up prices and it will be worthwhile for the young to work harder to produce more output. Price will also depend on the quantity of money that passes from one generation to the next. Lucas allows this, also, to be a random variable in that he proposes that the government issues periodically additional currency to current holders of currency and that the size of this monetary injection, say x, is random. Finally, he assumes that agents know the probability distributions of x and θ and the structure of the model in which they are located and that, in deciding what to do, they form their expectations rationally.

Lucas shows that, when $\theta = 1$ with probability 1, money is neutral in the sense that prices are proportional to the quantity of money while output and employment are independent of the quantity of money. If x = 1 with probability 1, then prices, employment and consumption will be depend on θ. However – and this is Lucas's crucial point – when x and θ *both* fluctuate, current prices inform agents only about the *ratio x/θ*. 'Higher than average' values of x will appear to both the 'old' and the 'young' as 'good times': an observer, sampling prices and output, will detect a 'Phillips curve' and yet, as Lucas also shows, there will be no exploitable trade-off between inflation and unemployment available to the government.

Despite its abstract nature, the impact of this argument was immense. If empirical data that suggested Phillips curve effects were fully compatible with the rational expectations hypothesis then there seemed no reason to retain the intellectually much less satisfying adaptive expectations assumption. Moreover, applying the rational expectations hypothesis to standard monetarist models, such as those put forward by Friedman and Phelps, produced the result that there was no unemployment–inflation trade-off, even in the short run.

It is often suggested that this makes the rational expectations or 'Wave II'[15] monetarists extreme pessimists about macroeconomic policy, in comparison with the earlier 'Wave I' monetarists who admitted some role for policy and hence were only moderately pessimistic about policy effectiveness. However, this is to misunderstand what monetarists believe the aim of policy should be. Wave II monetarists are not pessimistic due to the fact that they think that an expansionary policy will have little (positive) impact on real variables while it has a large impact on the rate at which prices increase. Rather they are *optimistic* because they believe that a deflationary policy will have little (negative) effect on real variables while it has a large impact on reducing inflation. In other words, they believe that the unemployment cost of reducing inflation will be low, unlike Wave I monetarists who tended to admit that reducing inflation would require maintaining higher levels of unemployment for some time as people slowly readjusted their inflationary expectations downwards. This is illustrated in Fig. 5.2. According to Wave I monetarists, to reduce inflation from, say, 10 to 5 per cent, it is necessary to allow unemployment to rise well above U_N to somewhere near B and to maintain it there while expectations are adjusted downwards. Once this occurs there will

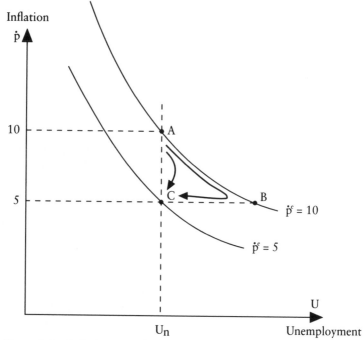

Figure 5.2 Deflationary policy with adaptive and rational expectations.

be a movement back towards C, but in the meantime there will a substantial amount of lost output. Wave II monetarists, on the other hand, believe that it is possible to move from A directly to C, as long as the government's commitment to reduce inflation from 10 to 5 per cent is fully credible. Clearly, if this is possible the output loss is much smaller.

Keynesian responses

The continuities between economic theory before Keynes and present-day monetarism raise a question about the thoroughness with which Keynes's theory displaced pre-Keynesian ideas. Did Keynesianism collapse so quickly and so completely because of theoretical weaknesses that had been there all along? Had the whole Keynesian episode been a mistake, based on the coincidence of a new economic theory and the post-World War II economic boom? Monetarists tend to give affirmative answers to both these questions and to welcome the end of Keynesianism. There are others, however, who, while criticising the way in which Keynesian concepts where introduced into mainstream economic analysis in the first few years following the publication of the *General Theory*, have responded by offering a more thorough, better grounded version of Keynes's analysis.

Arguments along these lines begin with the observation that the 'neo-classical synthesis' between standard neoclassical microeconomics and Keynesian macroeconomics that constituted textbook economics in the 1940s, 1950s and 1960s, was not a synthesis at all but rather the juxtaposition of two quite different theories. Microeconomics was taught in a way which assumed that markets usually work well to allocate resources and that state intervention in the market was justified only in a small number of well-defined cases. Macroeconomists, on the other hand, argued that the market usually failed to secure an optimal level of output and employment. Theoretical peace was maintained between the two groups on the basis of an esoteric debate about which particular rigidity, when imposed on a model built up from a number of well-behaved micro markets, would produce 'Keynesian' effects at the macro level. This debate had begun with Keynes's own claim that his theory was more 'general' than that of his classical opponents since they always assumed the 'special' case of full employment while his analysis took full employment as one possible case among many. Subsequently, Keynesians found this 'general versus specific' argument turned against them when it was pointed out that the special assumption of say, wage or price rigidity, could turn a well-behaved neoclassical model into a less well-behaved 'Keynesian' one; this made the Keynesian models special cases of more general neoclassical ones. In this debate it never quite clear *why* these rigidities were present but, from a practical point of view, this did not matter, since most economists agreed that the empirically relevant case was the one described by Keynes in which the appropriate rigidities were present.

This was hardly satisfactory, however, especially when opponents of Keynesian analysis questioned the empirical relevance of the Keynesian case. After all, it was hard to argue with those who called for the more consistent application of the key shared assumptions of microeconomics: rational optimising individuals and instantly clearing markets. Two solutions offered themselves: start with standard microeconomics and construct rigorous micro-foundations for Keynesian macroeconomics or start at the other end with Keynesian macroeconomics and abandon the idealised assumptions of the microeconomist. These two strategies are exemplified in the work in the UK of two Cambridge economists who attempted to resist the monetarist counter-revolution: Frank Hahn and Nicholas Kaldor.[16] Hahn shared many of the assumptions and modelling techniques of his monetarist opponents, but reached opposite conclusions which he supported by positing models in which 'unsatisfactory' or 'Keynesian' outcomes emerge as equilibrium solutions. Kaldor took a more radical view. He saw monetarism as simply Keynesianism in reverse. For him, monetarism was a theory designed to cloak with some respectability the deliberate creation of unemployment. To the extent that monetarism worked as an anti-inflationary policy it did so by exploiting the fear of unemployment; it was truly a scourge. However, these views, while forcefully put, failed to win widespread support, either inside or outside the economics profession. It seemed that both strategies underestimated the appeal of simple monetarist doctrines. Sophisticated models built along lines suggested by Hahn in which there were multiple rational expectations equilibria which could be ranked in a welfare sense were treated as curious, while Kaldor's polemics were dismissed or ignored.

Empirical issues
By the beginning of the 1980s the ground had been staked out fairly clearly. There was widespread agreement in both the US and the UK that deflationary policies were necessary, although there was disagreement about how costly this would prove. Rational expectations or 'Wave II' monetarists thought the cost would be low – in the extreme case, zero. This view fitted well with the approach to policy choices that emerged in the Reagan administration in the US. Monetarists of the older school thought the cost of reducing inflation might be high, but it was a cost worth bearing. Supporters of the Thatcher government in the UK seemed to take this view, though they too seem to have been surprised by the extent by which unemployment rose between 1979 and 1983.

There was also widespread agreement that controlling monetary aggregates was necessary and sufficient in order to control inflation. Agreement on this issue was based on two different foundations. On the one hand, many simple monetarist models had this 'money is neutral' property and, despite the models' abstract nature, a large number of economists and policy-markers were persuaded by arguments based upon them. On the other hand, there did appear to be some support from empirical studies showing links between the rate of growth of particular monetary aggregates and inflation using data from the post-war period.

It was understood that there are difficulties in interpreting data of this type, since monetary aggregates and nominal incomes might be expected to grow in step with one another even if monetarism as a doctrine proved to be false. However, one feature of UK data seemed almost to settle the matter. It so happened that Sterling M3, the government's preferred measure of broad money, had expanded rapidly in 1971, 1972 and 1973, while retail prices had accelerated in 1974, 1975 and 1976. This lag, reminiscent of that suggested by Friedman, seemed to prove that the causal relation ran from money to prices. Unfortunately (for monetarists) empirical support for the link between money and prices weakened when later data were included. Also, it was clear that M3 growth in the early 1970s was due in part to changes in financial regulation associated with the policy of Competition and Credit Control, while inflation in the mid-1970s was associated with the first oil shock. It may well be that these two policy shocks, coming three years apart, produced the regularities in the data that empirical studies carried out in the late 1970s found so convincing. This was the very time when many economists, commentators and policy-makers were persuaded that monetarism had strong empirical foundations.

Finally, there was agreement that an important link existed between fiscal and monetary policy. Fiscal deficits, if they were not fully funded by sales of government debt to the non-bank private sector, would require the creation of additional central bank liabilities and, eventually, an expansion in the money supply. Since it was assumed that the potential for debt sales to the non-bank public was naturally limited, a commitment to slower monetary growth seemed to imply fiscal rectitude as well.

4 Thinking about microeconomics

Among economists debates about microeconomic issues tend to revolve around empirical issues and questions of emphasis, since there is general agreement about the advantages and limitations of market solutions to public policy dilemmas. All economists agree that improving microeconomic efficiency is an excellent aim, but many are sceptical about the potential for rapid improvements in the supply side of any given economy. The factors that seem to be important on the supply side – the economy's technical resources, the skills embodied in its workforce, the degree of labour mobility, public attitudes to labour force participation, to technical change, to authority within the firm – change very slowly. Also, the consensus is that there is little that policy-makers can do to accelerate change in these factors, though there is wide agreement that policy should be set to encourage rather than discourage favourable supply-side changes.

Outside the economics profession, on the other hand, there are many who believe passionately that rapid improvements on the supply side are possible, if only the right policies are put in place. A key policy involves raising labour force participation, by changing tax rates and benefit entitlements. Such thinking lay behind the US 'Economic Recovery Tax Act' of 1981[17] and the income tax cuts announced in the Thatcher government's 1979, 1986, 1987 and 1988 budgets.[18] While it is easy to collect arguments supporting the link between such tax cuts and improved incentives,[19] it is not clear that they will have a large impact. As is well known, cutting the marginal rate of income tax has both a substitution effect (it makes the consumption of goods and services more attractive than the consumption of leisure and so, perhaps, reduces leisure) and an income effect (it makes the individual better off, perhaps increasing leisure). The net effect can go either way.[20] In addition, it is clear that the decision to participate in the labour force or to supply more hours is one based on many considerations, among which the tax regime may play a small role. Finally, it should be noted that a policy of raising labour supply is only welfare increasing to the extent that the increased output produced more than compensates for the leisure forgone. The net welfare gain may be small and it will be overstated if it is measured simply by the increase in output.

Another way to improve the supply response of the economy that proved popular among conservatives in both the US and the UK involved reducing government involvement in industries where previously there had been extensive regulation or state ownership.

Deregulation and – in the UK – large-scale privatisation was carried through in a number of industries including transport, housing, telecommunications, electricity, gas and water supply, financial services, health and education.[21] While proposals for change in each of these areas provoked fierce debate and while assessments of the effects of the changes are still emerging, some degree of consensus exits about the main issues involved. First, it is clear that ownership matters less than many on both sides of the privatisation debate believe. Much more important is the competitive and regulatory framework within which state-owned or privately owned enterprises operate. Second, a crucial difference exists between industries involving natural monopoly – the situation in which, for technical reasons, it is sensible to have only one supplier – and industries into which entry by new firms is possible. Privatising natural monopolies does not lead to an efficient outcome; regulation is necessary to prevent the monopolist from exploiting the consumer. Third, regulation and competition policy is difficult to operate in situations where incumbent firms can influence and even 'capture' the regulator. As a consequence, the efficiency gains to which advocates of privatisation and deregulation point may prove smaller than they hoped.

5 Macroeconomic outcomes

As Tables 5.6 and 5.7 show, both the US and the UK registered some success against inflation during the 1980s compared to the 1970s, although on average inflation stood above the levels observed during the period 1948–73. On the other hand, unemployment was worse – in the UK much worse – than during the 1970s, let alone during the earlier period. The US's growth performance was slightly better than during the 1970s, but it fell short of what was achieved in 1948–73. The UK certainly grew faster in the 1980s than it had in the latter part of the 1970s, but here too, performance fell short of what had occurred in 1948–73.

These comparisons suggest that the reduction in inflation that was achieved in both the US and the UK had large costs in terms of unemployment and lost output. As such, they serve to undermine the more optimistic hopes of some monetarists, especially 'Wave II' monetarists of the New Classical school, that a clearly announced anti-inflationary policy would succeed at little cost if

Table 5.6 *US economic performance, 1979–91*

	Growth rate (% p.a)	Unemployment (%)	Inflation (% p.a)
1979	2.5	5.8	8.9
1980	−0.5	7.2	9.0
1981	1.8	7.6	9.7
1982	−2.2	9.7	6.4
1983	3.9	9.6	3.9
1984	6.2	7.5	3.7
1985	3.2	7.2	3.0
1986	2.9	7.0	2.6
1987	3.1	6.2	3.3
1988	3.9	5.5	3.4
1989	2.5	5.3	4.4
1990	1.0	5.5	4.1
1991	−0.7	6.7	3.7
Average 1981–88	2.85	7.5	4.5

Source: J. N. Smithin *Macroeconomics after Thatcher and Reagan* (Aldershot, Edward Elgar, 1990), p. 56 and OECD, *Economic Outlook*, June 1992, p. 49 and tables R1 and R19. Growth is measured by the annual change in real GDP and inflation by the change in the GDP implicit price deflator.

pursued consistently enough by a committed, credible government. The Reagan and Thatcher administrations were almost ideal cases for this 'credibility' hypothesis; if it did not work under these conditions, it could hardly work under any others.

Of course, matters are never so straightforward. Some conservative critics of the Reagan and Thatcher governments have argued that there was too much back-sliding, which undermined the credibility of anti-inflationary policy. This has some force, especially in the US case. By 1984, as a result of tax cuts and increases in expenditure, the standardised-employment deficit – a measure of the fiscal stance – stood at over 4 per cent of GDP. This represented a very dramatic loosening of fiscal policy. Monetary policy, on one measure,[22] had also loosened significantly by 1983. In any case, it was argued, the fiscal stance made the commitment to an anti-inflationary monetary policy literally incredible.[23]

In the UK policy was more consistent. Both fiscal and monetary policy were tight throughout the 1980s.[24] However what may have let the authorities down was the unpredictability of private sector

Table 5.7   *UK economic performance, 1979–91*

	Growth rate (% p.a)	Unemployment (%)	Inflation (% p.a)
1979	2.6	4.5	14.3
1980	−1.7	6.1	19.7
1981	−1.0	9.1	11.5
1982	1.5	10.4	7.6
1983	3.5	11.2	5.1
1984	2.2	11.4	4.8
1985	3.6	11.6	5.6
1986	3.9	11.8	3.6
1987	4.8	10.4	4.9
1988	4.3	8.2	6.0
1989	2.3	6.2	7.1
1990	1.0	5.9	6.4
1991	−2.2	8.3	6.9
Average 1980–90	2.44	10.2	8.2

Source: J. N. Smithin, *Macroeconomics after Thatcher and Reagan* (Aldershot Edward Elgar, 1990), p. 58 and OECD, *Economic Outlook*, June 1992, p. 78 and tables R1 and R19. Growth is measured by the annual change in real GDP and inflation by the change in the GDP implicit price deflator.

behaviour. This showed itself in two ways. First, serious difficulties were encountered in targeting the government's preferred measure of broad money, sterling M3. This aggregate grew at a rate well outside the government's target range; in fact, by the late 1980s it was growing at over 20 per cent a year. It became clear that any relationship between the growth of this aggregate and inflation based on data from before 1980 must have broken down. There were attempts to look for other aggregates where the money growth–inflation relationship appeared sounder, but in the end monetary targeting was quietly abandoned and an attempt was made to 'borrow' the anti-inflationary credibility of the Bundesbank by targeting the pound–DM exchange rate within the Exchange Rate Mechanism of the European Monetary System.[26] The second source of private sector unpredictability involved attitudes to saving. As noted above, the personal savings ratio in the UK collapsed in the late 1980s. The corresponding growth in consumer expenditure seemed to take the authorities by surprise. This meant that, despite tight fiscal and monetary policy, output grew rapidly between

Table 5.8 *GDP growth for the US and UK, 1948–73, 1974–80 and 1981–88 (US) and 1980–90 (UK)*

	1948–73	1974–80	1980s
US	3.86	2.20	2.85
UK	3.33	0.93	2.44

Source: Tables 5.1, 5.2 and 5.6 above.

1985 and 1988. This helped to reduce unemployment, but it also led to higher inflation, forcing a further tightening of policy at the end of the decade.

These events in the UK, together with the impact of expansionary fiscal policy on growth and employment in the US, showed that Keynesian mechanisms were still at work, though the authorities were hardly acting in a deliberately 'Keynesian' way. Within the economics profession, Keynesians became slightly more assertive and monetarists slightly less so. There were also attempts to explore the links between 'Keynesian' and 'supply-side' effects. It was noted, for example, that the 'natural' or 'Non-Accelerating-Inflation' rate of unemployment (the NAIRU) itself seemed to rise if actual unemployment rose. Models incorporating this 'hysteresis' effect seemed to explain why the dis-inflationary policies of the 1980s had proved so costly in terms of foregone output and why inflationary pressures re-emerged so soon after employment started to grow again.[27]

6 Conclusion

Conservatives wanted to reduce inflation and to secure a more predictable macroeconomic environment – that is, one in which government played a less activist role – as means to an end: the intention was to secure the best possible conditions for individuals and firms to exploit market opportunities and so increase their own welfare. Despite the problems macroeconomic policy encountered under Reagan and Thatcher, was it nevertheless the case that their market-oriented policies had a significant positive effect?

Unfortunately, there is little agreement about the criteria that should be used to judge this question. As noted above (and reproduced in Table 5.8), US data on GDP growth show modest im-

Table 5.9 *Annual average labour productivity growth for the US and UK, 1963–73, 1974–81 and 1981–88 (US) and 1980–90 (UK)*

	1963–73	1974–81	1980–89
US	1.9	0.0	1.0
UK	3.0	0.8	1.7

Source: Table 5.3 above and calculations based on OECD *Economic Outlook*, June 1992, tables R1 and R17.

provement over the 1970s but not over 1948–73. UK growth in the 1980s was much better than in the disastrous 1970s but was not as good as in the 1948–73 period. Data on labour productivity in Table 5.9 show a similar picture: improvement over the 1970s, but not over earlier years, though here it is the UK rather than the US that performs better.[28]

Other perspectives on the legacy of the Reagan–Thatcher era are given by Tables 5.4 and 5.5, above. Table 5.4 shows that total outlays of government as a percentage of GDP decreased only a little in the UK between 1979 and 1989 and actually rose in the US. Table 5.5 shows that, far from seeing an increase in national saving, the 1980s as a whole saw a large fall in national and household saving in both the US and the UK. Finally, it should be mentioned that, according to OECD data, the US went from having a net stock of foreign assets of $95 billion in 1980 to having net liabilities of $674 billion in 1989; the UK, on the other hand, increased its net assets from $34 billion to $127 billion.[29]

On the basis of this evidence it is clear that a number of the goals of the Reagan and Thatcher governments were far from achieved. Where successes *were* recorded the mechanisms responsible may well have been quite unlike those proposed by conservative economists. Where a conservative consensus has emerged – for example, over the case for market solutions in situations where competitive markets can be established – this consensus has been built on propositions about market efficiency that are very widely shared among economists. When conservatives have attempted to go further than this by arguing for market solutions in contexts where natural monopolies or externalities are present or where the product has the character of a public good, they have found that these same widely shared propositions can be deployed to make a good case for regulation or some other form of state intervention.

In macroeconomics matters were less clear. For a start, the issues were more complex, the intellectual and practical stakes were very high and there was little agreement about what constituted a good theory or what counted as compelling evidence for or against an hypothesis. Nevertheless, theoretical issues were clarified in the course of macroeconomic debates during the 1970s and 1980s[30] so that when the Reagan–Thatcher experiment took place it was possible to draw lessons and settle some issues. Not everyone was convinced – or, rather, different observers were convinced about different things on the basis of the same data – since prior commitments to particular paradigms and favourite models play a large role in debates within economics. Still, some minds were changed, especially about the costs of reducing inflation, though perhaps this was too late for those who paid the cost.[31]

Notes

1 J. M. Keynes, *The General Theory of Employment Interest and Money* (London: Macmillan, 1936).

2 The classic account is W. A. H. Phillips, 'The relation between unemployment and the rate of change of money wage rates in the UK, 1861–1957', *Economica*, 25 (1985) 283–99. See also M. Desai (1984), 'Wages, prices and unemployment a quarter century after the Phillips curve', in D. Hendry and K. Wallace, *Econometrics and Quantitative Economics* (Oxford, Blackwell, 1984), pp. 253–74.

3 J. Robinson was characteristically scathing: 'From a hasty run over the statistics . . . is derived an econometric law relating the level of unemployment . . . to changes in wage rates. From this can be read off the amount of unemployment associated with a constant level of prices, and then policy can be framed in terms of the 'trade-off' between unemployment and inflation. The simplicity of this faith in the econometrician's magic numbers is matched by the remarkable cynicism of the proposals derived from it' ('What has become of the Keynesian revolution'? (1973), reprinted in J. Robinson, *Collected Economic* Papers, vol. 5 (Oxford, Blackwell, 1979).

4 See D. Worswick and J. Trevithick, *Keynes and the Modern World* (Cambridge, Cambridge University Press, 1983), p. 219.

5 See M. Friedman, 'The role of monetary policy', *American Economic Review* (1968).

6 Evidence from the UK in the late 1980s does not fit this account very well, since fast growth in 1987 and 1988 was associated with a dramatic fall in household (though not in national) saving. Various

explanations have been put forward for this phenomenon, including demographic changes and innovations in the financial sector which reduced the number of credit-constrained households. See J. Muellbauer and T. A. Murphy (1989), 'Why has UK personal saving collapsed?', *Credit Suisse First Boston Economics.*

7 H. C. Johnson (1971), 'The Keynesian revolution and the monetarist counter-revolution', *American Economic Review, Papers and Proceedings*, 61(2), pp. 1–14.

8 In accounts of the history of economic doctrines, the terms 'classical' and 'neoclassical' are used in contested ways. Keynes himself was partly responsible, as he explains at the very beginning of the *General Theory*: ' "The classical economists" was a name invented by Marx to cover Ricardo and James Mill and their *predecessors*, that is to say for the founders of the theory which culminated in the Ricardian economics. I have become accustomed, perhaps perpetrating a solecism, to include in "the classical school" the *followers* of Ricardo, those, that is to say, who adopted and perfected the theory of the Ricardian economics, including (for example) J. S. Mill, Marshall, Edgeworth and Prof. Pigou' (Keynes, *General Theory*, p. 3, n. 1) The more usual terminology is to use 'classical' to describe pre-marginalist economists such as Smith, Ricardo, Malthus and the Mills while referring to marginalist economists like Marshall, Edgeworth and Pigou as 'neoclassical'. It should be noted that Keynes's terminology was designed to emphasise the similarity between the two groups based on what he claimed was a common assumption that an economy would nearly always operate at a point where its productive resources were fully utilised.

9 The distinction between voluntary and involuntary unemployment was made by Keynes: 'Men are involuntarily unemployed if, in the event of a small rise in the price of wage–goods relatively to the money wage, both the aggregate supply of labour willing to work for the current money-wage and the aggregate demand for it at that wage would be greater than the existing volume of employment' (Keynes, *General Theory*, p. 15) If the labour market is clearing, in the sense that all unemployment is voluntary, the same thought experiment (a rise in the price of wage goods) will yield the result that, while the demand for labour at the existing money wage would be greater than the existing volume of employment, the aggregate supply of labour willing to work at that wage would be less.

10 E. S. Phelps, *Microeconomic Foundations of Employment and Inflation Theory* (1970) and Lucas, 'Expectations and the neutrality of money', *Journal of Economic Theory* (1972).

11 The reason this result is counter-intuitive is that most of us think of unemployment as *involuntary*, as in the Keynesian tradition. Reducing involuntary unemployment is an example, perhaps *the* classic example, of a welfare improving macroeconomic policy move, but if unemployment is the result of optimal behaviour, as in Phelps' model, reducing it involves moving to a sub-optimal situation.

12 The main argument for preferring rational to adaptive expectations is that any scheme of adaptive expectations will be essentially arbitrary:

such schemes involve giving 'weights' to past changes in the variable under investigation and there is no way to decide what the best weighting scheme should be.

13 Lucas, '*Expectations and the neutrality of money*'.

14 Strictly speaking, the old are allocated in such a way to produce the same total monetary demand in the two regions.

15 The terminology is Tobin's *Asset Accumulation and Economic Activity* (Oxford Blackwell, 1980).

16 See Hahn, *Money and Inflation* (Oxford, Blackwell, 1982) and Kaldor *The Scourge of Monetarism* (Oxford, Oxford University Press, 1982).

17 The Kemp-Roth Act. A key provision was a 30 per cent tax cut for individuals, spread over three years.

18 The 1979 budget cut the top rate of income tax from 83 to 60 per cent and the basic rate from 33 to 30 per cent. The basic rate was further reduced to 29 per cent in 1986, 27 per cent in 1987 and 25 per cent in 1988 when the top rate was also reduced to 40 per cent.

19 For the US see D. A. Stockman, *The Triumph of Politics* (London, Bodley Head, 1986) and J. D. Savage, *Balanced Budgets and American Politics* (Ithaca, Cornell University Press, 1988); for the UK see P. Robins, 'Government policy, taxation and supply-side economics', in N. M. Healey (1993), *Britain's Economic Miracle: Myth or Reality* (London, Routledge, 1993).

20 M. Beenstock and A. Dalziel, in their survey of UK research into work incentives and labour supply, conclude that few firm conclusions can be drawn about the impact of the tax-benefit system and that serious areas of disagreement remain among researchers in this field ('Econometric analysis of labour supply and work incentives', in Beenstock, *Work, Welfare and Taxation* (London, Allen and Unwin, 1986). Recent US studies by Triest ('The effect of income taxation on labour supply in the United States', *Journal of Human Resources*, 25: 3 (Summer 1990), 491–516) and MaCurdy, Green and Paarsch ('Assessing empirical approaches for analysing taxes and labour supply', *Journal of Human Resources*, 25: 3 (Summer 1990), 415–90) support the view that the incentive effects and deadweight losses of progressive income tax are small.

21 See D. Swann, *The Retreat of the State* (New York, Harvester, 1988); J. Vickers and G. Yarrow, *Privatization: an Economic Analysis* (Cambridge, Mass., MIT Press, 1988); C. Veljanovski, *Privatisation and Competition* (London, Institute of Economic Affairs, 1989); D. Helm, *The Economic Borders of the State* (Oxford, Clarendon Press, 1989) and J. Kay, C. Mayer and D. Thompson, *Privatisation and Regulation – the UK Experience* (Oxford, Clarendon Press, 1986).

22 One measure of the impact of monetary policy is the difference between short-term and long-term interest rates. The monetary authorities have much more control over the former than the latter. Since long-term interest rates tend to embody inflationary expectations, subtracting the short-term from the long-term interest rate gives an indication of expected *real* interest rates, and hence of the stance of monetary policy.

23 This argument was based on the fact that the government deficit had to be financed by either bond sales or money creation; if the potential for bond sales was limited, a large deficit would require inflationary financing sooner or later. In fact, the growth rate of the monetary base in the US was relatively modest during the 1980s, though in 1986 it reached 10.2 per cent.

24 See A. J. C. Britton *Macroeconomic Policy in Britain, 1974–1987* (Cambridge, Cambridge University Press, 1991), pp. 167–230.

26 Subsequently this, too, proved an incredible policy, as the events of September 1992 showed.

27 See R. Layard, S. Nickell and R. Jackman, *Unemployment: Macroeconomic Performance and the Labour Market* (Oxford, Oxford University Press, 1991) and J. H. Drèze and C. R. Bean, *Europe's Unemployment Problem* (Cambridge, Mass., MIT Press, 1990). Two sources of hysteresis have been identified. One derives from the loss of skills and motivation experienced by the long-term unemployed, so that they cease to compete with the currently employed or recently unemployed. When the short-term unemployed have found jobs inflationary pressures begin again; the longer unemployment persists the fewer short-term unemployed there are and the earlier this effect sets in. The second source of hysteresis arises from the scrapping of capital equipment during the recession. Again, when demand picks up, capacity constraints are reached long before unemployment has disappeared and this leads to inflationary pressures.

28 Interpreting labour productivity data over these relatively short periods is difficult, since very large cyclical effects are present. See G. Maynard, 'Britain's economic recovery', in H. M. Healey, *Britains Economic Miracle*; D. H. Blackaby and L. C. Hunt, 'An assessment of Britain's productivity record in the 1980s: has there been a Miracle?', in Healey, *Britain's Economic Miracle* and J. Muellbauer, 'Productivity and competitiveness in British manufacturing', *Oxford Review of Economic* Policy, 2: 3 (1986).

29 OECD, *Economic Outlook*, June 1992, table 75.

30 An example involves the rational expectations hypothesis. This was first discussed in the context of well-behaved 'classical' models and, for many observers, is still associated with the 'New Classical' school. However it soon became clear that the rational expectations assumption can be incorporated into 'Keynesian' models. When this is done the assumption, far from undermining the effectiveness of policy, actually can serve to make policy *more* effective.

31 These issues are explored in more detail in J. N. Swithin, *Macroeconomics after Thatcher and Reagan* (Alchershot, Edward Elgar, 1990).

The special relationship

Introduction

The United States and Britain have together been the greatest alliance in the defence of liberty and justice that the world has ever known.
Margaret Thatcher, Speech in New York, August 1991.[1]

Throughout the eight years of my presidency, no alliance we had was stronger than the one between the United States and the United Kingdom.
Ronald Reagan, An American Life, 1990.[2]

Any analysis of the Reagan–Thatcher interaction in foreign and defence policy finds itself obliged to deal with that mysterious element in Anglo-American politics, the 'special relationship'. This analysis is no different. The meaning and value of that relationship has been the subject of exhaustive academic dispute for some decades now and its ambiguous nature means such debate will inevitably continue.

However, to assess what, if anything, made the Reagan–Thatcher double act in this area somehow different four interrelated questions need to be asked. First, what exactly is the special relationship and has it had the same meaning to both participants? Second, how did this relationship affect the conduct of Anglo–American foreign and defence policy in the period between 1945 and Margaret Thatcher's coming to power in 1979? Third, how did the special relationship operate during Margaret Thatcher and Ronald Reagan's joint occupation of their respective offices? Finally, did Margaret Thatcher so alter the nature of Anglo-American foreign policy that those changes would continue to affect the special relationship not only after Ronald Reagan's passage from office but also her own?

This chapter will argue that the distinctive features of the special relationship has been the differing meanings placed on it by the two parties. Put simply, as a concept the special relationship meant much more to the British than the Americans – the content of this chapter will reflect that by focusing heavily on the British side of the compact. As a result of this misunderstanding there were major misinterpretations by British actors in both the Policy Scope and Geo-political domains. A highly belated realisation of this led to the abandonment by Britain of its east of Suez role, the attempted and finally successful entry into the EEC, and a subsequent downgrading of the special relationship. This will be illustrated by reference to the Anglo-American alliance between 1945 and 1979.

It will then be argued that during the Reagan–Thatcher era Margaret Thatcher attempted to revive the Anglo-American accord. She enjoyed considerable success in this but success that was limited by the same Policy Scope and Geo-political factors that had constrained her predecessors from Churchill to Callaghan. Furthermore, the new consensus for Europe that had been reached in the 1970s proved durable through the 1980s much to her displeasure. As a result the period between Ronald Reagan's voluntary retirement and her involuntary one highlighted the limitations of her special relationship through a predictable switch of America's attentions to the EC in general and West Germany in particular. That switch is, however, only partial because of a continued military and intelligence cooperation between Britain and the United States which was clearly demonstrated during the Gulf War. Nevertheless, it will be concluded that despite Mrs Thatcher's best efforts the Anglo-American relationship in the 1990s will be largely predicated on the EC–American relationship.

The nature of the special relationship

The special relationship was essentially the product of World War II. Although commentators have attempted to date it from the nineteenth century – the settlement of the Alabama claims in 1872 or the Anglo-Venezualan border dispute of 1895 both being offered as candidates[3] – the relationship was not especially close. Neither did World War I produce the understanding between the two countries that World War II would. However, the United

States's decisive contribution in 1918 did raise British estimation of the US's role in international politics. The British accepted naval parity with the US from 1921 and backed away from their alliance with the Japanese in 1922 as a consequence of American pressure. Nevertheless, the two countries rivalry for sea power and increasing trade friction in the 1920s combined to keep their relationship distinctly formal, although the preconditions for the special relationship may have existed in this era. Indeed, during the interwar period the US navy devised its war plan 'Red' for execution in the event of a clash with the British fleet and Austen Chamberlain, then Foreign Secretary, informed the Committee on Imperial Defence that while war with Germany, Italy and Japan was inconceivable, war with the United States was not.[4]

During the 1930s matters improved only marginally. Chamberlain snubbed Roosevelt's offer of a meeting between the two in 1937 and killed FDR's efforts to convene an international peace conference in Washington the next year. As a result, David Watt is almost certainly right to argue that 'Anglo-American relations at the outbreak of World War II were about as distant as it is possible to imagine between "friendly" powers . . .'.[5]

The subsequent improvement in relations was the product of joint struggle during the war and of Churchill's enormous efforts. It may not be far wrong to ascribe, as Sir Michael Howard does, the special relationship as Churchill's personal creation.[6] It was certainly Churchill who coined the phrase in a less-reported part of his 'Iron Curtain' address at Fulton, Missouri, in March 1946, when he called for 'A special relationship between the British Commonwealth and Empire and the United States'.

The Anglo-American accord that Churchill called for emerged as a consequence of Soviet adventurism in Europe. Churchill had perceived the relationship as one of equal partners, a mistake that his successors would regularly repeat. As Frankel notes of the Anglo-American alliance, 'The three important characteristics were first, its asymmetry, second, the different conceptualisations of it by the British and Americans, and third, the misunderstandings between the two sides.'[7]

This asymmetry evident from the start has, of course, widened much further since 1946. So much further that, as Robin Edmonds points out,[8] it is quite amazing that the relationship is still so energetically discussed. Asymmetry certainly continued during Mrs

Thatcher's premiership. Although her liaison with Ronald Reagan is given significant coverage in most accounts of her period in office, that is not true of most American accounts of Reagan. Nathan Glazer has argued that even among well-informed American citizens little is known of Mrs Thatcher other than the Falklands victory, her electoral triumphs, and her staunchly pro-American foreign policy.[9] More important though are the differing conceptualisations of the relationship between the parties and the misunderstandings they engendered. These misunderstandings can best be gathered in two categories – 'policy scope' differences, and 'geopolitical' differences.

Policy scope differences
Post-war Anglo-American co-operation was the product of the self-interest of both countries and its central forum was in military and, especially, military-intelligence collaboration. This was obviously reinforced by cultural and linguistic ties. Throughout this period the British held a much more expansive view of the special relationship and the policy areas it should operate in. American participants were much more coy about the relationship's domain. Dean Acheson once discovered that diplomats from both sides had produced a paper on the special relationship and, fearful of the British side's broad definition, had all copies destroyed. The British regularly brushed over certain crucial facts, namely:

1 Where US and British interests clashed, even in the military sector (for example over nuclear technology), the US would uphold its national interest and policy with little compromise.
2 While the British could have influence over American policy in the military sphere it was most likely to be successful when the Administration itself was divided. Invariably, British pressure was for a more moderate diplomatic approach to the communists.
3 British attempts to conduct a special relationship outside of military matters (for example, economic policy) usually failed.

Far from these limitations of the special relationship leading Britain to reassess its value or balance it with other alliances, they led to an excessive British zeal to impress the Americans by maintaining a global role and pursuing an independent nuclear deterrent, hence winning influence over them, i.e. to try and expand the special relationship to fit the British conception of it.

Geo-political differences

Europe was the main theatre for Anglo-American co-operation but the two nations saw Europe in very different ways. For the Americans Europe was the frontline in an ideologically based Cold War. A front line that must remain strong but, increasingly, at a not unduly burdensome financial cost. For the UK the basis of its security rested on retaining the US military (especially nuclear) presence in Europe to maintain the balance of power. To do so the British believed that they had to commit substantial troops to Europe themselves, spend a relatively high proportion of GDP on defence, and be willing to support the Americans outside the European domain. The two partners had very different conceptions of the British relationship with continental Europe. The UK influenced by Churchill's three circles of influence – Common wealth, Europe and the United States – saw itself as a non-European power operating inside Europe for security reasons. As Herbert Nicholas put it: 'Seen from Downing Street there are two Europes. There is the Europe of defence . . . and then there is the Europe of everything else.'[10] The United States saw Britain as a European power not unlike other countries of the continent and continuously pushed an extremely reluctant Britain towards closer contacts with Europe.

The next section will illustrate how these basic misunderstandings affected the Anglo-American relationship from 1945 onwards. How they led Britain to engage in expensive commitments outside of Western Europe and to remain aloof from the European Community. This unsustainable situation finally collapsed with the withdrawal from east of Suez and application for EEC membership in the late 1960s. This led in turn to a widespread consensus among commentators by the 1970s that a permanent downgrading of the special relationship had occurred.

The Anglo-American relationship, 1945–1979

World War II drastically increased the asymmetry between Britain and the United States. In 1938 although Britain's GNP was only about a third that of the United States, per capita income was only slightly lower and in military terms the British had over one hundred thousand more men under arms. Had the term been in vogue, the United Kingdom was a superpower. The war saw Britain lose about one quarter of its pre-war national wealth as well as the decimation of much of its industry and infrastructure. Britain was still a major power, albeit clearly third behind the US and USSR, and retained that status until the 1960s. Nonetheless, after the war any partnership between the UK and the US could not be one of equals. As will become evident, it took successive British Governments some time to appreciate this fact.

Policy scope differences
As David Sanders has cited[11] as early as VE day the special relationship was much more special in the military and technical theatres than either the economic or political ones. Over the next two decades co-operation even in the military dimension was strained. The main area of contention was nuclear policy. In 1946 Congress passed, and Truman signed, the MacMahon Act terminating Anglo-American co-operation in atomic weapons research. Britain struggled vigorously for the repeal of this Act and in the interim pressed ahead with its own atomic efforts. In the 1950s this led to an independent attempt to produce the H-Bomb which was nearly curtailled by an Eisenhower Administration plan to end fissile production known as the 'cut off' proposal.

However, once the launch of Sputnik by the USSR in 1957 raised the possibility that the United States itself could be struck by nuclear weapons, the Administration's attitude underwent a remarkable transformation. The Americans now wanted to deploy Intermediate Range Ballistic Missiles (IRBMs) in Europe and the British government willingly obliged. This in turn led to much closer collaboration on nuclear questions generally and the repeal of the much detested MacMahon Act in 1958. However, as will be noted later, the United States remained cool about the British independent deterrent.

In other areas of Cold War policy-making British influence remained modest. Attlee's dramatic visit to Washington in 1950 may have had some impact on Truman's decision to restrain and ultimately terminate Douglas MacArthur's conduct in Asia but opinion within the administration was already shifting in that direction. Throughout the 1950s Britain pushed for a Cold War summit to reduce tensions but the United States largely regarded this as an irritating side-show and only moved towards such a summit when it deemed it appropriate to American interests. Britain was persistently more moderate than the US in the negotiations both for the Comprehensive Test Ban Treaty and the Non-Proliferation Treaty (where the UK agreed with the Russians that such a treaty should preclude the Germans getting even an indirect finger on the nuclear trigger). Such moderation was only a marginal factor in American thinking on either question.

Despite British aspirations to the contrary, the special relationship barely operated beyond a narrow military sphere. This was especially true in economic policy. The two years after 1945 saw the abrupt ending of Lend–Lease, an American campaign against the UK's Imperial Preference system, the disbanding of the wartime Combined Board for raw materials, production and resources, an attempt to submerge the sterling area into the dollar area, American domination of the Bretton-Woods institutions, and an American loan on terms widely seen as draconian by the British. Together these actions led the *Economist* of 23 August 1947 to comment: '. . . not many people in this country believe the communist thesis that it is the deliberate and conscious aim of American policy to ruin Britain and everything that Britain stands for in the world. But the evidence can certainly be read that way'.[12]

In return the US government appeared almost callously dismissive of the British. Distaste for the domestic programme of the Attlee administation enhanced this. By 1949 the *Wall Street Journal* reported that State Department officials believed the British economy to be finished and floated the notion that the best strategy for the British would be to become the forty-ninth state.[13] Although economic relations improved in the 1950s they remained distant. Legislation such as the Cargo Protection Act of 1954 was deemed as a direct attack on British interests and Britain's attempts to coax the US in some form of free trade agreement made no progress.

Despite all this, the special relationship remained central to British strategic thinking and impressing the Americans became the chief foreign policy goal. This impressing came in two forms, Britain's ability to operate as a worldwide power and the pursuit – than possession – of an independent British nuclear capability.

Thus the Chiefs of Staff argued in 1949 that the UK government had to act in Libya to display Britain's world power status and duly impress the United States. Failure to do so would mean 'We should join the ranks of other European powers and be treated as such by the United States.'[14] The Government's 'Global Strategy' paper three years later argued that the UK would only have an imput into American nuclear strategy if the UK itself was a nuclear power. This view was reasserted in 1954 in favour of producing the Hydrogen Bomb by the Chiefs of Staff. 'If therefore we were to maintain our influence in the counsels of the world it was essential that we should join the H-Bomb club.'[15]

Any thoughts of changing strategy, and there were not many, were set back by the one policy adventure of the 1950s attempted without and in opposition to the United States, the Suez débâcle. Within two years of that fiasco Britain gained the H-Bomb and Harold Macmillan proudly explained to the House of Commons: 'The fact that we have it makes the United States pay a greater regard to our point of view, and that is of great importance.'[16]

Yet the cost of the independent deterrent and the failure of the British Blue Streak missile system eventually forced Macmillan to turn to the United States for the weapon's missile delivery system. This left Britain in the odd situation of attempting to impress the United States by a weapon that would only be credible if the United States could be persuaded to contribute towards it. Regardless of this, Britain entered the 1960s jealously guarding its concept of a special relationship that was much more limited in its scope than the UK cared to accept. British policy was also driven by the fear of any other nation acquiring a similar relationship with the United States or displacing Britain. After 1960 when its armed forces first became the largest Western European component of NATO, and more so after 1964 when its total armed forces exceeded Britain's, that potential rival was West Germany. As will be outlined in the next section fears of being left out of the United States' favour finally decided the other area of UK–US misunderstanding, the Geo-political domain.

Geo-political differences
Britain's central security strategy for the post-war era was to gain and maintain the American military commitment to Europe. This posed a significant challenge to British policy-makers given

America's previous isolationism. It also left a quandry for Britain's relationship with continental Europe that continues to this day. How to present the unity of Europe so that it was sufficient to justify America's military support without appearing so unified as to make the Americans feel that support was unwanted or unnecessary. During the war Eden had fretted over America's post-war role and rejected Duff Cooper's suggestion of a 'Western Union' between Britain and the continent for fear that it would encourage American isolationism.[17] From 1945 to 1949 Britain tried to entice the United States to remain in Europe and, through a combination of Stalin's actions and Bevin's skill, succeeded in creating NATO which British governments have struggled to preserve ever since.

Ensuring the American commitment to European defence required Attlee's government to reassess its own military priorities. The immediate priority for British defence planners in the late 1940s had been the Middle East not Europe. It was not until 1948 that, in support of Bevin's diplomacy, Bernard Montgomery proposed a new continentalist strategy gravitating British defence efforts towards Western Europe. This was initially opposed by the Navy, Air Force and Attlee himself before carrying the day.[18]

Once NATO had been created it had to be protected. Attlee's fear of alienating the Americans led his government to pursue an expensive rearmament programme and throw full military backing to the American effort in Korea. This increase in defence expenditure had a highly detrimental affect on the domestic economy and meant that Britain's defence outlays exceeded that of any European state. These actions probably cost Attlee the 1951 election. The collapse of the proposed European Defence Community in the mid-1950s led to further fears of an American withdrawal from Europe. In response, Churchill and Eden felt obliged to reverse British military strategy entirely and commit over 50,000 troops to Europe. Not, ironically, as part of a commitment to Europe but as part of one to the United States.

British policy-makers were also convinced that if the Americans were to assist Britain through NATO then the UK would have to reciprocate by assisting the US in other parts of the globe. This factor plus the hankering for 'Great Power' status led the British to make a major commitment to policing the Indian Ocean. Hence, bases in Aden and Singapore initially designed for the seapower defence of India remained in use two decades after Indian independence. The incoming Labour Government of 1964 was asked to retain footholds in Hong Kong, Malaya and the Gulf region and initially agreed. Given Wilson's then opposition to entering the EEC, Labour had little left but the special relationship as the basis of its external strategy. The cost of this strategy was substantial, amounting to 55,000 troops and 15 per cent of the defence budget – a bloated one by European standards. Over £30,000,000 was spend enhancing the Aden base in the four years before Britain finally decided it would withdraw. The combination of that decision to quit the east of Suez role plus Wilson's failure to send even a token force to support the Americans in Vietnam, effectively ended the special relationship as Bevin or Eden would have understood it.

Throughout this period the greatest source of friction in Anglo-American politics was the strikingly different attitudes of the two governments towards Britain's links with Europe. After the war Britain's aim was, as Brian White says, '. . . claiming a special position . . . just below the United States and the Soviet Union perhaps but definately "above" the other European allies'.[19]

This was not at all how the Americans perceived matters. The United States desired Western Europe as a whole – preferably led by Britain – not the United Kingdom alone as its partner in the Cold War. Although the United States position was primarily affected by Cold War thinking – the belief that a more united Europe would be more militarily credible – it was also affected by cultural factors as well. American observers found it difficult to believe that Britain's geographical proximity to Western Europe did not feed through into her attitudes towards it. Whatever the reason, Secretary of State George Marshall geared his European Recovery Programme to the pursuit of Western European unity, and expressed his sympathy with Senator Fulbright's resolution of March 1947 favouring the creation of a United States of Europe. US sentiment was made more explicit still through the European Co-operation Act of 1949 which squarely declared that it was American policy to encourage the unification of Europe.

There then followed a pattern of clashes over Europe between the Truman and Attlee Governments. Labour scuppered a series of European initiatives: the European Customs Union; the European Payments Union; a meaningful OEEC; a strong WEU: the Council of Europe; the Schuman Plan; and the European Defence Community, by a combination of non-participation or wrecking from the inside. Bevin's tactics were often quite subtle. Once it became apparent that the Americans would demand some kind of European mechanism for channelling Marshall Plan money, Bevin created one, the Organisation for European Economic Cooperation (OEEC). Having created it and ensured the dollars would flow, Britain vetoed Paul-Henri Spaak, a leading member of the European Movement, as Director-General and quashed an American plan to give it a strong secretariat instead creating a strong Executive Committee to be headed by a British official. Similarly, Bevin devised the Western European Union as part of his strategy for gaining an American commitment to Europe, spoke of it as a bridge between Britain and Europe (for Secretary Marshall's consumption) and then all but dumped it once NATO had been created.

Bevin's view throughout this period was that expressed in a memorandum to the cabinet in October 1949: '... we must remain, as we have always in the past, different in character from other European nations and fundamentally incapable of wholehearted integration with them ...'.[20]

Ironically, part of Bevin's reasoning for avoiding European commitment was Britain's relationship with the United States. Bevin's strategy worked in the sense that by 1951 an exhausted America accepted that the UK would not take on the leadership of Western Europe. Bevin had thus committed his country to the role of junior partner to the United States in a relationship with, as has been outlined, marked differences in perceptions of policy scope. Bevin's victory was short-lived. The incoming Eisenhower administration, and especially Secretary of State John Foster-Dulles, was particularly enthusiastic for European integration in general and the European Defence Community concept in particular. Dulles, like most of the 'Asia First' lobby within the Administration, regarded the EDC as a quick fix to the problem of manpower in Europe freeing resources for Asian operations. Dulles' threat of an 'agonising reappraisal' of American security commitments should the EDC fail forced Eden to agree to an indefinite British military presence in West Germany.

Britain's disagreement with the US over Europe continued throughout the 1950s as another set of European initiatives encountered British indifference. The United States opposed Britain's attempts in 1955 to use the OEEC to kill off the proposed European Economic Community and regarded Britain's reaction to the EEC – EFTA – as ill-conceived and divisive. Worse was to come under the Kennedy Administration, whose 'Grand Design' plan for an enhanced European pillar for NATO offered Britain the choice of either taking the European route or having no clear role at all. Kennedy had been influenced by a committee under Dean Acheson (whose speech about Britain's failure to find a post-imperial role caused such a sensation at this time) that recommended the Europeanisation of NATO. In practice this meant the Europeans taking on the conventional defence role while the Americans concentrated on the nuclear dimension. Acheson influenced a 'Europeanist' lobby inside the State Department led by George Ball which strongly opposed the British independent deterrent and was willing to virtually force Britain into Europe. Macmillan won that battle at Nassau in December 1962 although the agreement reached there contained ambiguities between the British desire for Polaris to be independent and American efforts to promote multilateralism. After Nassau, Macmillan still faced American proposals for a Multilateral Force (MLF) to which Britain's nuclear arsenal would be pooled.

All of this, coupled with Kennedy's assurance that the special relationship would be enhanced by Britain's membership of the EEC, strongly influenced Macmillan's application to join despite Britain's continuing distaste for its supranational aspirations. Ignoring the reality that Anglo-American nuclear collaboration made a French veto probable Britain made its first attempt to enter the European Community. Yet that decision was still influenced by special relationship considerations. As Northedge puts it: 'No British Government in the early 1960s . . . could fail to see that a hostile attitude towards European integration was likely to transform the old Anglo-American special relationship into a far more unpredictable and formidable American–German special relationship'[21]

During the Johnson and Nixon presidencies the special relationship came to be substantially redefined. This was somewhat paradoxical as these were the first two post-war US presidents who actually used the words special relationship.[22] After the decision to abandon the East of Suez role the Wilson government began to use NATO as an institution seriously for the first time, Defence Secretary Healey promoting the Eurogroup of leading

European nations. This process was accelerated under Edward Heath who finally succeeded in making Britain a member of the EEC. Heath took the European side in the EEC–US economic disputes of the early 1970s and ostentatiously distanced himself from the United States in foreign policy generally. He was obliged, however, to turn to the Americans for co-operation in the Polaris Improvement Programme in 1973 having tried and failed to establish Anglo-French collaboration on the matter.

This winding down of the Anglo-American accord was symbolised in many ways. In 1971 a separate North American Desk was created at the Foreign Office implying a much more conventional relationship between the two countries. In the same year a *Times* survey of *Who's Who* entrants showed only 30 per cent believing that the special relationship was very valuable to Britain (down from 53 per cent in 1963) compared with 62 per cent willing to give the Common Market that ranking (up from 42 per cent in 1963).[23] Europe now seemed to command a new and dominant consensus in British foreign policy evaluation and in the 1975 EEC referendum the Foreign Office, so hostile to Europe twenty years earlier, '. . . were prepared to commit everything bar treason . . .'[24] to keep Britain in the community.

Although Callaghan's relations with both Kissinger when Foreign Secretary and Carter when Prime Minister were very warm, and co-ordination in the military-intelligence field remained wide, there seemed little doubt that there had been a fundamental and permanent shift in Britain's foreign and defence policy perspective. That was the reality that faced Margaret Thatcher when she became Prime Minister. As Michael Smith states:

Before the Conservative victory of that year (1979) it appeared that the 'special relationship' had largely disappeared, to be replaced by a more generalised condition of 'complex interdependence' such as those which can be said to exist between many of the advanced industrial societies.[25]

Mrs Thatcher's impact on this new consensus both in the short and longer terms will be the focus of the next section.

Anglo-American relations under Thatcher and Reagan

Inherited constraints made the revival of the special relationship improbable regardless of which party came to power in 1979.

Furthermore, Mrs Thatcher must have seemed an unlikely character to attempt any significant reorientation of British foreign policy in any direction, let alone one as central as the EEC–American balance. She became Prime Minister with virtually no background in foreign policy and made little contribution to foreign policy thinking while leader of the opposition bar a set of withering attacks on the Soviet Union, which were not perceived as representing any great strategic analysis. Her lack of experience in this area was compounded by a lack of enthusiasm. She wanted to get on with the job of reshaping Britain, the prospect of attending three major summits – the World Economic Summit in Tokyo, the Commonwealth Conference in Lusaka, Zambia, and the EEC Council in Dublin – during her first three months in power held scant attraction for her. Indeed, her first instinct had been to send the Foreign Secretary to them in her place,[26] a suggestion that was quickly quashed as impractical. Her participation at these gatherings appeared to do little to whet her appetite for foreign policy.

However, while she might have lacked a background in external policy she did have an intuitively pro-American bias that did not take long to surface. Like many of her generation who had come of age politically during World War II and the inauguration of the Cold War she naturally assumed that British interests lie with the continued good favour of the United States and that there was little Europe could do to replace that. Her first trip to Washington as premier, in December 1979, confirmed this. She took the opportunity to firmly ally herself with the United States in its hostage crisis predicament. Furthermore, whereas Wilson had described the relationship with the United States as 'close' and Heath more neutrally still as 'natural', Margaret Thatcher took the opportunity to describe it as 'extraordinary'.[27]

With the election of an ideological soulmate, Ronald Reagan, in November 1980 Thatcher was to upgrade the relationship further still. Reagan had a strong Anglophile element which one biographer dated to World War II when Hollywood was ardently pro-British and Reagan participated in the making of numerous training and propaganda films.[28] He had similarly strong sympathies for NATO as he was to demonstrate throughout his presidency. With Reagan in office Mrs Thatcher's passion for the American connection, and her interest in foreign policy matters, markedly increased. By 1985 she told the *Financial Times* that she had no inhibitions about describing the US relationship as '. . . very, very, special . . .'.[29]

To assess the impact of the Thatcher–Reagan *entente* two matters have to be determined. Was Mrs Thatcher any more successful at pushing back the limitations of the special relationship – in Policy Scope and Geo-politics – then her predecessors? Was Mrs Thatcher able to break the new consensus towards the EEC rather than the US that seemed to have taken root in the 1970s?

Policy scope constraints
Although the period since 1945 had witnessed intense Anglo-American co-operation in the military and military-intelligence field the relationship had also been characterised by the British tendency to overestimate their own importance and to look for the relationship to operate in more areas than the Americans were willing to permit. It is difficult to say at what point, if any, Mrs Thatcher became guilty of repeating that mistake. Both Peter Jenkins and Sir Anthony Parsons[30] argue that Mrs Thatcher did not entertain delusions of grandeur about the relationship, although Jenkins weakens this by saying that she was no more deluded than many of her predecessors, which would still offer considerable room for the weakness.

Certainly, towards the end of the Reagan presidency Mrs Thatcher seems to have believed that the revival of the Anglo-American alliance she created would last during the next American administration. She told the *Sunday Express* that 'One really has established a kind of relationship with the American people. I believe it will outlast any changes.'[31]

Furthermore, Mrs Thatcher's occasional attempts to set herself up as a go-between for Reagan and Gorbachev, and her apparent attempt to intervene in the Middle-East by encouraging contacts between Shimon Peres and King Hussein – both of whom she was personally very friendly with – do smack of a foreign policy much more akin to Harold Macmillan than Edward Heath. Set against that, while she could not overcome the Policy Scope restraints of the special relationship she succeeded in stretching them on many occasions and could lay claim to be the most influential foreign figure in Washington during much of the Reagan presidency.

Anglo-American intimacy in military-intelligence matters, always great, became if anything more intense during the Thatcher–Reagan period. This intimacy was highlighted by two particular incidents. The first was the renegotiation of the Trident package from the C4 to the D5 format in 1981 where Mrs Thatcher's known charm over President Reagan led the American side to offer the missile system on distinctly generous terms. More spectacularly still was the level of collaboration during the Falklands Islands conflict which made British operations substantially easier. This collaboration started while the United States was technically an honest broker with Secretary Haig on his ill-fated attempt at shuttle diplomacy and with a significant lobby inside the Administration, led by Jeane Kirkpatrick, opposing any such co-operation at all.

Such co-operation was not strikingly new. It did not mean, as it never has, that on issues of fundamental military importance to the US Britain had any kind of veto over American activity. That was demonstrated most clearly by the American invasion of Grenada where Mrs Thatcher was not consulted until late in the day and then ignored when she opposed the intervention. In other matters too, such as her failed attempt to persuade the Administration to buy the British firm Plessey's battlefield telecommunication system 'Ptarmigan' over the French company Thomson CSF's alternative, Mrs Thatcher tried to play the special relationship card without success.

In many other areas of military or military–political decisions when the Reagan Administration demonstrated its oft-presented capacity for internal division, Mrs Thatcher attempted, with some success, to influence Washington. Despite her reputation as a hawk Mrs Thatcher followed her predecessors in regularly taking the more moderate position on relations with the Soviet Union and Arms Control. This usually meant allying with (indeed occasionally being drafted by) the State Department against the Department of Defence and in particular the hardline Richard Perle.

Within months of Reagan taking office a huge row flared within Washington over arms control stategy. At the time of the NATO decision to deploy Cruise and Pershing missiles in Europe the US had pledged a 'dual track' strategy of deployment and negotiations. The anti-arms control lobby within the Pentagon favoured withdrawing from any dialogue with the Soviets on the issue, and were opposed by the State Department who feared the effect this posture would have on European opinion. Mrs Thatcher lobbied heavily for continued negotiations which, given her reputation as no appeaser of the USSR must have counted for something. Having said that hers was not the only voice articulating this message nor was her opinion the only political factor. The swelling anti-nuclear movement in West Germany and pressure to outflank the domestic Nuclear Freeze lobby may have been far more powerful influences on the Reagan Administration. Certainly the negotiating position that emerged – the 'Zero Option' – was never to Mrs Thatcher's taste. Curiously that option was supported by the US Department of Defence who had now become so convinced that the Europeans did not have the will to actually deploy that they saw little harm in offering it.

Similarly, after the Soviet inspired military crackdown in Poland elements in the Defence Department favoured massively raising the stakes by calling in Poland's debt. Alexander Haig enlisted Mrs Thatcher to the State Department's position and she urged restrain on the President.

The area in which she made the most strenuous efforts to influence the United States was over the Strategic Defence Initiative (SDI). Twice she felt obliged to hurtle across the Atlantic and correct the President's desire to use SDI as a route to achieving the abolition of nuclear weapons. Such a shift in US policy, bypassing the principle of deterrence and exposing the vast conventional superiority of the Soviet Union as well as increasing the prospect of an American withdrawl from Europe, so offended the principles on which British policy had been based since 1945 that it is highly probable Churchill, Attlee, Eden or Macmillan would have opposed it in precisely the terms she did.

At Camp David in December 1984 she achieved a major policy coup by getting Reagan's agreement to a four-point accord that, at least on paper, significantly limited the American freedom to manoevre on SDI. That coup was described by the Institute for Strategic Studies as 'Europe's most important political accomplishment since the President raised the SDI issue in 1983.'[32]

However, whether this triumph on parchment could actually restrain Reagan in practise was much more problematic. Over the next two years the administration inconsistently swayed between abrogating the SALT II limitations (Thatcher favoured remaining within them) and its position at the Rekjavik Summit in 1986 when Reagan seemed on the edge of agreeing to the elimination of all nuclear weapons within a decade. Horrified, Thatcher flew to a hastily convened meeting at Camp David in December 1986: there she recommitted Reagan, again on paper, to the principle of deterrence and assured his commitment to the modernisation of western nuclear weapons.

President Reagan's instinctive distaste for nuclear weapons and hence embrace of SDI appears to have shocked and concerned Margaret Thatcher more than any other element of his presidency. In her own memoirs (*The Downing Street Years*, London, Harper Collins, 1993) she recalls: 'I did not share President Reagan's view that it [SDI] was a means of ridding the world entirely of nuclear weapons. This seemed to me an unattainable dream – you could not disinvent the knowledge of how to make such weapons.'

This direct rejection of the presidential preference is even more striking when compared with the generally eulogenic tone of her other remarks towards him. Indeed it is noteworthy that her memoirs contain many more references to her interaction with him than he gives towards her in his own book. The disagreement is also stark given that, as she records elsewhere in her memoirs, she saw it as her 'duty to do everything I could to reinforce and further President Reagan's bold strategy to win the Cold War which the West had been slowly but surely losing.'

Ultimately her objectives in 1986 were realised in that SDI did not turn into the centrepiece of American defence strategy thus undermining the centrepiece of British defence policy. This result was achieved, however, because of a combination of technical difficulties with the whole project and a deep distrust of the whole idea on Capitol Hill. It did not meet its fate because Margaret Thatcher exercised any kind of veto over its development. She opposed the possibility of negotiating away ballistic missiles and formed an effective alliance with Admiral William Crowe, Chairman of the Joint Chiefs of Staff, to prevent Reagan tabling such a suggestion at the Geneva arms talks.[33]

Camp David also provides the one clear example of Thatcher overturning a policy on which the Reagan Administration was united and reasonably determined. The issue was arms sales to Argentina. Once democracy had been restored in Argentina, neither the State nor Defence departments could see any good arguments against resuming arms supplies. Mrs Thatcher, on the other hand, could see plenty of good reasons and sweetly bounced

Reagan into a commitment not to resume them – to the clear anguish of his officials.

However, where she tried to expand the special relationship beyond military and diplomatic questions Thatcher's record was much more patchy. She achieved a victory in extricating British Airways from lengthy American judicial battles that could have delayed BA's privatisation. She also saw legislation easing the way for the extradition of IRA suspects passed in 1986, although this was almost certainly passed because of pro-British sentiment in the aftermath of the Libyan bombing. But on the really big issues of American economic policy at home and abroad her impact was minimal – for all her efforts. She had little sympathy for Reaganomics regarding his large budget deficits as fundamentally destabilising but she found her advice to cure the deficit by raising taxes made no progress. As her Chancellor, Nigel Lawson, fell in with Treasury Secretary Baker's attempts to control world exchange rates she found that the administration's ability to affect her economic programme was far greater then her ability to influence his.

Overall then, while Mrs Thatcher clearly had an influence in certain sectors of Washington policy-making not seen since Macmillan's tenure in Downing Street, it would be difficult to say that she escaped the policy scope constraints of the special relationship. Intimacy continued to be greatest in military-intelligence concerns, her influence was at its greatest when the US government was divided (fortunately for her a commonplace event), and the relationship could not be extended to the sort of across-the-board understanding that she clearly would have liked.

Geo-political constraints
Since World War II British foreign policy has been based on keeping the American presence in Europe. As a result Britain felt obliged to keep large numbers of troops in Europe herself, spend a relatively high sum on defence, and assist the Americans outside of the European sector. These factors continued during the Thatcher–Reagan years. A further distinguishing feature had been significant disagreements between the two states on Britain's relationship with the European continent. This did not surface directly during the 1981–88 period but, as will later be illustrated, this source of tension in Anglo-American activities did not go away.

Britain's desire to keep the Americans in Europe was retained and if anything strengthened during Mrs Thatcher's premiership. The UK was more sensitive to American concerns of being unappreciated and issues such as the Nunn Amendment of 1984 (which called for the withdrawal of one-quarter of US troops in Europe if no progress was made on burden sharing) seemed to cause greater consternation in London then in other European capitals. Similarly, fear of pushing the Americans out of Europe by appearing too keen on European defence co-ordination also affected UK policy. It led to caution over European defence collaboration (thus provoking the Thatcher–Heseltine split over Westland in 1986) and also led Britain to oppose François Mitterrand's bid to reinvigorate the Western European Union in 1985.

The view also dictated Britain's stategy in dealing with the Strategic Defence Initiative. At heart Thatcher opposed the project root-and-branch as did most other Western European leaders, but given the need not to antagonise the US Thatcher rejected the approach of clear opposition followed by Mitterrand and others. Her strategy was to take the inside track: to offer nominal support for the project; get as large a share of the research contracts as possible; but put constant pressure on Reagan to use SDI as a bargaining tool.

In the aftermath of the Rekjavik summit, when the limitations of this strategy became apparent, Thatcher again reacted differently to the Europeans. Mitterrand and Kohl announced the formation of a joint Franco-German brigade of 4,200 men stationed in West Germany under the alternating command of French and German Generals. Mitterrand also resurrected his plans for an upgraded Western European Union. This represented, in a highly embryonic form admittedly, the beginnings of a European insurance policy in the event of a serious breach with the Americans over security issues. Thatcher opposed it as likely to increase the chances of that breach occurring. Given the contempt with which many in the American political elite had for so many of the Europeans, Margaret Thatcher's analysis may well have been valid in all of these instances, but her actions did not come without a price in terms of relationships in Europe.

High British defence spending (as a proportion of GDP) continued as a distinctive feature of UK policy again influenced by the need to pacify American sentiment. By 1987, Britain spent 5.5 per cent of GDP on defence compared with 3.8 per cent by the average European NATO country. This was despite a major – although ultimately partially implemented – set of cuts in 1981 from which the British Army on the Rhine was left broadly exempt. Interestingly, under Thatcher Britain resumed its willingness to support the United States outside the European quarter. David Sanders[34] identifies three specific instances: the revival of the Royal Navy's Armilla patrols in the Gulf of Oman in 1980; the UK contingent in the Lebanon in 1982–84; and the dispatch of Royal Navy minesweepers in the Persian Gulf in 1987.

To these three another two can perhaps be added. The use of British bases for the American raid on Libya in April 1986 effectively made the UK a *de facto* partner, albeit a reluctant one, in this particular enterprise. Finally, the speedy dispatch of British forces to the Gulf in support of the American-led coalition in Autumn 1990. The fact that all five operations were in the Middle East might be considered more than a coincidence given Britain's policy between 1945 and 1948 of considering that region the most vital one for British interests. Put together this support meant that, as David Sanders outlines, 'While this shift in posture did not amount to Britain playing anything resembling an "active world role" in the 1980s, it was certainly associated with a more active role than that pursued in the 1970s.'[35]

The desire to be seen as the best friend of the United States – and the US often needed and wanted vocal supporters – also affected Britain's diplomatic dealings with the Third World. While much of Europe opposed US policy towards Nicaragua and the Reagan Doctrine of aiding centre-right insurgency movements in the Third World, Britain broadly tolerated it. The exception to this was Mozambique on which the Administration was divided over the question of backing RENAMO against the Frelimo regime. Thatcher was on good terms with the Mozambique leadership and, given the split in the Administration, felt able to oppose the pro-rebel lobby. On South Africa, although for reasons much wider than just the American connection, Thatcher outdid Reagan in support for 'constructive engagement' with Pretoria. Britain also followed the US in withdrawing from UNESCO.

One area where there was notably little American pressure on Britain was over policy towards the European Community. Under Reagan the US had remarkably little interest in the European integration process and failed to appreciate the significance of the 1992 programme for some time. Within the State Department though there was an organised lobby that favoured a closer link to West Germany and this was to surface much more dramatically after Reagan's departure from the White House.

Overall, then, there appears to be a strong sense of continuity between the actions of the Thatcher Government and those of pre-1970s premiers, although not, it should be said on balance, with some of the 'Great Power' status-seeking they were motivated by. The extent of this was inevitably modest but, nonetheless, one is struck by how much more Mrs Thatcher might have agreed with Ernest Bevin then with the foreign secretaries she actually worked with.

The 'New Consensus' in the 1980s

The longer-run success of Margaret Thatcher's drive to put the special relationship closer to the centre of British foreign and defence thinking depends on two developments. First, how supportive of this goal post-Reagan American presidents are; and second, the extent to which she succeeded in moulding a consensus behind her objectives in Britain. The attitude of President Bush and the possible outlook of his successors will be examined in the next section but clearly if the British are unwilling to pursue the special relationship in the 1990s then it is unlikely to happen. This section will argue that for three reasons: the UK's resource base; the attitude of the Foreign Office; and the dynamics of events within the European Community. The 'New Consensus' on Britain's external role – centred on the EC – was battered but not broken during the Thatcher–Reagan period and is likely to command the attention of policy-makers in the 1990s.

The first restraint on any return to the special relationship is the continued wide asymmetry between the two parties. In the late 1960s, at the time when the East of Suez role was abandoned and the overture to Europe seriously made, Britain remained the world's second largest trading nation, was seventh in the GNP per capita pecking order, and in the worlds' top ten for: merchant shipping; shipbuilding; iron and steel production; coal output; automobile output; radio and television output; and cement output.[36] While there is scope for debate about whether the Thatcher years saw Britain's decline reversed in anything more than self-esteem terms there can be no doubt that Britain has not returned to the position it had in 1968. A position then believed to be too weak to sustain the special relationship as the pivot of British strategic thinking.

The reality therefore is that the economic preconditions that forced Britain to turn away, rather belatedly, from world power pretensions still hold. In that regard John Nott's defence review of 1981 with its focus on cutting the Navy's world patrolling capacity and concentrating on the Army in Europe is illuminating. Without an economic miracle on a German or Japanese scale Britain has very limited choices in its external policy dealings.

That is certainly how the British Foreign Office perceives matters. One of the distinctive features of the Thatcher premiership was the frosty relationship between Number 10 and the Foreign and Commonwealth Office (FCO). She quickly grew to detest the FCO's approach to politics (particularly in matters pertaining to the EC) with its perennial stress on accommodation and compromise, as much as its actual policy output. By 1982 she decided she needed independent foreign policy advice and used it to rigorously scrutinise the FCO. The professionals there barely disguised their dislike for her. Insults were traded between Number 10's categorisation of 'Eurofreaks' at the Foreign Office and the FCO's tendency to refer to (pro-American) 'poodlism' over at Downing Street.[37]

Mrs Thatcher's Foreign Secretaries tended to agree with their department's line. Her first, Lord Carrington (1979–82), became convinced of Britain's European destiny while serving as High Commissioner in Australia in the 1950s. Describing himself as a 'passionate' European he characterised Mrs Thatcher's approach to the EC as 'intransigent'.[38] Her second, Francis Pym (1982–83), referred to himself as an 'idealist for Europe'[39] and repeated the charge of intransigence against Mrs Thatcher. The memoirs of her third Foreign Secretary, Sir Geoffrey Howe (1983–89), have yet to enter print but everything about the circumstances of his departure from the Government in 1990 – a year after being abruptly shifted from the Foreign Office – would lead one to believe that his views matched those of Carrington and Pym. Her last Foreign Secretary, Douglas Hurd (1989–), has thus far been the soul of discretion but enthused for Europe in an article published a decade ago when he was a junior Minister at the FCO.[40]

All this meant that Mrs Thatcher's instinct to support the United States was often watered down in practice by the Foreign Office.

While she supported the American line on Iran, Afghanistan, and the Rapid Deployment Force British policy in action did not reflect those commitments. According to one account[41] Lord Carrington spent up to 80 per cent of his time on EC-related activities hoping that through his industry he could smooth the feathers that she had ruffled. Sir Geoffrey Howe reflected the FCO's hostility to Reagan's SDI in a hard-hitting speech in March 1985 virtually undermining Thatcher's attempt to achieve the same ends by stealth. In dealings with Europe from the middle 1980s onwards the Foreign Office strove to give the impression that Britain's bark on Europe was far worse then its bite.

Finally, of course, developments within the EC undermined the special relationship strategy. Britain was part of a European Community fast losing its Gaullist constraints. After the solution of Britain's long-standing row over its budgetary contribution in 1984 the UK began to act more in tune with the community as a whole. Britain participated vigorously in the debate over the single market, and Mrs Thatcher signed the Single European Act of 1985 despite the extension of powers to European institutions and hints of a common foreign policy contained within it. By the time of the skirmishes over European Monetary and Political Union Britain was so far into the European Community as to make Mrs Thatcher's options in opposing these proposals extremely limited. A retreat to the special relationship was certainly not an avenue available to her.

In summary, Mrs Thatcher's desire to shift the balance of British foreign policy towards a more Atlantic orientation had relatively few allies within the British political elite and Europe remained an issue capable of bedevilling both domestic politics and the transatlantic relationship. Just how can be seen through an examination of developments since Ronald Reagan left the White House.

Anglo-American relations since 1989

Anglo-American relations seemed to take a distinct turn with the arrival of George Bush to the presidency. Devoid of the sentimentality that had often appeared to characterise Reagan's dealing with Thatcher, those elements in the State Department that argued for a realpolitik reorganisation of policy towards France and, especially, West Germany appeared to get their head. Thus, as

Geoffrey Smith noted,[42] while Margaret Thatcher was the first European leader invited to Washington in 1981, Helmut Kohl had that honour in 1989.

West German concerns now appeared to dominate the Bush administration's dealings with Europe. When Bonn wanted to defer a decision on replacing the short-range Lance missile system and for the West to make a significant attempt to reduce conventional troops in Europe, Bush reversed policy and agreed. Mrs Thatcher had opposed both German initiatives. The first she thought smacked of backsliding and weakness, the second was likely to lead to the reduction of American force levels in Europe. Crucially, Washington was notably more sympathetic than London to the notion and timetable of German reunification.

Matters deteriorated further with Bush's call in December 1989 for a continued, possibly intensified, push for European integration. Such remarks had to be toned down after anxious protests from Downing Street acutely aware of the differences between Bush's comments and Thatcher's speech in Bruges on the subject just the previous year. This change in American thinking was partly a reaction to the reality that the German question remained the central one in the security future of Europe. There were also economic motivations as well. After realising that the EC's 1992 programme was serious and important, American officials began to feel acutely concerned about the implications for European–American trade relations. In practice they shared many of Margaret Thatcher's concerns about the whole enterprise. However, an alliance with her – the *bête noire* of the European integration lobby – on these issues was thought likely to reduce American influence not increase it. For American policy-makers it seemed far better to try and reach an accommodation with West Germany, clearly the central actor in the evolution of the EC, and use that relationship to gain an imput into the development of the Community.

Hence at the time of Margaret Thatcher's fall from power in Britain it looked as if her conception of the special relationship had fallen already. There also appeared to be a generational shift inside the Conservative Party. Mrs Thatcher, growing up in wartime Lincolnshire surrounded by American military personnel, had not ventured abroad until her honeymoon at the age of 26, hardly surprising given that it was unusual for young single women to travel alone at this time. Her experience contrasted with that of the previous generation, represented politically by Heath, Wilson and Callaghan, which grew up in the 1930s when questions of European policy were at the centre of domestic politics. Mrs Thatcher's successor came from a different background too. John Major's pre-parliamentary experience abroad had been in Africa. Much of what parliamentary contacts he had encountered from overseas were European. Indeed he had only visited the United States once before he became Foreign Secretary in 1989.

This analysis proved to be flawed. It ignored the cultural bonds between the US and UK. It also ignored the difficulties the United States would face in its bilateral dealings with the Germans. America's relationship with West Germany over the last twenty years has been frequently uncomfortable. Many of those difficulties have been the consequences of sharply differing ideas on how to deal with the Soviet Union with the Germans usually taking a much more dovish position. In their attempt to exert influence over EC policy via West Germany American officials forgot both the deep seated commitment to Europe in Germany's political culture and elites and ignored the fact that West Germany already had a special relationship – with the pro-integrationist French.

Commentators also underestimated the continuing importance of the military and military-intelligence links between Britain and the United States, which, after all, had always been the core component of the two countries' deep relationship. Three out of the five floors of the British embassy in Washington remain committed to military and intelligence purposes. That co-operation came into its own during the Gulf crisis and ultimate conflict where Britain sent the largest contingent of troops from any European source while Germany remained on the sidelines protesting that constitutional restrictions prevented it from acting. Germany's position during the Gulf War, and subsequent German–American disagreements over aid to the Soviet Union seems to have led the United States to draw back from its German experiment. By August 1991, the British appeared to have regained their pre-eminence in American sentiments, with President Bush eulogising the 'extraordinarily special relationship'.[43] Whether this pre-eminence can be retained under President Clinton is surely more doubtful.

The US has concerns about the development of the European Community both out of a fear that the new Europe will be protectionist and that it may take an isolationist stance over issues affecting present British anxieties. Nevertheless, neither party appears to be in much of a position to shape the evolution of the European Monetary and Political debate. The Maastricht Summit and treaty indicates that the United Kingdom may well find itself forced along by these events even if it dislikes them and even if they appear overtly hostile to American interests. Furthermore, Britain's problem remains that its popularity with the United States is purchased by its willingness to support American foreign policy to preserve the American military machine in Europe. It is also dependent on an enthusiasm for spending a relatively high sum on defence, and its readiness at times to operate outside of Europe in concert with the United States. For all the personal warmth between political leaders, in a world without the cold war, and with the EC and United States possibly moving in differing directions, the price of popularity with the Americans might be deemed excessively high.

Despite the considerable force that Mrs Thatcher placed behind the special relationship it would appear that those factors which reorientated British external thinking in the late 1960s and 1970s have held firm. The revival of the accord between the United States and Britain during the 1980s will not predetermine British or American attitudes in coming decades. Anglo-American relations in the 1990s will be heavily determined by the state of EC-American relations. The course of that relationship – special or otherwise – cannot yet be anticipated. That Margaret Thatcher will strongly disapprove of such an interdependence between Britain, the European Community, and the United States can be taken for granted.

Notes

1 Reported in the *Financial Times*, August 31st 1991.

2 Ronald Reagan, An American Life (New York, Hutchinson, 1990).

3 David Watt in W. Louis and H. Bull (eds), *The Special Relationship* (Oxford, Clarendon, 1986) and D. Vital, *The Making of British Foreign Policy* (London, Allen & Unwin, 1968) respectively.

4 G. Moorhouse, *The Diplomats: the Foreign Office Today* (London, Cape, 1977).

5 David Watt in W. Louis and H. Bull (eds), *The Special Relationship* (Oxford, Clarendon, 1986).

6 Sir Michael Howard in Louis and Bull (eds), *The Special Relationship* (Oxford, Clarendon, 1986).

7   J. Frankel, *British Foreign Policy 1945–1973* (London, RIIA, 1975).
8   R. Edmonds, *Setting the Mould* (Oxford, Clarendon, 1986).
9   Nathan Glazer in J. Clark (ed.), *Ideas and Politics in Modern Britain* (London, Macmillan, 1990).
10   H. Nicholas, *Britain and the United States* (London, Chatto & Windus 1963).
11   D. Sanders, *Losing an Empire, Finding a Role* (London, Macmillan, 1990).
12   Quoted in R. Edmonds, *Setting the Mould* (Oxford, Clarendon, 1986).
13   R. Manderson-Jones, *The Special Relationship* (London, Weidenfeld & Nicholson, 1972).
14   W. Roger Louis in Louis and Bull (eds), *The Special Relationship* (Oxford, Clarendon, 1986).
15   Nigel Wheeler, British nuclear weapons and Anglo-American relations, 1945–1954, *International Affairs*, 62.
16   Reported in *the Times*, 24 February 1958.
17   E. Barker, *Britain in a Divided Europe 1945–1970* (London, Weidenfeld & Nicholson, 1971).
18   J. Baylis, *British Defence Policy* (London, Macmillan, 1989).
19   Brian White in S. Smith, M. Smith & B. White (eds), *British Foreign Policy* (London, Unwin Hyman, 1988).
20   R. Edmonds, *Setting the Mould* (Oxford, Clarendon, 1986).
21   F. Northedge, *Descent from Power* (London, Allen & Unwin, 1974).
22   J. Frankel, *British Foreign Policy 1945–1973* (London, RIIA, 1975).
23   Frankel, *British Foreign Policy*.
24   G. Moorhouse, *The Diplomats: the Foreign Office Today* (London, Cape, 1977).
25   Michael Smith in P. Byrd (ed.), *British Foreign Policy under Thatcher* (Oxford, Philip Allen, 1988).
26   G. Smith, *Reagan and Thatcher* (London, Bodley Head, 1990).
27   J. Baylis, *British Defence Policy* (London, Macmillan, 1989).
28   L. Cannon, *Reagan* (New York, Simon & Schuster, 1991).
29   *Financial Times*, 23 March 1985.
30   Noted by P. Jenkins, *Mrs Thatcher's Revolution* (London, Pan, 1988) and Sir Anthony Parsons in Kavanagh and Selsdon (eds), *The Thatcher Effect* (Oxford, Oxford University Press, 1989).
31   Quoted in G. Smith, *Reagan and Thatcher* (London, Bodley Head, 1990).
32   Quoted in P. Jenkins, *Mrs Thatcher's Revolution* (London, Pan, 1988).
33   L. Cannon, *Reagan* (New York, Simon & Schuster, 1991).
34   D. Sanders, *Losing an Empire, Finding a Role* (London, Macmillan, 1990).
35   Sanders, *Losing an Empire*.
36   D. Vital, *The Making of British Foreign Policy* (London, Allen & Unwin, 1968).

37   Cited in P. Cosgrove, *Carrington: a Life and a Policy* (London, Dent & Sons, 1985) and P. Jenkins, *Mrs Thatcher's Revolution* (London, Pan, 1988).

38   Lord Carrington, *Reflect on Things Past* (London, Collins, 1988).

39   F. Pym, *The Politics of Consent* (London, Hamish Hamilton, 1984).

40   D. Hurd, 'Political co-operation', *International Affairs*, 57.

41   P. Cosgrove, *Carrington: a Life and a Policy* (London, Dent & Sons, 1985).

42   Observed by G. Smith, *Reagan and Thatcher* (London, Bodley Head, 1990).

43   Quoted in *The Times*, 31 August 1991.

Part II
Elites

The transformation of the Conservative Party in the 1980s

It will be interesting to be the last of the Conservatives. I foresee that will be our fate.

Lord Salisbury, 1882[1]

[A colleague in 1975] prepared a paper arguing that the 'middle way' was the pragmatic path for the Conservative Party to take, avoiding the extremes of Left and Right. Before he had finished speaking to his paper, the new party leader reached into her briefcase and took out a book. It was Friedrich von Hayek's *The Constitution of Liberty*. Interrupting our pragmatist, she held up the book for all of us to see. 'This', she said sternly, 'is what we believe,' and banged Hayek down on the table.

John Ranelagh, *Thatcher's People*[2]

When Lady Gwendolyn Cecil, daughter and biographer of the Marquess of Salisbury, the most successful Tory leader before Margaret Thatcher, was attributing blame for appeasement in the 1930s, she heaped it on Viscount Halifax, Neville Chamberlain's Foreign Secretary. Her argument: that Chamberlain himself was 'a poor middle-class monster who could not be expected to know any better'.[3]

Fifty years ago, the Tories reluctantly tolerated upper-middle-class leaders. Nowadays inverse snobbery reigns supreme, though not until 'classless' John Major defeated 'toff' Douglas Hurd for the succession to Margaret Thatcher in 1990 did attendance at Eton become a positive disqualification for leadership. The quip of the 1980s was that the Conservative Party had passed from the estates to the estate agents.

The broad outlines of the social transformation in the Tory elite are well known; so are the main features of the shift in Tory ideology which accompanied it. Less explored, but crucial to an understanding of the Conservative party of the 1980s, is an assessment of the interrelation between the two. To shed some light on that issue, and on the development of modern British conservatism more generally, this essay explores three aspects of the Conservative party under Thatcher: its values, its electoral geography, and its elite. Analysing the character of all three in a broad historical context, and the connections between them, it argues that far from leading the Conservatives into *terra incognita*, Thatcher largely reaffirmed traditional Tory values and reinforced the traditional Tory electorate; only the new elite spawned in the Thatcher years marked a distinctly new force, and even that, by leavening the Conservative parliamentary party with MPs more closely attuned to the populace than ever before, served mainly to generate the self-confidence crucial to the reaffirmation of traditional values. In other words, it was new elite, old ideology – though stripped of its former 'aristocratic defence' baggage; a make-up not dissimilar to that of Ronald Reagan's Republican Party, as the essays by Nicol Rae and Jack Pitney testify.

For Thatcher, as for all democratic leaders, electoral success was the prerequisite for power. In the 1980s the Tories established an electoral base stronger, and perceived by its MPs as stronger, than any since Salisbury's day. In the words of that great post-war Tory pragmatist R. A. Butler, politics is the art of the possible. But the 'possible' is no more immutable than the fabled 'centre ground' from which pre-Thatcher politicians were supposed to stray at their peril. Under Thatcher, the Tories came, for the first time since the mass franchise, to regard themselves as naturally Britain's dominant party. This gave them, for the first time in a century and a half, the actual and psychological freedom to say and do what the heart of the party had always believed but feared to express, let alone to implement. That, working in tandem with a new, more populist, Tory elite, constitutes the fundamental transformation of the Conservative Party in the 1980s.

Tory values

The Conservative Party, as an organised political force worth the name 'party', was established in the 1780s by William Pitt and had its ideology articulated in the following decade by Edmund

Burke in his *Reflections on the Revolution in France*. The Tory party of Pitt and Burke stood for the landed aristocracy, the existing social and political order, discipline, sound finance and the established Church. Before democracy threatened, it relied on the monarchy and its dominance of state institutions to protect those interests. However, a distinct wariness of the state soon developed. The treble trauma of the wars against revolutionary France (1793–1815) imposing the heaviest taxation ever remembered, the Great Reform Act (1832) extending the vote downwards and eliminating the Crown as an independent political force, and the repeal of the Corn Laws (1846), legislation which, more than any other, symbolised the landlord state, led the party towards a *laissez-faire* economic stance early in its life. It sat – still sits – uneasily with a strong étatist tradition, deriving from the party's Pittite origins as an instrument of government and from its inherited assumptions about hierarchy and authority. *The Free Economy and the Strong State* (1988), the title of Andrew Gamble's influential study of Thatcherism, could entitle a study of Conservatism in any period since Sir Robert Peel's premiership (1841–46). By the 1870s the Tories were a broadly anti-collectivist, 'small government', nationalist, free-market (if not always free trade) party, spiced by Benjamin Disraeli with a mild social conscience ('one nation') and a lot of imperial flag-waving.

However, the Tories were never simply the party of the landed aristocracy. The City supported Pitt from the beginning, and from the 1870s onwards – particularly after Gladstone's espousal of Home Rule for Ireland in 1886 – the Conservative Party's status as the 'Establishment', plus its hostility to collectivism, brought strong infusions of support from industrial capital and the professions.[4] The Liberals retained a fair slice of business support – particularly business run by 'nonconformist' Protestants – until its demise after the World War I; but by the time mass politics had arrived in 1880s, the Tories were a recognisably pro-business party, albeit tempered by the dominance of traditional aristocratic forces in the party's leadership. Significantly, it was only after the 1880s that British Tories began to look on America and its Republicans with anything approaching enthusiasm.

Yet if forging alliances with rising financial and industrial elites proved fairly straightforward for the Tories, embracing the mass electorate was a far more fraught endeavour. Adapting to the quasi-democracy introduced by a series of statutes to extend the vote enacted between 1832 and 1884 caused the aristocracy deep *angst*, personified in the extraordinary progress of Lord Salisbury (1830–1903), thrice prime minister between 1885 and 1902, from passionate reactionary to fatalistic master of the democracy he despised.[5] In truth, Salisbury's most valuable ally was W. E. Gladstone, the Liberal leader to whose genius Britain's smooth and peaceful transition to mass politics may be largely attributed. Gladstone's intense conservatism in matters social, married to an extraordinary rapport with the 'labouring classes' (as he called them), kept the pace of change manageable, and left its management largely in the hands of the landed elite – so much so that the desertion of the influential Whig segment of that elite from the Liberals to the Tories in the mid-1880s proved to be the foundation for a generation of Tory rule. But the subsequent rise of the 'New Liberalism', a socially-oriented brand of progressivism associated with Welsh radical David Lloyd George, wrong-footed the Tories, who in the run up to World War I lost three elections in a row (one in 1906 and two in 1910) fighting mildly progressive social reforms and defending to the hilt regressive tariffs and the privileges of the Established Church and landed aristocracy.[6] Lord Hugh Cecil, Salisbury's son, went so far as to make church and lords pillars of the Conservative creed.[7]

In its blind opposition to New Liberalism in the Edwardian decade the Tory party sacrificed electoral expediency to 'principle' for the first time since the Great Reform Act,[8] and the memory of the consequences died hard. Without pressing the analogy too far, the experience of New Liberalism and World War I made an impression on British Tories commensurate with the impact of Roosevelt's New Deal on US Republicans thirty years later. A decade of fierce combat with populist collectivism had yielded bitter defeat and impotence. By the end of it, the moral seemed unambiguous: accommodate or perish. To Stanley Baldwin, the most successful Tory leader between Salisbury and Thatcher,[9] it meant 'facing leftwards in opposition to socialism'; Eisenhower called it 'dynamic conservatism'.[10] They were separated by two decades, and the degree of accommodation was different, as were the Lloyd George/Roosevelt reforms to which they were reacting. But the approach was the same; and it was the same whether couched in the emollient tones of Baldwin and Eisenhower or the more pugnacious rhetoric of Neville Chamberlain and Richard Nixon.

Accordingly, from the Lloyd George coalition (1916–22) until the Selsdon conference (1970) the Tory leadership continuously and consciously appeased its opponents. The Unionist Party surrendered the Union; the Imperial party sacrificed the Empire; the party of the aristocracy hastened its political demise; the Conservative Party accepted, even pioneered, greater state intervention and welfare provision; the party of Pitt and Disraeli even wobbled dangerously on the necessity for strength abroad in the face of European fascism rampant. Indeed, many of the Tories' most dynamic leaders – Chamberlain in the 1920s and 1930s, Butler in the 1940s, Macmillan in the 1950s and Macleod in the 1960s – positively gloried in beating Labour at their own game. Public utilities in the 1920s? The state would create and regulate them as readily as its opponents. Public housing in the 1950s? The Tories would build more and faster than Labour. Nationalisation from the 1940s to the 1970s? Attlee's legacy left untouched, save for a few token reversals. Taxation? No cuts, save just before elections.

The mistake, however, is to view Thatcherism as simply a rejection of this phase in Tory development. It was, of course, such a rejection, given deep emotional intensity by the experience of the so-called 'Heath U-turn' of 1972/3. The conviction that there should be no repetition was a central tenet of Thatcherism. But equally, Thatcherism marked a *reaction*, a return to values deeply rooted in the party's history, values the party had never wholly foresaken even when most compromised by accommodation. 'The puzzle to be recognised', two leading political scientists assert, 'is that despite the British Conservative party's long-standing distaste for dogma, it has spawned a new ideology, "Thatcherism".'[11] There is no puzzle: the dogma of Thatcherism was, refurbished and in certain respects reformed, the dogma of Burke and Salisbury. All they would have found distasteful was the use of that word to describe it.

An appreciation of the reactionary nature of Thatcherism is crucial to understanding why the Conservative Party accepted it so readily. Once put forward by the party leadership with the authority of an electoral mandate, Tories could no more oppose tax and public spending reductions, privatisation and the curbing of trade union power, to take but four controversial policies of the first

two Thatcher terms, than could Labour MPs oppose their oppo-
sites when similarly proposed. The so-called 'wets' who opposed
Thatcher in the early 1980s were bereft not just of back-bone but
of principles amounting to more than a commitment to 'social
peace' (which the *status quo ante* had manifestly failed to guarantee) and a 'middle way' between two poles, one of which was
free-market conservatism itself. In this context it is important that
statements of official ideology are separated from underlying
beliefs and commitments. Because in the 1950s successive Tory
ministries pursued pro-welfare and colonial withdrawal policies,
it does not follow that the Tory outlook had become essentially
collectivist and 'little England'. In fact, Tory language, and the
underlying convictions it expressed, remained remarkably un-
changed throughout. 'Conservative Freedom Works' was the party's
election slogan at the height of 'Butskellism' in 1955. Harold
Macmillan, Tory prime minister from 1957 to 1963, gave great
emphasis to the need for accommodation, but even he was always
careful to differentiate his vision of the welfare state from Labour's.
'We believe that unless we give opportunity to the strong and able,
we shall never have the means to provide real protection for the
old and weak', he told the party meeting that confirmed him as
leader.[12] Setting out *The Conservative Case* in 1959, Lord Hailsham
was far blunter: 'In fighting socialism in the twentieth, as they
fought liberalism in the nineteenth century, Conservatives will be
found to have changed their front to meet a new danger, but not
the ground they are defending.'[13] Iain Macleod had no doubt that
the essence of modern conservatism was 'to see that men had an
equal chance to maker themselves unequal'.[14]

Thatcherism was largely a change of front, not of ground. It
was not a straightforward return to the world before 'socialism'.
Britain was no longer an empire, and not even the Falklands War
(1982) could delude Conservatives otherwise. Even in social policy,
the Thatcherite emphasis on Victorian self-help and Christian
individualism did not signal an assault on the welfare state, much
though many ardent Thatcherites wished to launch one. Electoral
exigencies had not relaxed to that extent – as Table 7.1, comparing
popular attitudes to government intervention in Britain and the
United States in 1985, demonstrates graphically. For the rest,
though, the values of Thatcher were the values of Salisbury, once
he had come to terms with political democracy in the 1880s,

Table 7.1 *Attitudes to state responsibilities, 1985*

per centage saying the government definitely should:	*Britain*	*USA*
Provide health care for the sick	86	35
Provide a decent standard of living for the old	78	40
Reduce income difference between rich and poor	45	16
Provide a decent standard of living for the unemployed	43	15

Source: J. A. Davis, 'British and American Attitudes', in R. Jowell (ed.), *British Social Attitudes* (Aldershot, Gower, 1986).

discounting at least partially his notions of imperial, aristocratic and racial ascendancy. Small government, low taxes, free markets, property large and small, self-reliance, Christian charity, limited intervention – the same principles applied to different circumstances. As David Willetts writes insightfully of his party's history:

There has always been a strong free-market element in conservatism, going back to Edmund Burke himself. [And] Conservatives have always understood that there is more to life than free markets – the ties of history, community and nationhood. Those two propositions remain as true of the Conservative party in the 1980s and the 1990s as throughout its history. Mrs Thatcher may have expounded those principles with a rare conviction and emotional force, and thus given them a distinctive personal tone, but it was still conservatism she was expounding.[15]

But if much in 'conservatism' is constant, the Tories' perception of their ability to marry it with politically marketable programmes has changed greatly over the century. Electoral exigencies lie behind the changes. Once the vote had been extended to the working classes, the Tory-dominated House of Lords had been curbed and New Liberalism had launched the political left firmly on the collectivist road, those exigencies meant one thing: the devising of programmes appealing to a sufficient section of the mass, predominantly working-class electorate to enable the party to win elections.

To sum up, for Conservatives the sixty years after World War I witnessed a fairly continuous process of appeasement. Tory governments contended for the 'centre ground' in what they conceived to be Downsian party system. Macmillan actually dubbed his 1930s Tory programme 'The Middle Way'. On the domestic front it was largely the political left which defined what was the centre; only when it came to imperial and foreign policy, and the more general facets of 'statecraft' – the way government in Britain should be conducted – were Tories able to impose their will with any confidence. In comparative European (though not US) terms the Labour party was a moderate, barely socialist, force, which made accommodation more palatable than it might otherwise have been. But that made the necessity for it only more imperative in Tory eyes. Under Baldwin and Macmillan the imperative was acknowledged with flourish; under others – notably Heath and Chamberlain – it was done with evident distate; either way, it was done with an inner conviction which, for most Tories, rarely extended much beyond an appreciation of the exigencies of 'modern politics'. Under Thatcher, however, the Tories discovered that they did not need to do it to anything like the same degree. The next section starts to explain why.

Electoral geography

The late 1970s and 1980s saw the composition of the English electorate, and the electoral geography of England, shift dramatically in the Conservatives' favour. It is important to stress 'English' and 'England'. In Scotland and Wales ostensibly similar changes did not work to the Tories' advantage, but in 1987 those countries together comprised only 14 per cent of the UK electorate (Northern Ireland, with its idiosyncratic party system, accounted for only a further 2 per cent), and the party proved more than able to compensate through strength in the union's 'predominant partner'.

Social change was an important factor in the Tories' increased English strength. In 1964 the 'salariat' comprised 18 per cent of the electorate and the manual working class 47 per cent; by 1983 the proportions were 27 per cent and 34 per cent respectively.[16] Owner-occupiers accounted for 39 per cent of the residential housing stock in 1961, 63 per cent in 1986.[17] The litany of statistics could go on to educational qualifications, council house sales, real disposable income, mobility – all tell a similar story. There is no simple correlation between support for the Conservatives and the growth of the salariat, the decline of the manual working class, or more affluence/ownership/education. In Scotland the correlations are weak or even negative. Throughout the 1980s students of electoral behaviour were reluctant to admit their strength in England either: writing after the 1983 election, Anthony Heath and his colleagues saw a 'trendless fluctuation' in the movement of votes between elections since 1964,[18] while Ivor Crewe, highlighting the rising number of voters declaring themselves uncommitted to a party and the failure (according to opinion surveys) of Thatcherism to refashion public attitudes to the role of the state, concluded that the 'committed electorate' had given way to the 'hesitant electorate'.[19] If opinion polls are the yardstick, volatility there certainly was – enough to convince one and all by the end of the 1992 election campaign that the English electorate, depressed by recession and alienated from the Tories by a succession of extraordinary public policy débâcles, was about to fluctuate decisively in Labour's direction. But when the votes were counted, the fluctuation evaporated, and Labour recorded a significantly lower percentage of the vote than that with which it lost office in 1979. Surveying English electoral politics in the last thirty years as a whole, the fluctuations appear anything but trendless: the most significant hesitation in the electorate between 1979 and 1992 was the evident unwillingness of a steady 46 per cent of it to vote anything but Conservative.

The Tories' post-1979 parliamentary strength was built on a virtually hegemonic grip over the constituencies of southern England. In 1987, of the 260 seats south of the midlands, constituting 41 per cent of the mainland total, the Conservatives won 227 (or 87 per cent), polling an average of 52 per cent of the popular vote across them. Taking England as a whole, in 1987 the Tories won 358 of the nation's 523 seats (67 per cent) with an average poll of 46 per cent, in spite of three-party contests throughout. The proportions of the vote were similar in 1992, though higher than average swings in marginal seats gave the Tories 38 seats fewer than in 1987. The party nonetheless secured 61 per cent of England's seats, losing only a handful in the south outside London, with 45.5 per cent of the vote across the country.

This regional dimension to the Tories' electoral strength was not new to the 1980s. The Tories' electoral base centred on the home counties and 'respectable' suburbs of the major cities long before class politics clearly asserted itself in the early part of this century. There is nothing new in dubbing the Tory party the English National Party: they have been doing it themselves for three centuries and more. 'My politics are described by one word, and that word is ENGLAND', Disraeli declared to his electors in 1832.[20] Yet in no run of three successive elections between 1830 and 1980 was Tory strength in its heartland so absolute,[21] nor previously was Tory strength, especially in terms of parliamentary seats, so disproportionately concentrated on its heartland as it was in the 1980s. Indeed, had it been, given the party's 1980s decline in Scotland, Wales and the north, the electoral consequences would have been dire. Taking the period 1955 to 1987 as a whole, the two-party (i.e. Labour-Tory) swing to the Tories was 8.9 per cent in the south and 5.9 per cent in the Midlands, ample compensation for swings to Labour of 8.6 per cent in the north and 19.1 per cent in Scotland. Wales offered a meagre swing of 0.6 per cent to the Tories.[22]

Statistical analysis of the 1987 election reinforces this by revealing a strong correlation in Scotland, the north and the west between the social composition of constituencies and their voting behaviour, but at best only weak correlations between those variables in the south and the east.[23] In the first three areas, the higher the proportion of unemployed, manual and skilled non-professional workers, the better Labour performed at the expense of both the SDP/Liberal Alliance and the Tories; in the south and west, however, it was location and, particularly, distance from London and certain lines of communication from the metropolis which appear to account for much of the variation in voting behaviour. In 1992 the picture was less clear: the impact of the early 1990s recession was evident in results in both halves of the country, but in the south-east triangle bounded by East Anglia, the south-east Midlands, the West Country and the south coast (Greater London excepted) Conservatives performance did not correlate with unemployment trends, and within much of the triangle, particularly the areas north and east of the capital, Tory performance was distinctly stronger than would have been expected from the national result.[24]

Thus under Thatcher the electoral base of Conservatism was not only large and growing, but increasingly socially homogeneous and geographically concentrated. In the 1970s and 1980s Tory England was expanding England – just as in the same period in the US, Republican-inclined states were expanding America. By the mid-1980s half of Britain's population lived south of Birmingham. In 1935, southern English counties outside the inner

London area elected 165 MPs; in 1987 the region returned 235; after the next boundary revision, due in 1994, it will be around 250, an increase of almost 50 per cent in sixty years.

It was not, though, only a matter of the strength of the Tory electoral base: the *perception* of that strength counted just as much. Between 1982 and 1989 Tory support, as recorded in opinion polls, remained consistently higher and less volatile than that for any other party not only at, but also between elections. For 33 of the 47 months of the 1983 to 1987 parliament the party led the polls, a remarkable record; and for the entire 1983–87 parliament its registered support rarely dipped below 35 per cent and was usually nearer 40 per cent, a figure neither Labour nor the SDP/ Liberal Alliance proved able to reach – or at least, in Labour's case, to sustain. It was a different story in the first two years of the 1979–83 parliament and the last two of the 1987–92 parliament. But the intervening eight years was a period when the Tories were not merely dominant, but consistently exhibited their electoral dominance. Moreover, that dominance appeared – and was so considered by the party's leadership – to be almost entirely due to national factors and efforts. In their own perception of the forces significant to their holding power nationally, local government became decreasingly important to the Tories; even local constituency parties came to be seen as less important than hitherto – although they continued to play a crucial role in the selection of candidates. Ironically, perhaps, the Tories' first impressive result in local elections across the country after Mrs Thatcher entered Downing Street came in May 1992, a month after the party's surprise fourth parliamentary victory.

One final factor must be noted before drawing conclusions. The electoral collapse of the Labour party in the early 1980s, and the failure of the SDP/Liberal Alliance to concentrate it support sufficiently to pose a serious electoral challenge to the Tories in more than some four dozen seats, gave Tory MPs elected in 1983 and 1987 extraordinarily large majorities in their own constituencies, even though the Conservative party's national share of the vote was unimpressive in historic terms. At 42.2 per cent, the Tories' 1987 percentage of the vote was the lowest won by any Conservative government since 1922. But 300 of the 376 Tory MPs returned in 1987 had leads over their nearest rivals of more than 10 per cent of the vote: for the 76 MPs with majorities of less than 10 per cent

to have lost their seats at the subsequent election would have required a uniform swing of a size equal to the largest recorded
in any post-1945 election – and that was the 1979 swing to the
Tories.

To be sure, such a swing seemed entirely plausible in the depth
of the Tories' 1990 poll tax trauma; it even appeared possible
during the 1992 election campaign. In the event barely half the 76
seats actually fell. However, more to the point, until the poll tax
crisis only a very small proportion of Tory MPs elected in 1987
actually believed themselves vulnerable to defeat at the next
election, even allowing for a comparatively respectable Labour
performance at the polls. For most of the decade most Tory MPs
believed themselves to be well-nigh electorally invulnerable. This
had a double effect: it helped to give radicals among the Tory
leadership – Mrs Thatcher first and foremost – the courage of
their private convictions; and it rendered the Conservative parliamentary party maleable in their hands. The fact that most Tory
MPs considered themselves 'non-ideological',[25] far from slowing
this process, only served to hasten it.

To underline this argument, compare the elections of 1959 and
1987, both of which yielded Tory majorities of around 100 seats
in the Commons. In 1987 the Conservative lead over Labour, 11.5
per cent, was more than twice as large as the 1959 margin. The
comparison is equally stark if one looks back to the 1920s, the
last period when the Tories were the largest, and usually governing, party in a three-party electoral contest. Both the 1922 and
1924 elections resulted in decisive Conservative victories, on
a scale to match 1983 and 1987 in terms of seats won. However,
taking the two sets of elections together, a study of the results
in a representative sample of 50 Tory seats from each election
in both decades indicates that around 28 per cent of Tory MPs
in the 1920s had constituency majorities of less than 10 per
cent of the votes cast, whereas for the 1980s the figure was around
19 per cent – suggesting that in the 1980s there were a third fewer
marginal seats.

The comparison with the 1920s can be taken further by applying to the Conservative vote in the 1980s an analytical technique
employed the historian Ross McKibbin in his study of inter-war
Conservatism[26] – namely the 'two-party preferred vote', ascertained
by supposing that all voters who did not vote for the two largest

parties were required to chose between them. There are obvious problems in calculating this vote, and it can only be done crudely from the broad pattern of polls and surveys of the Liberal – SDP/ Liberal Alliance in the 1980s – vote. There are also clear limitations in the usefulness of the preferred vote, since in Britain electoral outcomes depend upon first preferences alone. Even so, the preferred vote helps illuminate the dynamics of electoral change and the realignments to which they give rise. If we apply the McKibbin model to elections since 1964, assuming a roughly equal division of Liberal second preferences between the two major parties, for the five elections between 1964 and 1974 the mean Conservative preferred vote was about 47.5 per cent. On the same assumption, the mean Conservative preferred vote for the three elections between 1979 and 1987 was about 53.3 per cent. In fact, even that may underestimate the Tory preferred vote: a survey of the 1987 vote[27] suggests that SDP/Liberal Alliance voters divided Tory: Labour in their second choices in the ratio 51:33 – suggesting a higher Tory vote still had the third party's voters been obliged to make the choice. In elections between 1922 and 1935, the Conservatives' preferred vote is calculated by McKibbin[28] at consistently between 55 and 59 per cent (apart from the highly exceptional 1931 election when it rose to 67 per cent).

But if the level of the preferred Tory support was similar in the 1920s/1930s and 1980s, its quality was altogether different, in two respects in particular. First, its distribution, as noted above, was less consistently favourable to the Conservatives in the earlier period. Second, Tory leaders in the inter-war years regarded their electoral position as critically dependent not only on the divisions of their opponents (as in the 1980s), but on their ability to accommodate the 'moderates' among the leaders of their opponents – just as forty years earlier Salisbury's strategy had depended upon drawing over the Whig leaders to break the Gladstonian majority. The 1931 election saw the return of 473 Tories in a House of Commons of 615, yet the post-election reconstruction of the 'National' government saw the former Labour Prime Minister, Ramsay MacDonald, retain his post, with the foreign and home secretaryships both in the hands of Liberals. Imagine Mrs Thatcher after the 1987 election yielding her post to, say, Denis Healey, and the Tories accepting David Owen and David Steel as respectively Home Secretary and Foreign Secretary in the same government, and you get a sense of the difference in the Tories' underlying confidence in the strength of their position.

It is important, then, to distinguish between the Tories' electoral record, and the party's belief in its electoral vulnerability. As every student of modern British politics knows, Britain is generally governed by the Tories. Should the current parliament run its course, by the next election the Conservatives will have governed for some 59 of the 79 years since the modern party system emerged in the 1918. They won outright (with or without close allies) four of the ten elections held between 1867 and 1914, four of the six between the wars, and eight of the 14 held since 1945. But in all periods prior to the 1980s, the Tories invariably regarded their position as highly vulnerable. Until then, most Tory leaders conceived their party to be, naturally, a minority force, able to secure power only by working largely within the programmatic constraints of its opponents. As often as not, they went further still and embraced as many of their parliamentary opponents as they could with a modicum of self-respect and without splitting their own party. As Sir Michael Hicks Beach lamented to Lord Salisbury in the late-1880s: 'I confess to much doubt whether the country can be governed, nowadays, by persons holding opinions which you and I should call even moderately Conservative'[29] – a situation which Salisbury, for all his electoral success, once likened to tobogganing down a pre-arranged course 'though you may have the profoundest conviction that it was not the wisest course to select'. From Salisbury to Heath, excepting the aberrant decade running up to World War I, all Conservative leaders articulated similar sentiments, whatever the language in which they couched it.

Both the language and the sentiments changed in the 1980s. Not that the art of compromise was foreign to Mrs Thatcher. Until the final débâcle over the European Community and the poll tax, she showed herself sensitive to political currents and quite prepared to make strategic withdrawals as circumstances demanded.[30] But circumstances demanded it far less of her than of her Tory predecessors. That was partly because her position was stronger than theirs; but partly because, until 1990, the party's elite was more determined than previously to use that strength. The third aspect of our study, the changing character of the Tory elite under Thatcher, is thus integral to understanding the transformation of the Conservative party in the 1980s.

The Tory Elite

Between the early 1920s and 1974 the social background of the Tory elite changed remarkably little. Even the post-war Maxwell-Fyfe reforms, a deliberate attempt to broaden the social basis of the parliamentary party, had, in practice, more impact on party organisation, in particular the role and funding of constituency parties, than on the candidates and MPs they selected. True, the period saw the retreat of the landed aristocracy from the Tory benches in the Commons: 'Duchess's kisses aren't what they used to be', complained Loelia Westminster when in 1944 the Duke of Devonshire's eldest son lost a by-election in the Cavendishes's once impregnable Derbyshire fiefdom.[31] Yet in other respects little was different: the solid upper-middle class remained dominant in the party's ranks in the Commons; even the Tory aristocracy, its parliamentary base in the Lords unimpaired, continued to feature prominently in Conservative governments. (Devonshire's second son, who succeeded to the dukedom, served as a minister under Macmillan – who was married to his aunt. As Macmillan told his biographer: 'Andrew [Devonshire] is awfully good with the natives. The Devonshires have always been good with the natives.'[32]) Indeed, perhaps the most remarkable feature of the two decades either side of the war was the continued predilection of the party for being led by peers and their MP relations long after the peerage had ceased to be a significant political force in the country at large. As late as 1951 Churchill could include five peers in his Cabinet of sixteen; in 1962, a substantial proportion of Macmillan's government was related to the forementioned Duke of Devonshire; and a year later the party leadership itself went to a 14th earl, who took advantage of recently enacted legislation to disclaim his title, enter the Commons, and so become the first 'peer' premier since Lord Salisbury's retirement in 1902.

Of the Tory MPs elected in 1923,[33] 79 per cent were educated at leading public schools; in 1974 the figure had declined only to 74 per cent, with the proportion of Etonians falling only from a quarter to 17 per cent. The occupational balance within the party also remained broadly constant over that period: the proportion drawn from the civil service, the professions and the armed forces, taken together, was 56 per cent in 1923, 57 per cent in 1939 and 49 per cent in 1974, with businessmen constituting about one third throughout.

On the face of it, little changed between 1974 and 1987 – for all Peregrine Worsthorne's congratulations to Mrs Thatcher for having introduced 'the brutal energies of the C2s and Essex Man into the party'. Of the Tory MPs elected in 1987, two-thirds were public school educated, 42 per cent professionals and 37 per cent hailed from a business background. But below the surface a significant shift had occurred. The businessmen elected in 1987–37 per cent of the party's MPs – represented a broader spectrum of business and financial interests than their 1974, let alone 1923, forebears. Of the 1987 contingent, only 11 per cent were Etonians (down from 17 per cent in 1974), typical of the general shift away from the Clarendon boarding schools towards the 'minor' public schools, independent day schools and, increasingly, the ex direct-grant day schools. A comparable broadening was evident in the university background of Tory MPs: over the same 13 year period the proportion from Oxbridge declined sharply (from 56 per cent to 44 per cent), while the proportion educated at provincial universities doubled, from 13 to 26 per cent – rising further to 28 per cent among the 1992 contingent. Even the still-large Oxbridge contingent was radically different in character to that of the previous generation: the 'Cambridge mafia' which entered the Commons in the 1970s and worked its way up the Tory hierarchy in the 1980s, was largely the product of the meritocratic lower-middle-classes. Its members mostly got to Cambridge with scholarships from provincial grammar schools – Kenneth Clarke from Nottingham High, Michael Howard from Llanelli Grammar, Norman Fowler from King Edward VI Grammar, Chelmsford. Only Norman Lamont hailed from a public school – but even that, Loretto in Scotland, was not one of the famous 'Clarendon' schools.[34]

'When the call came to me to form a government', recalled Stanley Baldwin, a Harrovian, 'one of my first thoughts was that it should be a government of which Harrow should not be ashamed.'[35] Neither Margaret Thatcher (Grantham High) nor John Major (Rutlish Grammar) were much concerned at the shame of Harrow and Eton. Nor were the parliamentary parties they led, in which the sons (and a few daughters) of teachers, doctors, even small tradesmen increasingly replaced the sons of landowners, business leaders and wealthy profesionals – though the last two of those groups still retain a firm foothold.

John Major's background – son of an impoverished trapeze artist with no further or higher education – is still exceptional: the Tory road from Coldharbour Lane, Brixton, to Huntingdon and Whitehall is not well trodden. More significant for this study is the fact under Thatcher Tory MPs were coming in increasing numbers from those sections of the salariat which formed the core of the party' support, making the Tory elite far more representative of its electorate than at any time in the party's modern history. In 1939 one critic remarked, noting that out of the 400-plus Tory MPs of the day there were but 10 solicitors, 8 accountants and 4 teachers: 'The Conservative Party is indeed exclusive, excluding entirely members of nearly all the main occupations from becoming Conservative Members of Parliament.'[36] By 1969 the solicitors and accountants were not quite so rare. By 1989 they and their kin were running the party.

Two further novel aspects to the occupational background of Tory MPs in the 1980s should be noted: about half of the new intake of 1983 and 1987 had been local councillors before their election, and 13 per cent of those returned in 1987 were ex-journalists and/or political organisers[37] – that is, more or less professional politicians, more or less steeped in the party outside Parliament well before reaching Westminster in their own right. Until well into the twentieth century only aristocrats could afford to make politics their career from youth; by the 1980s, with the financial entry barriers to politics eroded on the one hand, and a stock of well-paid political adviserships, Central Office posts and media openings available on the other, a new breed of full-timers emerged, many hailing from the lower-middle-class backgrounds described above. To take one rising star, Michael Portillo, son of Spanish *émigré* intellectual, was educated at Harrow County Grammar (a state day school, not Baldwin's alma mater) and Cambridge; after a brief spell as an oil industry consultant and TV political researcher, he became special adviser first at the department of trade and industry then to Nigel Lawson at the Treasury; within a year of that he won a by-election nomination for suburban Enfield in north London, entering the Commons at the age of 31. After a string of junior posts, John Major appointed him Chief

Secretary to the Treasury in 1992, taking him to the Cabinet at the age of 39 and back to the department at which he was a political adviser only nine years previously. Portillo was a leader of Thatcher's Praetorian Guard. By upbringing an economic liberal with a populist streak, he is one of the most professional politicians of the day, certain that his creed represents the aspirations of middle-class middle-England, and supremely confident of his rapport with that class. In all those respects that makes him a model of the 1980s 'new Tory'.

So far it is changes to the social character of the Tory parliamentary party under Thatcher that have been highlighted. In his accompanying essay on the Republican elite, Jack Pitney emphasises the importance of generational change, stressing the different style, values and priorities of a rising 1980s generation of Republican leaders born after Roosevelt and World War II.

In the 1980s the British Conservative Party underwent a generation shift at least, if not more, pronounced than that described by Pitney. Under Thatcher, the parliamentary party changed guard precipitately. Of the 376 Tory MPs returned in the 1987 election, 211 (56 per cent) were first elected to the Commons after Thatcher became party leader – that is, they had been in the Commons only since 1975, and in most cases only since 1979. If the 1974 elections are included, fully 276 (73 per cent) of the 1987 contingent had virtually no experience of parliamentary life before Thatcher became party leader. It was not just the roll of the wheel of time: the success of the party whips, armed with honours and other blandishments, in persuading Tory MPs pushing retirement age to stand down in 1983 and 1987, fearful as they were of by-election losses, hastened the shift; also significant was the influx of Tory MPs as a result of the 1983 landslide (which inflated the parliamentary party from 339 to 397 in one bound, an increase of 17 per cent), most of whom held their seats in 1987. Mrs Thatcher's demise, resulting as it did in a large number of 'old-timers' retiring at the following election, provided a further impetus: more than half of the parliamentary party returned in the 1992 election had been first elected only within the previous ten years.

In Britain, however, it is difficult to identify a single Tory generational attitude to specific policy issues. Take Europe. True, many Tories with memories of the war – and not only Tories

– became strong Europhiles. It was not just Edward Heath who put the European Community on a elevated pedestal: so, in his government, did the likes of Carrington, Whitelaw, Pym, Prior, and Gilmour. Whitelaw speaks for them all in his memoirs:

> Personally, my strong support for joining Europe [note 'Europe' – not the 'EEC', which is what Britain actually joined] was based more on broad foreign policy than on economic grounds. Having lived through the 1939–45 war, I was desperately keen to ensure that no further world war would start through the quarrels in Western Europe . . . Britain's membership of the European Community clearly makes a significant contribution to this ideal. I still hold this view today [i.e. 1989], and I only hope that the great gains of a united Europe will not be submerged in petty disagreement about economic details.[38]

But Mrs Thatcher, too, was of that generation. Her wartime experience, however, was not of liberating occupied villages and advancing in tanks down the Rhine. It was of the isolated home front, of a mild xenophobia which embraced most Europeans and fully excluded only the Americans. The first time Thatcher went abroad was on her honeymoon at the age of 26; she never once visited Germany before becoming party leader in 1975, and until well into her premiership was profoundly ignorant of European politics.[39] That was at least as authentic a generational experience as Whitelaw's. A generational divide at least as significant (though of course conditioned by different forces) animated the succeeding generation; and an appreciation of the divide is crucial to understanding Tory divisions on the European issue in the late 1980s and early 1990s. Were one to move to welfare, no less significant generational cleavages could be exposed.

That is not, however, to say that the changing of the guard in the Conservative Party mattered little. One the contrary, it was of the greatest consequence, but not so much because of the translation of specific 'generational experiences' into specific policies, but because it entailed the social change discussed earlier, which had a dramatic impact on the general style and approach of the party. It brought to the fore a Tory elite more assured in its rapport with its electorate, and more confident in its ability to sustain its support, than any in the party's modern history.

Thatcher personified that new self-confidence par excellence. As she told Hugo Young: 'Deep in their instincts people find what I am saying and doing right. And I know it is because it is the way

I was brought up. I'm eternally grateful for the way I was brought up in a small town. We knew everyone, we knew what people thought. I sort of regard myself as a very normal, ordinary person with all the right instinctive antennae.'[40] The Majors, Clarkes and Portillos around her felt – feel – equally 'normal', equipped with the same 'instinctive antennae'. Indeed, at the end of the Thatcher premiership, Thatcher's belief in the invincibility of her antennae played a large part in her downfall. Thatcher believed the poll tax would secure the Tories among the home-owning mass, while closer European union offended against the gut British instinct to preserve national identity from external assault. The more concrete evidence of opinion polls, plus the demands of maintaining a 'governing competence', made the mainstream of the party nervous on both fronts. 'It was not that the party as a whole shared Geoffrey Howe's ... Euro enthusiasm,' Lawson recalls of the events precipitating her fall, 'it was rather that they sensed she was handling Europe badly, and feared that she would split the party over it.'[41]

In other words, where principles conflicted, the outcome was uncertain – particularly since the Tory's key Pittite principle, antedating Burke's *Reflections*, is the cardinal importance of the party *governing*. Twas ever thus, of course. The difference in the 1980s was that the commitment to the basic values described at the outset was firmer; the party's perception of its ability to give effect to them in government greater; and its deference to the demands of its electorate more complete. Every party has a class it cannot desert without dishonour. For Salisbury's Conservatives, the landed aristocracy was that class; for Thatcher's, it was the struggling salariat, mortgaged, respectable, nationalistic, and acutely mindful of its taxes and state handouts. When Mrs Thatcher's perception of her electoral invincibility outgrew that of her colleagues, she was forced out. But equally, Thatcher herself was, until her last 18 months, alive to the need to marry Tory values to the maintenance of a Pittite 'governing competence' – even if that meant selling out to the miners (1981), abandoning thoughts of reigning back the National Health Service (1983/4) and signing the Single European Act (1985).

The legacy? For the first two years of the Major premiership, it was fashionable to hail a return to the old 'centre', and to predict a do-nothing administration temporising *à al* Harold Wilson. There has been temporising aplenty; with a Commons majority of twenty-one, it could hardly be otherwise. But looking at the government's agenda, the most striking feature is the continuity with the 1980s. At the time of writing, railway privatisation is heading for the statute book, and the Post Office looks set to follow; so is the Maastricht treaty, but shorn of its 'social chapter' and accompanied by much bad-mouthing of the Germans; low interest rates are the priority of macro-economic policy; 'law and order' is trumpeted from the rooftops; and a full-scale public expenditure review is under way, in the hope, at least, that an electorally saleable path can be found out of the welfare morass.

It was said of Lord Salisbury, that as an intelligent aristocrat who inspired confidence, he was the kind of leader the Victorian Tories had always wanted but rarely been able to find. Plain John Major was the kind of Tory Thatcher's Conservative party wanted; henceforth, his type will be anything but hard to find.

Notes

1   Robert Taylor, *Lord Salisbury* (London, Allen Laue, 1975), p. 73. (All works cited are published in the United Kingdom.)

2   John Ranelagh, *Thatcher's People* (London, Fontana, 1992), p. ix.

3   Andrew Roberts, *The Holy Fox: a Biography of Lord Halifax* (London, Weidenfeld and Nicolson, 1991), p. 85.

4   The best introductions are B Coleman, *Conservatism and the Conservative Party in Nineteenth Century Britain* (London Edward Arnold, 1988) and F O'Gorman, *British Conservatism* (London, Longman, 1986).

5   Peter Marsh, *The Discipline of Popular Government: Lord Salisbury's Domestic Statecraft 1881–1902* (Hassocks, Harvester Press, 1978).

6   A. Adonis, *Making Aristocracy Work: the Peerage and the Political System in Britain 1884–1914* (Oxford University Press, 1993), chs 5, 6 & 9.

7   In his *Conservatism* (1912).

8   Or, arguably, since the repeal of the Corn Laws: Peel's commitment to repeal was motivated largely by expediency, but those opposed to him (most of them on principle) succeeded in splitting the party, which kept it in opposition for most of the following 25 years.

9   Prime Minister 1923–24, 1924–29, 1935–37.

10   Compare S. Ball, *Baldwin and the Conservative Party* (New Haven, Conn., Yale University Press, 1988), and A. L. Hamby, *Liberalism and Its Challengers* (Oxford University Press, 1992 edn), ch. 3.

11   Ivor Crewe and Donald D Searing, 'Ideological change in the British Conservative Party', *American Political Science Review*, 82:2 (1988), 361.

12   Alistair Horne, *Macmillan 1957–1986* (London, Macmillan, 1989), p. 17.

13   Viscount Hailsham, *The Conservative Case* (Harmondsworth, Penguin, 1959), p. 59.

14   Nigel Fisher, *Ian Macleod* (London, Deutsch, 1973), p. 73.

15   David Willetts, *Modern Conservatism* (London, Penguin, 1992), p. 47.

16   A. Heath, R. Jowell & J. Curtice, *How Britain Votes* (Oxford, Pergamon, 1985), p. 36.

17   A Heath, *Understanding Political Change* (Oxford. Pergamon, 1991), p. 207.

18   Heath *et al.*, *How Britain Votes*, p. 35.

19   Ivor Crewe, 'The electorate', in H Berrington (ed.), *Change in British Politics* (London, Frank Cass, 1984), p. 204.

20   J. Vincent, *Disraeli* (1990), p. 68.

21   In terms of seats, that is.

22   J. Curtice & M. Steed, appendix 2 to D. Butler and D. Kavanagh, *The British General Election of 1987* (London, Macmillan, 1988), pp. 330–1.

23   Ibid., pp. 330–1.

24   J. Curtice & M. Steed, Appendix 2 to Butler and Kavanagh, *The General Election of 1992* (London, Macmillan, 1992), pp. 324–32.

25   Crewe and Searing, 'Ideological change', 364; Philip Norton, 'The Lady's Not for Turning: but what about the rest of the party?' unpublished paper, 1989.

26   R. McKibbin, *Ideologies of Class* (Oxford University Press, 1990), pp. 259–284.

27   Heath, *Understanding Political Change*, p. 58.

28   McKibbin, *Ideologies*, p. 260.

29   Beach to Salisbury, 25 December 1885, Hatfield House papers.

30   A fact well documented in the memoirs of her long-serving Chancellor of the Exchequer Lord Lawson: *The View from Number Eleven* (London, Bantam Press, 1992).

31   D. Cannadine, *The Decline and Fall of the British Aristocracy* (New Haven, Conn., Yale University Press, 1990), p. 634.

32   Horne, *Macmillan 1957–1986*, p. 244.

33   The statistics in this and the following paragraphs and drawn from David Butler & Michael Pinto-Duschinsky, 'The Conservative Elite 1918–78', in Zig Layton-Henry (ed.), *Conservative Party Politics* (London, Macmillan, 1980), and Byron Criddle's analysis of candidates in the 1987 and 1992 elections in David Butler & Dennis Kavanagh, *The British General Election of 1987* (1988) and *The British General Election of 1992* (1992).

34   Chapter 3 of Peter Riddell's *Honest Opportunism* (1993) contains fascinating insights into 'becoming active' in modern British politics.

35   Simon Haxey, *Tory MP* (London, Macmillan, 1939), p. 180.

36   Haxey, *Tory MP*, pp. 190/1.

37   Butler & Kavanagh, *Election of 1987*, pp. 204–5.

38 Viscount Whitelaw, *The Whitelaw Memoirs* (London, Hurum Press, 1989), p. 94.
39 Hugo Young, *One of Us* (London, Macmillan 1991 edn), pp. 168–71.
40 Young, *One of Us*, p. 208.
41 Lawson, *View from Number 11*, p. 1001.

Republican elites under Reagan and Bush

In *Changing of the Guard*, American political columnist David Broder wrote: 'In the 1980s the custody of the nation's leadership will be transferred from the World War II veterans, who have held sway for a generation, to a new set of men and women.'[1] Subsequent events seemed to mock this forecast. Soon after the book's first edition reached the stands in 1980, American voters chose 69-year-old Ronald Reagan, the oldest man ever to win the presidency. More than a decade later, the national GOP was headed by President George Bush, Senate Republican Leader Robert Dole and House Republican Leader Robert Michel – all combat veterans of World War II.

Yet just beneath this topmost layer, the Republican Party's elite was indeed changing. The passage of time was deposing the people who remembered the Great Depression, the New Deal, and Pearl Harbor. Taking their place were those who had come of age amid the Great Society, the urban riots, and the Vietnam War. As of 1993:

- Dole and Michel were the *only* Republican congressional leaders old enough to have served in World War II (that is, born before 1927). Indeed, the Republican leadership of both the House and Senate included law-makers born *after* the war ended.
- Less than one-eighth of House Republicans and one-third of Senate Republicans had begun their tenure before the 1978 election. Over forty House Republicans entered in the 1992 elections alone.

- In both the House and Senate there had been a major shift in geographical base from the traditional North-East/Mid West to the West/South.
- President Bush's cabinet secretaries were all younger than he, with age differences ranging from two to seventeen years. Only one was a fellow World War II veteran, Secretary of Veterans' Affairs Edward Derwinski. Defense Secretary Richard Cheney was ten months old when Pearl Harbor was attacked. Lynn Martin, the fourth woman to serve as Labour Secretary, came into the world in 1939, six years after Frances Perkins became the first.

An era hardly stamps all members of a generation with the same views and habits, for class, race, religion, and other social characteristics all create divisions among members of each age group. Nevertheless, the calendar does leave its signature. As Arthur Schlesinger says: 'Different individuals respond differently to the same stimuli. But shared stimuli give each generation, if not a uniform ideology, at least a collective identity. Members of the same generation, in Karl Mannheim's words, occupy "a common location in the historical dimension of the social process". '[2]

Within the GOP, the generational shift has taken many forms. At Republican national headquarters, Chairman Lee Atwater (born 1951) brought rock music to hallways that had once been filled with Perry Como. More important, the Reagan–Bush years saw an evolution of the party elite's world view and style. 'World view' is their way of seeing: lasting ideas about governmental mechanics and the political conflicts. 'Style' is their way of acting: habitual ways of handling rhetoric, personal relations and homework.[3] World view and style are coloured by the historical setting of a political leader's youth and early career. In some ways, President Bush (born 1924) had more in common with Democratic Representative Dan Rostenkowski (born 1928) than with his own party's House whip, Newt Gingrich (born 1943). Conversely, Gingrich bears a closer stylistic likeness to one-time Democratic whip Tony Coelho (born 1942) than to his own leader, Robert Michel (born 1923).

So as we shall see, the new Republican elite is making way for a different kind of politics from that practised by the World War II generation.

The old old guard and the old new guard

In 1984, Representative Barber Conable – a star of the World War II generation of House Republicans – reflected upon generational change: 'Old as I am, I recall being a "young turk" at one point and participating noisily in a successful effort to change House rules which the then Establishment found adequate. I learned a lot about the institution from the effort, vented my frustrations, and gradually became part of the Establishment myself.'[4] Conable's remarks remind us that the Bushes, Michels and Doles once made up the party's new guard. To understand their world view and style, one should start by looking at the older Republican order that they replaced.

Through the mid-1940s, the GOP had a distinct 'congressional' wing, consisting largely of Midwestern law-makers who espoused isolationism in foreign policy and opposed innovation in domestic policy. On the other side stood the 'presidential' wing, based in Northeast, which favored internationalism and moderately liberal policies at home. Senator Robert Taft and Representative Joseph Martin (House Speaker during the 80th and 83d Congresses) led the former, while GOP presidential nominees Werdell Willkie, Thomas Dewey and Dwight Eisenhower led the latter.

The party's 1952 sweep did not close the rift. Eisenhower and other presidential Republicans sought strong executive power, particularly in foreign policy. The congressional wing clung to the attitude voiced by Joseph Martin when he first assumed the Speakership in 1947: 'Our American concept of government rests upon the idea of a dominant Congress . . . which will protect the liberties of the people and not delegate its power either to the executive or to arrogant bureaucrats.'[5] This faction proposed a constitutional amendment to curb the president's treaty-making power. The proposal failed, but not before irking President Eisenhower, who privately sneered at the congressional Republicans as 'stupid'.

Meanwhile, every new class of Republican law-makers included veterans who split with the 'congressional' wing. In 1948, a young lawyer and former Navy lieutenant commander named Gerald Ford defeated an isolationist congressman in a Republican primary campaign that focused on aid to Europe. 'Before the war, I'd been an isolationist,' Ford wrote in his memoirs, '. . . but now I had become an ardent internationalist. My wartime experiences had given me an entirely new perspective.'[6] In 1956, another Midwestern district sent Army veteran Robert Michel to the House. Three decades later, Michel recalled:

> I'll tell you, we had some doggone good conversations sitting there in the old doggone foxholes and just gassing with one another. 'If we don't keep a force in Europe for a good, long time, to prevent these birds from shooting it up again, by God, we're missing a bet.' That stuck with me, you know, because our fathers had to fight World War I. We went to fight World War II. And we said, 'By God, we can't let it happen again'.[7]

By the early 1960s, old-style Republican isolationism ebbed as people of Michel's age began to fill up Republican ranks. All major elements of the party supported internationalism, though with different emphases: followers of New York Governor Nelson Rockefeller championed foreign economic assistance, while Goldwaterites called for military assertiveness.

Republican domestic positions also changed. Notwithstanding Goldwater's musings about scrapping mandatory social security, the new Republicans generally accepted Roosevelt-era social programs. Even the 1964 Republican Platform endorsed a 'strong, sound system of Social Security, with improved benefits to our people'. Younger Republicans had grown up when the welfare state was becoming part of American life – and many of them had personally gained from it. Maimed in combat, Kansas Representative (and later Senator) Robert Dole acknowledged that he had been able to resume an active life because of a 'generous government' that provided benefits under the GI Bill.[8]

Republicans did disagree about *extending* the welfare state: Lyndon Johnson's Great Society program evoked less hostility from some Republicans than from others. They also clashed over the emerging social issues, particularly civil rights. But in spite of the ugly 1964 nomination mêlée between Goldwater (who voted against the 1964 Civil Rights Act) and Rockefeller (who supported it), Republicans shared some common ground on domestic policy. 'We resisted these new laws for things like aid to education and urban renewal,' said Goldwater in 1967, 'but now we must recognise that they are here to stay and make them work.'[9] Liberal and conservative Republicans often co-operated on issues such as revenue sharing and community service.

The GI generation of Republicans also sought a heartier leadership that would challenge the ruling Democrats with positive GOP policy stands. In 1959, they ousted House Republican Leader Joseph Martin for his lethargy. Six years later, they sacked Charles Halleck, Martin's successor, for carping at popular Democratic initiatives without offering Republican alternatives. Both times, Democratic sweeps in congressional elections had strengthened the younger House Republicans by decimating their senior colleagues. The new House Republican Leader Gerald Ford (born 1913) and Republican Conference Chair Melvin Laird (born 1922) were both World War II Navy veterans who promised to jump-start the party. According to Hess and Broder: 'The revolution that put them in power was not a revolution of ideas but one of generations . . .'.[10]

Although these Republicans were called 'Young Turks', they were fundamentally 'Organization Men'. When they beat Martin and Halleck, they acted in accord with longstanding practices. And while they jousted with the majority over substance and procedure, they generally enjoyed collegial relationships with Democratic leaders. Their gentlemanly style reflected their generation's 'other-directedness' and devotion to order; and they could afford civility because congressional Democrats reciprocated. John Rhodes, who succeeded Ford as House Republican Leader, recalled in 1976 that past Democratic leaders 'were capable of launching some of the most partisan attacks ever known to man [But] when it came to the real business of running the country – of choosing between legislative results or stalemate – they chose co-operation over confrontation virtually every time'.[11] The Democrats' co-operativeness resulted at least partially from their belief that the Republicans could regain control of Congress within an election or two – why inflict needless scars on a minority that could later turn into a majority and strike back?

Generational change came more slowly on the Senate side. Everett Dirksen (born 1896), who had delivered Robert Taft's nominating speech at the 1952 Republican convention, served as Republican leader from 1959 until his death in 1969, when he was followed by Hugh Scott. Though a World War II veteran, Scott was at age 69 more a man of Dirksen's generation. But the number-two Senate Republican, party whip Robert Griffin of Michigan, was Scott's junior by twenty-two years and had served in the House as a Ford

ally. Griffin and other younger senators, like their House counterparts, held a world view that comprised internationalism and
maintenance of the welfare state, along with a political style that
stressed activity bounded by gentility.

The year 1969 brought the generation's first Republican President: former Navy Lieutenant Richard M. Nixon (born 1913). He
too came home from World War II as an earnest internationalist:
even as a freshman House member, he lent key support to the
Marshall Plan. Though he repeatedly damned the Washington
bureaucracy, he joined most people of his age in accepting the
basic New Deal order. On the other hand, elements of his political
style were unusual. Indeed, allegations about Watergate abuses
finally cost him the backing of his age peers in Congress: a climactic
meeting with Scott, Rhodes (born 1916) and Goldwater (born
1909) persuaded him to resign.

Gerald Ford replaced Nixon. Two and a half years later, Hugh
Scott was succeeded by yet another former Navy officer, Howard
Baker (born 1925). Within the GOP, as in the country as a whole,
the World War II generation was at its peak of power – and past
its prime of life. The first-born of the GIs were already starting to
retire and the last-born were slouching into middle age. Looking
down the greasy pole, they could see the next elite making its
inevitable climb.

Born in a different USA

Generations dissolve into one another. Men born in 1930 would
be a shade too young to serve legally in World War II, yet they
would always remember the war, as well as the Great Depression
(albeit through children's eyes). Thus their perspectives would blend
with those of people just a few years older. With each new cohort
of Americans, however, the shadows of this period would grow
fainter. More and more, the things that would shape their world
view and style would happen in the 1960s and 1970s. Several of
their shared experiences would color the politics of the 1980s and
1990s.

Taxes
Members of the World War II generation disliked taxes, yet com-
plaints about high taxation seldom led their political agenda. Even

the Kennedy–Johnson income tax cut of 1964 aimed more at macro-economic stimulus than at relief for the individual taxpayer. The late 1970s, by contrast, saw a burgeoning 'tax revolt'. What happened?

One obvious answer is that taxes went up. In 1946, when the veterans resumed civilian jobs, the average person worked one hour and fifty-seven minutes each day to pay federal, state and local taxes.[12] By 1976, that figure stood at two hours and forty minutes. Social security supplied one source of upward pressure: in 1976, the total social security tax rate was nearly *six times* higher than it had been three decades earlier.[13] Even worse, the regressivity of social security taxes meant that these increases hit hardest at people with modest incomes. Since younger people tend to earn less than older ones, the post-World War II generation felt the pinch more than the aging GIs.

At the same time, inflation was raising taxes in several ways. In the phenomenon called 'bracket creep', increases in nominal income pushed people into higher income tax brackets even when their inflation-adjusted incomes were stagnating. The personal exemption for dependents – a special concern of young families – lost nearly half of its inflation-adjusted value between 1946 and 1976. And in many communities, inflation was also increasing property taxes by bloating the assessed value of homes. The latter development ignited 1978 California ballot initiative, Proposition Thirteen, which cut the state's property taxes and served as an omen of national sentiment.

High taxes, usually a side issue in the world view of the World War II generation, now loomed large to younger politicians.

The 'Sickness of Government'

In the 1930s and 1940s, 'Big Government' defeated the Depression and the Axis. For years afterward, most Americans applauded government's growth, while those who opposed it fell on the defensive. Barry Goldwater voiced concern 'that so many people today with Conservative instincts feel compelled to apologise for them'; William Buckley cited 'the failure of the conservative demonstration' – the right's inability to convince the public of the welfare state's shortcomings.[14] With some exceptions (Goldwater, Buckley, and of course, Reagan), conservatives of the World War II generation never quite shook their ambivalence. They liked the idea of 'the end of ideology', for they feared that liberal Democrats would always win ideological conflicts.

The next generation grew up when the New Deal order seemed to be going senile. As Peter Drucker said in his essay 'The Sickness of Government', the welfare state promised a new and happy society, but 'the more we expand the welfare state the less capable even of routine mediocrity does it seem to become'.[15] Growing inflation and taxation offered just two symptoms of ailing government. Others abounded. After Congress passed laws to protect civil rights and aid the poor, race riots broke out in many central cities and progress against poverty began to slow down. After the Medicare and Medicaid programs made the federal government a major player in health care, medical costs outran overall inflation. It was the same story with education: as spending took off, standardised test scores tumbled.

None of these developments *proved* the failure of Democratic social policy, but they did supply younger conservatives with intellectual ammunition – and confidence. In their world view, the 'liberal welfare state' was not a popular hope, but a discredited relic. And just as the perceived failure of the Great Society tinted their vision of domestic policy, the Vietnam War influenced their view of national security policy. Whether hawks or doves, they agreed that the previous generation had turned the war into a disaster. Few became isolationists, but many became intrigued with 'military reform' writers such as James Fallows who argued that America's armed forces were suffering from the same diseases as the welfare state: bureaucratisation and centralisation.

Inside games and outside games

The post-war years were the high-water mark not just for Big Government, but Big Business and Big Labour as well. The returning veterans respected authority and hierarchy; and even when they fought for power, they observed well-defined rules of engagement in which battles were fought largely indoors (e.g., the Martin and Halleck overthrows).

Their daughters and sons grew up 'inner directed', with a strong desire for quick personal gratification. Vietnam, Watergate and other upheavals both deepened their dissatisfaction with existing institutions and highlighted alternatives to hack politics. Ralph Nader humbled General Motors not through quiet negotiations but through books, articles and public hearings. Such examples helped teach young politicians about message and media skill: rather than patiently gathering seniority and cultivating colleagues, they could instead make a name by touting ideas and building constituencies outside the institution. During the 1970s and 1980s, the latter course was fostered by increased legislative staff, C-SPAN television coverage of Congress, and improved communication technology.

The old style of politics encouraged comity. Politicians who entered the House of Representatives under Speaker Sam Rayburn (1882–1961) often heard his famous saying: 'You got to go along to get along.' When invited to appear on a television interview show, Rayburn replied: 'I never go on programs such as yours because twenty or more years ago I did go on a panel program on the radio and all the folks on the panel got in such an argument that I had enough.'[16] In the new style of politics, politicians often *seek* opportunities for televised arguments, since heated exchanges get more airtime than friendly discussion.

The new style of politics encouraged rancor, and the younger politicians showed sharper elbows. They first appeared in large numbers during the late 1970s.

The next generation's first wave

In the 1974 midterm elections, dominated by Watergate and an economic recession, Republicans absorbed a net loss of forty-eight House seats and five Senate seats. One immediate consequence was the 'Class of 1974' a huge cohort of new Democratic lawmakers who shook up the congressional majority, particularly in the House. They began by ousting three powerful committee chairs, thus serving notice to the rest of the party hierarchy both to respect their power and to take a harder line against the Republicans. They sneered at Speaker Carl Albert for being too weak, and he retired just two years later. To replace him, they joined with their colleagues to support Tip O'Neill, who belonged to the older generation (born 1912), but displayed extraordinary partisanship for a man of his age. As House Majority Leader, O'Neill had once said: 'Republicans are going to have to get it through their heads that they are not going to write legislation!'[17] O'Neill named all Democratic members of the House Rules Committee, and during his tenure, the Committee increasingly curbed Republicans' ability to offer floor amendments – a result that the Class of 1974 strongly desired.

As mentioned earlier, the fear of future retaliation had once restrained the Democratic majority. But as of 1975, the House Republicans had dwelt in the minority for twenty years – the longest such stretch in congressional history. And their 1974 disaster made it seem unlikely that they would ever regain control. Now Democrats had free rein to use the rules against Republicans.

The Watergate election altered the composition of the congressional GOP. During that year, more than one-fourth of House Republican incumbents left Capitol Hill: thirty-six through defeat in November, and twenty-one others through retirement, often under the threat of loss. This exodus cut deeply into the World War II generation, because all but eight of the departed Republicans were born before 1929. While the next election in 1976 saw little net change in either chamber, the 1978 election was pivotal for House Republicans. The GOP net gain of fifteen seats was slight by historical standards, but the freshman class rejuvenated the party. Of the thirty-six new members – nearly one-fourth of the GOP membership – only *two* were born before 1929.

Because of their relative youth and closeness to the electorate, the Republican freshmen of 1978 were sensitive to the tax problems of younger families. All had witnessed the passage of Proposition Thirteen and many had based their campaigns on a proposal to cut federal income tax rates by thirty percent. The proposal's author, Jack Kemp (born 1935, elected 1970), was a hero to the 1978 class, which in turn would produce leaders such as Newt Gingrich.

In several respects, the new Republican members provided a preview of the emerging politics. First, they continued to press the tax issue. With Kemp and Representative David Stockman (born 1946, elected 1976), they offered 'The Budget of Hope', a set of tax and spending cuts designed to put the Democrats on the defensive. Though it did not pass, it did gain thirty-nine Democratic votes, thus bolstering GOP morale and pointing the way for future legislative strategy.

Second, they broke with the old 'get-along-go-along' code by directly attacking congressional Democrats over ethics. Soon after taking the oath of office, they pushed to expel a Democratic House member who had been convicted of mail fraud. While the move fell short, the resulting publicity forced Democrats to support a censure motion.

Third, they pressed their own party's leadership to fight harder. During their first eighteen months in office, the freshmen held more than forty class meetings at which they criticised the leadership's passivity and discussed ways to seize majority status. Gingrich helped lead a task force on party strategy; as a former professor of contemporary European history, he took his cue from parliamentary parties. He was intrigued when Republican pollster Robert Teeter told the task force that television coverage of the Canadian Parliament's Question Hour had enabled the Progressive Conservatives to score points against the Liberals. With C-SPAN television coverage recently under way, Gingrich wondered aloud how Republicans could adapt the Tories' tactics to the US House floor.

The task force also pondered how to translate the expected GOP 1980 presidential victory into gains at the congressional level. A former Gingrich aide told the author:

Thatcher was elected in May of '79. Joe Clark was elected in May of '79. There was a sense of a tide out there. So our office not only brought in [Republican pollster] Bob Teeter to tell these members how to build a majority but also brought in people who'd worked with the British Conservatives [to tell them]: Here's how you run a national campaign, a party-wide campaign from top to bottom.[18]

In the 1960s, the World War II Republicans had also groped for a party-wide message, but were ultimately curbed by their own lack of boldness. The new generation regarded these men (except for Goldwater) as American equivalents of Macmillan and Heath. The younger Republicans instead looked to Margaret Thatcher not only for her campaign style but also by her programme of radical economic reform, and helped persuade Ronald Reagan and other party leaders to adopt a unified party message centered on supply-side economics. Although the message had far less specificity than Kemp and Gingrich had hoped, it did boost the GOP's fortunes.

While Young Turks may have supplied the party with intellectual fuel, older men still gripped the steering wheel. Six of the major candidates for the 1980 Republican presidential nomination (Anderson, Baker, Bush, Connally, Dole and Reagan) belonged to the World War II generation. The seventh, fifty-year-old Philip Crane, missed by only a couple of years. Crane fared most poorly among the seven, while the firstborn took the prize.

The Reagan revolution

The 1980 election represented a Republican triumph:

- Ronald Reagan won the electoral college by 489 to 49.
- Republicans realised a net gain of twelve Senate seats, which gave them control of the chamber for the first time in twenty-six years.
- In the House, a net pickup of thirty-three seats enabled the Republicans to exert leverage over floor proceedings even though they were still twenty-six seats shy of a majority.

The election also advanced the generational shift within the party – but hardly finished it. The transition would prove fitful and contentious, and it would still be under way a decade later.

The Administration

At first, the Young Turks thought that they would drive the new Reagan Administration. One of their own, David Stockman, landed what was apparently the key domestic-policy job in a budget-cutting regime: Director of the Office of Management and Budget. Stockman was only thirty-five years old in 1981, and he was a representative character of his generation. He scorned incrementalism, because he saw a need for radical action against taxes, spending and bureaucracy. And he had a deep contempt for the established power structure – of both parties. To him, Speaker O'Neill 'with his massive corpulence and scarlet, varicose nose, was a Hogarthian embodiment of the superstate he had laboured for so long to maintain'. Traditional Republicans were 'ideological neuters, wrapped warmly in the cozy fog of country club Republicanism and faithfully murmuring its nostrums'.[19]

Stockman worked with Phil Gramm (born 1942), a conservative Democratic congressman from Texas, on a legislative strategy to bypass established procedures and force a single vote on a package of tax and spending cuts. In the short run, the strategy worked. Soon, however, Stockman saw that his package had too many special-interest tax loopholes and too few spending cuts. Stockman later blamed many culprits – including his reckless tongue and his feckless former colleagues – but much of his frustration came from World War II veterans in the Reagan circle.

Despite their personality scuffles, Secretary of State Alexander Haig (born 1924) and Defense Secretary Caspar Weinberger (born 1917) shared the perspective of men who had served Douglas MacArthur and who viewed the globe through the Munich lens. Like his hero Winston Churchill, Weinberger believed in a massive military buildup to deter a totalitarian foe. He artfully persuaded Reagan to disregard Stockman's 'military reform' arguments and agree to increases in defense spending. In his tangles with Weinberger, Stockman got no help from Treasury Secretary Donald Regan (born 1918). 'Whatever the President insisted on, he would try to get – without regard to the price', said Stockman of Regan, 'He had been a Marine, and this was the moral equivalent of taking a hill'.[20]

In 1985, Regan left Treasury to assume the more-powerful job of Chief of Staff, where his performance got poor notices. In the same year, Stockman was replaced by James C. Miller, an able economist who found little support in the Donald Regan White House. Would War II Marine George Shultz succeeded Haig at the State Department, while Weinberger stayed at the Pentagon until 1987.

The Senate

The Republican Senate class of 1980 included younger members such as Don Nickles of Oklahoma (born 1948). But with the GOP assumption of control, the seniority system came into play, raising older members to positions of power:

Majority Leader Howard Baker (born 1925)
Finance Committee Chairman Robert Dole (born 1923)
Appropriations Committee Chairman Mark Hatfield (born 1922)
Foreign Relations Committee Chairman Charles Percy (born 1919)
Armed Services Committee Chairman John Tower (born 1925)

The seniors tended to be more moderate than the new breed, who sometimes disdained their elders as 'country-club Republicans'.[21] During the 97th Congress (1981–82), those elected since

1972 had an average career vote rating of 74 per cent from the conservative Americans for Constitutional Action (ACA). Those elected before 1972 averaged only 57 per cent.

Even when the elders had conservative voting records, they still displayed their generation's world view and style. Tower sided with Weinberger on budget increases. Dole never fully embraced the tax-cut issue, and in 1982 he helped sponsor the Tax Equity and Fiscal Responsibility Act (TEFRA), then the largest peace-time tax increase in history. In 1984, when some Republicans proposed a national platform plank ruling out tax increases, he said that 'it would be a major mistake to attempt to box the president in by ruling out any particular option for tackling economic problems . . .' Dole had little use for the activist House Republicans. 'In the Senate, where we have a majority, we have less freedom to run around and stake out positions of our own. . . . While we're passing legislation, they're looking around for new ideas'.[22]

For the rest of the decade, the World War II generation held onto key committee posts. True, the Finance chair went to Robert Packwood (born 1932), who used it to reform the tax code. But Hatfield continued at Appropriations, while retiring John Tower was replaced at Armed Services first by Barry Goldwater, and then (as ranking minority member) by John Warner (born 1927). Republican leadership on Foreign Relations passed from Percy to Richard Lugar (born 1932) who then had to relinquish it to the more-senior Jesse Helms (born 1921).

Nevertheless, younger Republicans made headway in winning elected party positions. When Baker retired in 1984, the top leadership position went to fellow veteran Bob Dole. But four of the five other leadership positions went to men born in the 1930s. Meanwhile, the post-war generation was filling the back benches; before coming to the Senate, Dan Coats (born 1943) and Connie Mack (born 1940) had been prominent among the House Republicans that Dole had criticised.

The House of Representatives
The Mack and Coats examples reinforce a point made by Broder in *Changing of the Guard*: that the House is a 'key barometer of intergenerational tension because it is the point of entry to national politics for ambitious young leaders'.[23] During the 1980s, this barometer pointed toward increased influence for the Young

Turks. In the House, as in the Senate, Northeastern liberal Republicans were vanishing as the ranks of Southern and Western conservatives were swelling with newer, younger members. Old Rockefeller Republicans, such as Silvio Conte of Massachusetts, held positions as ranking minority members on legislative committees, but these posts had much less power than their analogues in the Senate.

As the House Republicans' campaign chairman, Guy Vander Jagt (born 1931) hoped that his relationship with the freshmen would win him the post of Republican Leader in 1980. He also thought that his relative youth would be an advantage. But opponent Robert Michel was only eight years older, and had greater aptitude for personal politicking. Michel won by a margin of 103–87. Several younger members did assume leadership positions: conference chair Jack Kemp, party whip Trent Lott (born 1941), and policy committee chair Richard Cheney (also born 1941).

Still remembering the tax-revolt fever that had helped them win office in the first place, the Young Turks acclaimed the tax-cut bill of 1981 and fought the TEFRA tax-increase bill of 1982. Although TEFRA passed with a majority of GOP votes, most members of the classes of 1978 and 1980 voted against it. The next year, a number of the younger members formed the Conservative Opportunity Society (COS), an informal group dedicated to 'guerilla war' against the House Democrats. COS tactics included 'special order' speeches directed at the C-SPAN television audience. One series of COS speeches provoked a confrontation in which Speaker O'Neill lost his temper with Newt Gingrich, causing the temporary chair to rule him out of order and making Gingrich an instant media star.

The World War II generation of House Republicans disliked the younger generation's tactics, but the Gingrich faction's influence was growing. Kemp, Lott and Cheney all worked with COS from the beginning. As the decade wore on, confrontationalism spread in GOP ranks as the House Democratic majority increasingly used its procedural powers to block Republican initiatives in committee and on the floor. When Gingrich launched an ethics attack against Speaker Jim Wright, most Republicans cheered him on. As a result, the Gingrich faction gained still more strength. In 1988 and 1989, four of the eight elected Republican leadership positions went to COS figures, including Gingrich, who became party whip.

Age clearly affected attitudes toward party activism: all four COS members of the leadership were born after 1940, while four non-COS leaders were born before 1940.

Several years before, Speaker Wright had laughed off the Gingrich followers as a group of 'gnats'.[24] In 1989, the Gingrich-led Republican war against Wright cost him the Speakership.

The Bush era

The Bush Administration's first fight was the nomination of John Tower to head the Pentagon. Tower fell prey to the 'hardball' politics that had become so prevalent in Washington. Whereas an older generation would have overlooked stories of drinking and womanising, a new set of senators made such rumors the centerpiece of their campaign against him. After the Senate rejected Tower, Bush turned to the Richard Cheney, sixteen years younger.

The age difference counted. Tower, like Weinberger, believed in the 'bigger-is-better' mentality of the World War II era. Cheney, though just as hawkish, viewed the Pentagon in the light of different experiences. He had spent his young adulthood not as a solider in the South Pacific but as a staffer in the Nixon and Ford Administrations. 'Having watched the final throes of the Vietnam war, having tried to fight poverty at OEO [Office of Economic Opportunity],' he told Broder, 'I saw how difficult it is to have government programs well designed to achieve any significant results.'[25] As Defense Secretary, he worked with Vietnam veterans such as Colin Powell to make the Pentagon put performance ahead of empire-building. While it had taken the Defense Department three million soldiers and 10 per cent of GNP to lose in Vietnam, it smashed Iraq with two million soldiers and 5 per cent of GNP.[26]

Elsewhere in the Bush Cabinet, some of the younger department heads were fighting the bureaucratic welfare state. Housing Secretary Jack Kemp sought to replace the traditional governance of public housing with tenant ownership and management. Education Secretary Lamar Alexander (born 1940) called for a complete restructuring of American schools, through devices such as parental choice.

To succeed, such proposals needed presidential leadership. Bush spent little time on domestic affairs. Like most Republican leaders of his generation, he had great interest in an activist foreign policy.

But on the home front, he generally felt content to leave the New Deal order alone: even when he praised fundamental reforms, his heart did not seem to be in the effort. He was particularly uneasy with supply-side economics. True, his 1988 campaign was immortalised by the phrase, 'Read my lips: no new taxes' – but those words were penned by speechwriter Peggy Noonan (born 1950) at the urging of Jack Kemp.[27] And in 1990, Bush broke that pledge by acceding to a major tax increase.

This issue illustrates the gap between Bush's world and that of the younger Republicans. Bush took his pledge lightly; and at one point in 1990 he even joked about it by jogging past reporters and shouting 'Read my hips!' Younger Republicans were dismayed. In the early stages of budget talks, Kemp openly called on Bush to rule out any tax increase, and House Republicans passed a resolution to the same effect. Columnist Paul Gigot explained:

The GOP is having a shootout at Generation Gap. . . . The generation lines aren't always pure, of course, and some of the older crowd cross over. [Budget Director Richard] Darman is only forty-seven, but politically he's considered a young fogey. HUD Secretary Jack Kemp is a gray fifty-four but his many ideas make him a new generation stalwart. At its roots the split is about confidence and temperament, more than ideology. Republicans who came to power before 1975, in an era of Democratic dominance, believe the Reagan years were an aberration. They think Mr. Darman is negotiating a necessary strategic retreat. The Young Turks liked the 1980s and want to build on them. They think Mr. Darman is Petain after the Democrats' latest blitzkrieg.[28]

When the 1990 deficit-reduction proposal first came to the House floor, 58 per cent of House Republicans elected before 1978 voted for it, while 65 per cent of those elected in 1978 and after voted against it. Significantly, the members of the tax-revolt classes of 1978 and 1980 were even more likely to vote no than more recently elected members.

Nine years earlier, the pre-1978 House Republicans had been numerous enough to win a majority of GOP votes for the TEFRA tax increase. Now the generational centre of power had shifted. With the post-1978 members dominating the ranks, the House Republicans rejected the first version of the budget agreement by a vote of 105–71. But while the Young Turks showed clout within the GOP, the Democrats still controlled the Congress. With time running out, Bush made even more tax concessions to swing

Democrats to his side. The final package passed both chambers with a majority of Democrats voting in favor and a majority of Republicans voting against.

A couple of weeks later came more signs that the younger generation was moving ahead. In a race for Chairman of the Senate Republican Conference, Thad Cochran (born 1937) edged out incumbent John Chafee (born 1922, served in the Marines 1942–45), leaving Dole as the only World War II veteran in the Senate GOP leadership. Pete Domenici (born 1932) lost a race for Chairman of the Policy Committee to Don Nickles (born 1948), who thus became the first holder of that position born after World War II. Nickles said that he would use the post 'to see a Republican Party that is united against tax increases'.[29]

Dole and Gramm

In the 1990 Senate leadership races, the chairmanship of the GOP's campaign committee went to Phil Gramm (born 1942). Although Gramm had supported the original budget agreement, he voted against the version that reached the Senate – and he personified the new Republican generation in other ways. It is fitting to compare Gramm with Bob Dole, since their careers parallel each other. Both are former House members who won GOP leadership posts in the Senate. Both have played a major role in fiscal policy. And both have been touched with White House fever: Dole twice sought the presidency, while Gramm is reportedly considering a race for 1996.

Regional roots

Dole was born, raised and educated in the Midwestern state of Kansas, home of GOP presidential candidates Alfred Landon and Dwight Eisenhower. The Midwest and Northeast once supplied the GOP with the bulk of its law-makers; but as noted earlier, newer Republicans have tended to come from the South and West. In the 102d Congress (1991–93), the latter regions accounted for 58 per cent of the GOP's senators and just over half of its House members. Gramm is part of this wave, since he was born in the Southern state of Georgia and now represents Texas, which straddles both the South and the West.

Formative experiences

Dole's poor origins and postwar experiences tempered his conservatism. He never completely trusted the free market that had been so hard on his desolate home town, and he never forgot that government programs had helped him recover from his war wounds. Gramm also grew up poor. As the son of a disabled war veteran, ironically, he too attended college on government subsidies; but then he earned a PhD in economics at a time when government programs seemed to be failing, and when the 'public choice' school was having a major influence on his chosen discipline. As a result, he came to believe that a top priority of politics was to restrain government from doing harm.

Style

Dole entered the House of Representatives during the Speakership of Sam Rayburn. In his early years on Capitol Hill, he learned the 'inside game' of compromising the issues and patiently rising through the ranks. In the Senate, he served on the Finance Committee and became immersed in the language of taxes, tariffs and transfer payments. As Finance Committee chairman and then as Senate Republican Leader, he earned high marks for coalition-building and attention to detail. As a vice-presidential and presidential candidate, however, he displayed far less aptitude for the 'outside game' of media politics.

Gramm entered the House during the Speakership of Tip O'Neill. As a conservative Democrat, he quickly learned that he could have more influence by playing the 'outside game' with like-minded Republicans such as David Stockman. The Gramm–Latta budget resolutions not only enacted President Reagan's fiscal program, but also disrupted the old ways of money politics in Congress. After fellow Democrats punished him for working too closely with the GOP, he switched parties. In 1984, he won John Tower's seat in the Senate. In his freshman year – without a seat on the Budget Committee – he seized upon public concern with the deficit to propose the Gramm–Rudman law, which embodied the public choice economics he had long espoused. In the process, he bypassed the committee system, overcame the reluctance of Dole and other leaders, and won passage of the measure two weeks after introducing it.[30] By 1990, he had gained seats on the Budget and Appropriations Committees, a sign not that he had fundamentally altered his style, but that the Senate was coming to accommodate it.

World View

'Bob waits to see which way the wind is blowing,' said his Kansas colleague Nancy Kassebaum in 1987. 'There's always a question: Does he have a vision? You won't see him creating an agenda.'[31] In his 1988 presidential campaign, Dole did take specific stands on a number of issues, but shied away from discussions of ideology or underlying principles. Gramm, on the other hand, often speaks of vision and grand ideas:

'The "American Empire" is an empire of ideas and vision, not an empire of conquest.'

'It is important that we [Republicans] define our vision in such a way that every American can understand it, and every American can feel part of it'.

'We need an American perestroika – the relentless empowerment of the individual and the family – for the 1990s'.

'I want to make sure we've changed government forever. If I don't do it, it might not get done'.[32]

It remains to be seen whether Gramm can change government forever. But members of his generation are changing the Republican Party. During the 1990s, they will inherit the last remaining leadership positions from Robert Dole's generation. This changing of the guard will then be complete – right in time for the next one.

The next generation

Just as the 'young turks' of the 1960s eventually grew old, so will Phil Gramm's generation. The college students and new workers of 1993 will become the first 'young turks' of the twenty-first century, impatiently viewing their elders as out of step with the times. Though it is impossible to make a complete forecast of this generation's politics, one thing is already clear: it will take a distinctly new view of international affairs.

For exactly fifty years – from the Pearl Harbor attack in December 1941 to the dissolution of the Soviet Union in December 1991 – military considerations dominated America's international perspective, as debates about foreign policy largely concerned troops and weapons. Should America send more men to Europe? To

Vietnam? Should the Nicaraguan rebels receive lethal military equipment? How many and what kind of nuclear arms should the Pentagon deploy?

To a generation that grew up watching Berliners tear down their Wall and Russians hoist their new flag, such questions may seem antiquated. Younger Americans no longer worry about the Soviet army; instead they worry about perceived 'economic threats' from immigrants and foreign competitors. Provided that new military foes do not arise, this generation will define international relations more as a matter of economics than armaments.

Within the Republican Party, the faint outlines of future debates are emerging. Isolationism, dormant since the 1950s, may be waking in a new form: some Republicans believe in protectionist trade policies and restrictive immigration laws. They say that the United States must bolt its doors against predatory trading practices and welfare-seeking foreigners. On the other side stand the new 'supply-siders' who believe that free trade and relatively open immigration policies will result in greater wealth for the country. While no one can say which side will dominate the party, one can make a good guess what the argument will be about.

Some of the older Republicans may try to shift the debate back to military preparedness. Aged hawks from the World War II generation will talk about Pearl Harbor. Aging hawks from the baby boom will talk about America's decline under Jimmy Carter. But these names will scarcely stir members of the next generation.

Notes

1   D. S. Broder, *Changing of the Guard: Power and Leadership in America* (Penguin, 1981), p. 11.

2   Arthur Schlesinger, *The Cycles of American History* (Houghton Mifflin, 1986), p. 30.

3   J. D. Barber, *The Presidential Character* (Prentice-Hall, 1985), p. 5.

4   B. B. Conable, 'Washington Report', 10 June 1984.

5   J. W. Martin, *My First Fifty Years in Politics* (McGraw-Hill, 1960), p. 190.

6   G. Ford, *A Time To Heal* (Harper & Row, 1979), p. 61.

7   R. H. Michel, remarks at the National Press Club awards for consumer journalism, Washington DC, 6 December 1989.

8   R. H. Dole & E. H. Dole, *The Doles* (Simon & Schuster, 1988), pp. 51, 56.

9   A. J. Reichley, 'Here come the Republicans', *Fortune*, 1 September 1967, 166.

10   S. Hess & D. S. Broder, *The Republican Establishment* (Harper & Row, 1967), p. 25.

11   J. J. Rhodes, *The Futile System* (Doubleday, 1976), p. 67.

12   Tax Foundation, *Facts and Figures on Government Finance* (Johns Hopkins University Press, 1990), p. 19.

13   Committee on Ways and Means, *Overview of the Federal Tax System* (1991), p. 179.

14   W. F. Buckley, *Up From Liberalism* (Bantam, 1968), pp. 139–65.

15   P. F. Drucker, *The Age of Discontinuity* (Harper & Row, 1969), p. 218.

16   R. B. Cheney & L. V. Cheney, *Kings of the Hill* (Continuum, 1983), p. 177.

17   Rhodes, *Futile System*, pp. 32–3.

18   J. J. Pitney, 'The Conservative Opportunity Society', paper presented to the annual conference of the Western Political Science Association, San Fransisco, 1988.

19   D. A. Stockman, *The Triumph of Politics* (Harper & Row, 1986), pp. 121, 231.

20   Stockman, *Triumph*, p. 235.

21   C. J. Bailey, *The Republican Party in the US Senate* (Manchester University Press, 1987), p. 79.

22   *Washington Post*, 19 November 1984, A5.

23   Broder, *Changing the Guard*, p. 33.

24   Pitney, 'Conservative Opportunity Society'.

25   Broder, *Changing the Guard*, p. 99.

26   J. P. Pinkerton, 'General Schwarzkopf's new paradigm', *Policy Review*, Summer 1991, 22–6.

27   P. Noonan, *What I Saw at the Revolution* (Random House, 1990), p. 307.

28   P. Gigot in *Wall Street Journal*, 19 October 1990, A14.

29   K. Mattingly, 'Cochran ousts Chafee for no. three leader post', *Roll Call*, 15 November 1990, 3.

30   B. Sinclair, *The Transformation of the US Senate* (Johns Hopkins University Press, 1989), p. 169.

31   M. Tolchin & J. Gerth in *New York Times Magazine*, 8 November 1987.

32   F. Gregorsky, interview with Gramm in *Far From Right* (May 1991), p. 1; A. Meyerson in *Policy Review* (1989), p. 12; *The Vision Thing* (1990), p. 20; P. Duncan (ed.), *Politics in America 1992* (Congressional Quarterly Press, 1991–2).

Moderates lost and found: centrists in the Conservative and Republican Parties

The salience of ideology was one of the most distinctive features of Anglo-American politics during the 1970s and 1980s. In the late 1950s it had appeared that ideology had become obsolete both as an instrument of political mobilization and as an agenda for governance, and that a politics based on technocracy and pragmatism would prevail.[1] These predictions proved false and on both sides of the Atlantic the intervening decades witnessed the rising importance of ideology on both the left and right of the political spectrum. The consensus politics of Eisenhower and the British Tory governments of the 1950s were rejected in favour of ideological prescriptions which had been regarded as outmoded and irrelevant, and the moderate establishments within both the Republican and Conservative parties were deposed by a new set of politicians who specifically emphasized ideology: most particularly Ronald Reagan and Margaret Thatcher. Even the British Conservative party, which had traditionally prided itself on its very lack of an 'ideology', became a vehicle for the politics of protest and principle.

This essay focuses on the predicament of the centrist elements within the Republican and Conservative Parties under Thatcher and Reagan. The reasons for the demise of consensus politics and the rise of the ideological right are discussed; there follows an analysis of the strategies adopted by the dissident moderates *vis à vis* the Thatcher/Reagan leadership. I conclude with a discussion of the future prospects for a new politics of 'moderation' within the Republican and Conservative Parties during the 1990s.

Who are the moderates?

It is first necessary, however, to define the phenomenon under discussion. 'Moderate', 'Centrist' and 'Pragmatic' are notoriously elusive and imprecise terms. In liberal-democratic political systems all major political parties have an element which is closer to the centre of the political spectrum, but that centre-point does not remain static. As the political debate evolves the moderate of yesteryear may become the 'Conservative' of today and *vice versa*. However, in describing the groups under discussion I prefer 'moderate' as a generic term rather than 'liberal', 'wet' or 'progressive' which carry rather different meanings on either side of the Atlantic.

'Moderate' is also the most apposite term because within both British Conservatism and American Republicanism there is a tradition which values 'moderation' and 'pragmatism' for their own sakes as enduring political virtues regardless of the specific issue under discussion. In this sense the concept of 'moderation' refers not to an ideology, but to a style of politics and a particular political temperament. It is this pragmatic tradition that I take as the defining characteristic of 'moderation' within the Conservative and Republican parties. These traditions have deep roots within both parties, but they have been discarded over the past quarter-century or so by new party elites which have wished to place more emphasis on adherence to specific doctrine (the 'conviction politician') and the arousal of electoral support through a populist political style.

British Conservative moderates have claimed the authority of Edmund Burke in their distrust of abstract and systematic reasoning in politics. Another frequently cited ancestor of Tory moderation is Benjamin Disraeli and his doctrine of 'one nation': a reformulation of the aristocratic tradition of *noblesse oblige*. Burke and Disraeli argued that the specific 'genius' of the British Constitution was its ability to adapt to a constantly changing socio-political environment, by contrast with the *ancien régimes* of continental Europe. Modern British Tory moderates therefore see themselves as the inheritors of this pragmatic and paternalistic, 'one nation' tradition.[2]

The United States lacks the tradition of aristocratic paternalism that has survived in Great Britain. Indeed historians of American political thought in the 1950s described American Conservatism as a 'thankless persuasion' in a society based on Lockean liberalism.[3] Nevertheless there are some parallels with the British moderate Conservative tradition within the GOP. As the party of the northern white Protestant elite, the Republicans incorporated the 'old-money' families of the Eastern Seaboard, whose scions – principally President Theodore Roosevelt – provided a critique of unbridled *laissez-faire* (with echoes of *noblesse oblige* and paternalism) during the Progressive Era (1900–16).[4] In addition to TR, Republican moderates also claimed descent from the Federalists and the *antebellum* Whig party, both of which had advocated governmental activism to bolster free market capitalism.[5] Moderate Republicans have also been the most consistent guardians of the party's Lincolnian heritage on civil rights. Their geographic base has traditionally been the areas of White, Protestant settlement outside the old confederacy – New England, the Upper Midwest, the Pacific Northwest, and the Border South.[6]

These then are the respective traditions within American and British Conservatism that I refer to as 'moderate' for the purposes of this paper. After 1945 the 'moderates' dominated both the Conservative and Republican Parties until the late 1960s. In each case there were two main sources of this dominance.

First, the 'moderates' on the right on either side of the Atlantic represented the traditional governing establishment within their parties: the British aristocracy in the case of the Conservatives, and the East Coast establishment in the American case. The British aristocrats still largely controlled the Conservative Party because Conservative activists were deferential towards the upper classes and celebrated aristocratic values.[7] In the American case East Coast domination was rooted more in control over the party's financial resources and strong influence over the Republican business community nationwide.[8]

The second factor in explaining the dominance of the moderates was the social and political impact of the Great Depression and the New Deal. To defeat the Labour party electorally in the 1950s the British Tories had to accept the premises of the Welfare State and government intervention in the economy, and the aristocratic element in the party – led by men such as Harold Macmillan who had been profoundly personally affected by the suffering of the 1930s – had little trouble in adapting itself once more to a changed political situation.[9]

In the United States the New Deal discredited traditional Republican economic doctrine, and Pearl Harbor discredited the isolationist foreign policy which the party had adopted during the 1930s. Republican elites saw that the party could only regain power nationally by accepting the New Deal and an interventionist foreign policy after 1945, and they strove mightily to keep the GOP nomination out of the hands of the conservative Robert Taft in the 1940–52 period. The moderates succeeded because they controlled the national convention delegations from the largest and most powerful states – New York, Pennsylvania, and California.[10]

Nevertheless during this period there were longer-term changes in the political environment in both countries which were working to undermine the moderate Tories and Republicans. These will be discussed in the following section.

The rise of ideology and the activists

The Republican and Conservative Parties in the immediate postwar years still operated according to the norms of 'traditional party politics'. Both parties had a clear leadership elite to which party activists deferred in intra-party affairs. The activists were generally 'professionals', in James Q. Wilson's sense of the term; motivated primarily by considerations of patronage and loyalty to the organization rather than matters of policy or ideology.[11] Party loyalties within the electorate were based on class, ethnicity or region, and were reinforced by the fact that in this period the parties were still the major sources of political information for most voters.[12]

Yet traditional party politics was already showing signs of erosion by the end of the 1950s. The major factors generating this change were: the changing composition of society, the development of new media of political communication, and the emergence of new kinds of party activists.

The social transformation is evidenced by the growth of the salaried, white-collar, middle-class in both Britain and the US.[13] This class not only did not fit into the class, ethnic, and regional categories that underlay traditional party loyalties, but they were also more likely to think of political activity in terms of issues or even ideology. At the same time the parties' roles as conduits of political communication were also eroded by the advent of new electronic news media. This had the effect of weakening loyalties to political parties, and the new media's treatment of politics reinforced the increasingly ideological orientation of the new middle-class.[14]

Unmotivated by the traditional rewards of social inclusiveness and patronage, the new middle-class entered political parties on both right and the left of the political spectrum, and imposed their own ideological and populistic style of politics on the parties. Even in the British Conservative Party which had almost prided itself on its lack of concern for ideology (reflecting the Burkean/Disraelian heritage) ideas and policies became increasingly important – particularly after the election defeat of 1964. In that same year the East Coast establishment lost control of the Republican Party to a coalition of conservative activists aroused by the candidacy of the explicitly ideological conservative Senator Barry Goldwater.

In Britain's case the country's seemingly endemic decline had the additional effect of discrediting the traditional, aristocratic, public-school and Oxbridge elites. Upwardly mobile, middle-class, activists within the Tory party no longer deferred so readily to those elites nor accepted their paternalistic approach to politics.[15]

While these changes affected the parties in both countries, the effects were much more profound in the United States than in Britain. In the latter the major political parties retained strong organizations, party loyalties stayed high, and parties remained the primary vehicles of governance. In the United States the political party as organization virtually disappeared, and ideology supplanted party as the primary means of political mobilization and governance. The parties survive as vote-structuring organizations, as fund-raisers, and to organize Congress and the state legislatures, but their role in the political system is much diminished relative to interest groups and the news media.

The trend towards party decomposition has been more pronounced in the US primarily because American parties have never been 'strong' relative to their European counterparts, although they were certainly once much more effectual organizations than they are today. The country's Lockean political heritage precluded the concentration of power implicit in the idea of strong parties, and the separation of powers itself makes party government on a national scale hard to realize. American parties never developed into the disciplined mass organizations depicted by Michels and typical of the political parties of Western Europe, but remained in a pre-modern, 'cadre-party', style of organization. Outrage at party corruption during the progressive era led to the passage of further measures restricting the parties' activities – principally the direct primary which even stripped them of the basic function of deciding the candidates who should bear the party label – and as the twentieth century progressed, the emergence of the new, 'non-partisan', ideologically-motivated middle-class finally killed off the American party as organization.[16]

The collapse of the centre and the rise of the right

The control of the moderates over the Conservative and Republican Parties during the post-war decades, however, was not only a consequence of traditional party structures which favoured non-ideological approaches to leadership, but also of the general level of consensus which prevailed within society and between both of the major political parties in Britain and the United States.

In Britain, the post-war decades were the years of social-democratic consensus, forged by the 1945–51 Labour government which established the welfare state and took key sections of the economy into state ownership. In opposition the Conservatives accommodated themselves to the new order of British politics, and during their thirteen years in government in 1951–64, they consolidated the edifice that Labour had built after the war. This required no major adjustment in party doctrine or leadership: the party was still governed by aristocrats, and welfarism and state planning accorded well with the Tory tradition of paternalism. Yet greater social mobility in Britain as educational opportunities increased, brought a new generation of 'meritocrats' into the Tory leadership. During the period of the social–democratic consensus these tended to be 'modernizers' or 'technocrats' who saw a vigorous governmental role as essential to restoring Britain's economic competitiveness. In the early 1960s, then, both the meritocrats – led by Edward Heath and Iain Macleod – and the aristocrats – best represented by Harold Macmillan and Alec Douglas-Home – were committed to the social-democratic consensus, though from different motivations.

In the 1951–64 period the Conservatives divested Britain of most of its Empire and with the modernizers in the vanguard they sought to re-orient British foreign policy around the European Community, which would assist the 'modernization' of British industry and provide Britain with a new international role. Despite De Gaulle's rejection of Britain's first application for membership in 1963, enthusiasm for Europe remained a major feature of the moderate wing of the Tory party.[17]

The only problem with the social democratic consensus was that it failed to reverse Britain's economic decline relative to its international competitors. During the 1960s this decline became more evident as the country was struck by a series of balance-of-payments crises and bouts of inflation. For the Conservatives there was the additional problem of what Sir Keith Joseph referred to as the 'ratchet effect' – as Conservatives conceded more and more ground on state intervention in pursuit of the elusive 'centre-ground' between themselves and Labour, they made concessions which later were politically impossible to reverse.[18] Conservatives once again had to face up to Disraeli's question in *Coningsby*: 'what will you conserve?'[19] In the mid-1960s they had no ready answer.

During the period in opposition under Edward Heath (1964–70) there were signs of a change in direction. Heath – the leading symbol of the new meritocratic politics within the party – espoused a more 'free-market' approach on economic issues specifically rejecting the incomes policies which had been resorted to by Conservative and Labour governments to conquer inflation during the 1960s. While committing the party even more firmly to EC membership, Heath continued to pursue the themes of 'modernization' and 'competitiveness'. Failing industries would no longer by bailed out by the state but would have to compete on their own terms. Others in the party wanted to go even further in a right-wing direction. Enoch Powell embraced a much more radical free-market approach on economics, combined with a populistic hostility towards non-white immigration into Britain, and opposition to EC membership.[20]

Within eighteen months of taking office in 1970, however, Heath abandoned much of his free-market manifesto. Failed companies such as Rolls-Royce were taken into state ownership, and incomes policies were reintroduced to curb inflation. While Heath did succeed in finally taking Britain into the EC in 1973, discontent on the right wing of the party simmered throughout his government. When his gamble of calling an early general election during the 1974 miners' strike backfired, and he lost another election in October of the same year, a change of direction seemed to be in order.[21]

Enoch Powell had abandoned the Conservatives in February of 1974 and none of Heath's senior cabinet colleagues wanted to challenge him. However during 1974–75, Sir Keith Joseph, a member of the Heath Cabinet, repudiated Heath's celebrated U-turn on economic policy, and called for a more radical free-market approach to the economy. When Joseph himself failed to stand it was left to his ally Margaret Thatcher to finally oust Heath in the spring of 1975.[22]

In Britain, then, moderate conservatism in both its aristocratic and technocratic versions failed to reverse relative economic decline in the postwar period. This undermined the authority of the traditional party elites and coincided with the arrival of the new middle-class to a position of power within the Conservative Party. The combination of economic failure and social change fatally undermined the moderate wing of the party, which was further damaged by its association with the failed Heath administration after 1974.

In the United States the sources of the decline in the power of the traditional establishment were not entirely dissimilar. Socio-economic change and concerns about America's international status also played a part in unraveling the New Deal political system to the benefit of the Republican right. The lessons of the 1930s and 1940s for the Republicans were that they could not win the White House again without making an accommodation with the New Deal political system. In domestic policy this entailed a commitment to the maintenance of the New Deal's welfare measures, and to intervene in the economy to prevent another Great Depression. In foreign policy the New Deal consensus was based on a global commitment to contain the Soviet Union and Communism in general.

During the 1950s the Eisenhower administration maintained the bipartisan consensus in domestic and foreign policy. But the Republican right did not disappear with Senator Taft's death in 1953, and during the Eisenhower years their ranks were expanded by the addition of McCarthyite Democrats and White Southerners increasingly disenchanted with their party's liberal turn on civil rights.[23]

As the New Deal consensus began to disintegrate during the 1960s, the power of the Republicans' eastern, moderate, establishment began to wane. As the grassroots of the party became increasingly conservative, the moderates found that they could no longer control the party's presidential nomination through their economic power. In 1940 Wall Street won the presidential nomination for Wendell Willkie, by putting financial pressure on the bankers and businessmen who controlled the state Republican parties that selected convention delegates. By 1964 the eastern establishment no longer held a monopoly on that kind of power – new centres of economic power had opened up in the South and West – and the new conservative activists were not disposed to pay much attention to the eastern establishment anyway.[24]

The Goldwater nomination in 1964 was the key sign that the party's establishment was in deep trouble, and the unraveling of the New Deal consensus which they represented during the 1960s confirmed their downfall. Moderate Republicanism had supported civil rights for blacks, but the racial violence of the mid-1960s destroyed the national consensus on civil rights and created a new electoral cleavage based on race. Moderate Republicanism represented anti-communist interventions overseas, but the Vietnam war and the domestic upheaval it brought in its wake, fatally undermined the national consensus on foreign policy issues that had existed since the late 1940s. Finally, state interventionism in the economy and the maintenance of the welfare system were undermined by the advent of higher rates of inflation in the late 1960s and the concomitant squeeze on middle-class incomes.[25]

In response to these developments, the GOP leadership moved towards the more populist conservatism of the new right in order to capture middle and working-class Democratic voters disenchanted by racial violence, falling incomes, and the antiwar movement. Richard Nixon's comeback in 1968 was as a 're-born' conservative rather than a moderate Republican, since Nixon was well-aware that he could not be nominated without the support of the Goldwater conservatives. As the disintegration of the New Deal political system continued through the 1970s, and as America's foreign policy seemed haunted by irresolution and the ghosts of

Vietnam, the more radical ideas of the Republican right – supply-side economics, monetarism, increased defence spending, and the restoration of traditional 'family' values – began to seem plausible as a means of forging a new electoral majority for the Republicans.[26] In these circumstances it is hardly surprising that the right's champion, Ronald Reagan should have had such an easy path to the Republican presidential nomination in 1980.

Moderate conservative strategies in the era of the new right

Having been dethroned from their positions of power within the Conservative and Republican parties, the moderates faced a choice between two strategies: accommodation or counter-attack. The former strategy implied that the battle for the ideological soul of the party had already been lost, and that moderate influence within the party could best be maintained by accommodating the ideas of the new right within the broader Conservative or Republican tradition. The risk here, however, was that the moderates would sell their political souls to an ideological leadership with which they disagreed fundamentally on most issues, without obtaining any significant concessions in return.

Counter-attack implied that the battle with the right over party doctrine had not been definitively lost and that it was still possible for the moderates to regain control over the party. The problem with counter-attack was that it risked bitterly dividing the party and thereby virtually excluding it from power. Counter-attack became doubly hazardous as a strategy for moderates, when the activist base of the party had moved so far to the right.

By examining each party in turn we can illustrate how and with what success these strategies were employed in both the Conservative and the Republican Parties.

Great Britain: moderate Toryism under Thatcher

Moderate Toryism remained very influential in the first phase of Mrs Thatcher's leadership – the period of opposition between 1975 and 1979. After having won the leadership in a bitterly fought contest, it was not in her interest to prolong party divisions. Moreover, while new right economic ideas had gained significant support in the party, most of its experienced leadership was firmly in the moderate camp. The moderates hoped that, like Heath, Mrs Thatcher could be won round to moderate ideas if the party gained power and she was faced with the exigencies of government. The accommodationist strategy was epitomized in the special role given to William Whitelaw, who had challenged Mrs Thatcher for the leadership after Edward Heath's withdrawal. As Deputy Leader Whitelaw gave Mrs Thatcher unswerving support, and most of the other moderates rallied behind him.[27]

Once the Conservatives were in office, however, it became apparent that Thatcher and her Chancellor Geoffrey Howe took their monetarist and free-market ideas seriously. After Howe's 1981 budget in which he deflated the economy in the midst of a recession and record unemployment, confrontation with the moderates became inevitable. In September 1981 Mrs Thatcher purged her Cabinet of several moderates such as Sir Ian Gilmour (whose book *Inside Right* had provided an eloquent restatement of Burkean/Disraelian Toryism), Christopher Soames and Mark Carlisle, and moved those who remained to positions well removed from economic policy-making, where the key ministries were headed by hard-line 'Thatcherites'.[28]

In early 1982 it seemed that with the economy in deep recession, three million unemployed, and the party in the doldrums in the opinion polls, a more confrontational approach to the Thatcher leadership might prevail. The formation of the new Social Democratic Party of disaffected Labour moderates, and its spectacular by-election successes in mainly Conservative seats, seemed to vindicate moderate forebodings about the dangers of rigid adherence to ideology. With signs of panic on the Tory backbenches, rumours of a challenge to Thatcher from the moderates began to circulate. These aspirations were dashed by Mrs Thatcher's triumph in the Falklands War and the first signs of economic success with a falling inflation-rate in 1982/83. The reaffirmation of Thatcherism in the landslide Tory election victory in 1983, effectively suppressed the moderates and consolidated the new right's grip on the Conservative party.

Yet that grip was never quite as firm as it appeared.[29] Thatcher herself displayed an ability to capitulate to moderate arguments when it was clear that her own views could not prevail in Cabinet. And while prominent moderates such as Francis Pym and James

Prior were gradually eased out of the Thatcher Cabinet, other accommodationists such as Douglas Hurd and Kenneth Baker replaced them. Two unreconstructed Heathite technocrats, Peter Walker and Michael Heseltine, also remained in the Thatcher Cabinet because the Prime Minister reckoned that they would be more dangerous on the backbenches than within the government. Moderate Tories' unease over the 'divisive' tone of Mrs Thatcher's regime revived briefly during the government's bitter and prolonged conflict with the National Union of Mineworkers in 1984/85. The most remarkable expression of Tory dissent over the government's conduct of the miners' dispute came from the former Prime Minister Harold Macmillan, now in his nineties and ennobled as the Earl of Stockton. Stockton was joined by Francis Pym, who had been sacked as Foreign Secretary after the 1983 election victory. Pym's political testament, *The Politics of Consent*, received considerable attention, and in May 1985 he attempted to capitalise on this by forming a moderate grouping called 'Conservative Centre Forward' within the parliamentary party.[30] While the criticisms of Stockton and Pym made some impression at the time, they inadvertently exposed a serious weakness of Tory moderation during the Thatcher years; namely that it was associated with the failed policies of an outdated and increasingly irrelevant social caste. Moreover, the critiques of Thatcher from the 'Wet' sections of the party contained more than a trace of paternalistic condescension for the 'bourgeois' nature of the government, which further reduced their chances of rallying support against her either inside or outside the party.

The growing importance of the European issue after Mrs Thatcher had signed the Single European Act in 1985, did, however, widen the scope of moderate dissent within the party, even into the ranks of the Thatcher camp, many of whose members – such as Chancellor Nigel Lawson – were less wary about European economic and political integration than the Prime Minister herself. And it was the Europe issue which precipitated the dispute between Thatcher and Defence Secretary Heseltine over the bailout of the Westland helicopter company that resulted in Heseltine's dramatic resignation from the Cabinet in 1986.[31] On the backbenches the charismatic Heseltine – untainted by associations with the upper classes, and who had a rapport with Conservative activists and the news media which the other leading Tory moderates conspicuously lacked – was a much more serious threat than in government, and he immediately marked himself as the leader of the opposition to 'Thatcherism' in terms of both style and substance within the Conservative Party.[32]

Thatcher recovered from the Westland débâcle to win a third term in office with a very comfortable majority in 1987, but as this term progressed the voices of dissent within the party became louder and more numerous. Mrs Thatcher's increasing scepticism about European integration collided with an extensive enthusiasm for the European Community that had persisted in sections of the party since the Macmillan era. The City of London and the business community which had hitherto been generally supportive of Thatcherism, were keen on European economic integration, and feared that Thatcher's disdain for Europe might damage London's position as a world commercial and financial centre relative to Paris or Frankfurt.[33]

Disagreements over European integration also caused the exits of first Nigel Lawson and Sir Geoffrey Howe from the Cabinet: resignations which played a crucial role in Thatcher's downfall.[34] Mrs Thatcher would not have fallen, however, had her economic policies still proven successful and had she not introduced the unpopular 'community charge' or poll tax to pay for local government services. The combined effects of rising inflation and the poll tax damaged the government's popularity as evidenced in by-elections and opinion polls, and dissent on the backbenches spread beyond the embittered Edward Heath and the handful of aristocratic 'wets' and into the broad centre of the Conservative party.

Accommodationists such as Douglas Hurd (Howe's replacement as foreign secretary) remained loyal, however, and Thatcher had successfully co-opted several younger moderates – Chris Patten, Kenneth Clarke and William Waldegrave – into the Cabinet. Heseltine thus remained the focus of a counter-attack strategy, but he was reluctant to move unless he could be certain of victory. An eccentric backbencher Sir Anthony Meyer did challenge Thatcher for the party leadership in 1989, and some sixty Conservative MPs either voted for him or abstained indicating an increasing level of overt dissent within the party.[35]

In 1990 with the economy still in the doldrums, the Poll Tax as unpopular as ever, and the Europe issue still dividing the

Conservatives, a more serious leadership challenge seemed likely. The chances increased after Geoffrey Howe's resignation from the government and his bitter resignation speech in which he denounced Thatcher's style of government from the floor of the Commons. After that Heseltine could no longer resist a challenge, and capitalizing on the discontent with Thatcher, he did well enough to prevent her winning the required number of votes on the first ballot. Thatcher's resignation two days later apparently indicated that moderate Toryism was about to regain control of the party after the Thatcher aberration, but, in fact, the outcome of the leadership election graphically demonstrated the impact of the Thatcher revolution on the Conservatives.[36]

After Thatcher's exit Heseltine and the moderates had virtually no chance of winning. His philosophy of energetic and interventionist government was too much at odds with the non-interventionist economics that was now broadly supported even on the moderate wing of the party, and Heseltine's enthusiasm for Europe in a party where scepticism about the Community was still widespread, was an additional liability. His chances diminished further, when another moderate candidate, Douglas Hurd, whose roots were in the paternalistic/Burkean Tory tradition rather than in the technocratic/modernizing vein characteristic of Heseltine, entered the contest after Thatcher's departure.

Further problems were created by the entry into the leadership contest of the Chancellor of the Exchequer, John Major. Major's 'Thatcherite' credentials were excellent. Having risen from a very humble background, he epitomized the ethic of the 'self-made' man and of the new meritocratic British middle-class. And while he held fairly orthodox free-market views on the economy, he was thought to be less antipathetic towards the EC, and less abrasive in his temperament and style than the deposed leader. As soon as he entered the race it was apparent that Major, who could command most of the votes of the Thatcher loyalists while not alienating the centre and left of the party, was the candidate best-placed to maintain party unity, and he easily defeated Heseltine and Hurd.[37]

During the fifteen years of Mrs Thatcher's leadership, moderate Conservatives thus pursued strategies of both accommodation and confrontation. In the first phase of her leadership the accommodation strategy was pursued in the hope of tempering the Prime

Minister's views and maintaining party unity. In those terms the strategy could claim some successes though on the essentials of economic policy, the moderate viewpoint was frozen out of the Thatcher government at a fairly early stage. In the midst of the 1981/82 recession and after Thatcher had sacked prominent moderates from her Cabinet, wider rumblings of discontent were heard, but moderate opposition dissipated in the wake of Thatcher's triumph in the Falklands War. Moderate opposition outside the Cabinet continued to be ineffectual during the second Thatcher term, but the resignation of Michael Heseltine provided moderate Toryism with a leader who had substantial appeal both within the Conservative party and among the wider public. His themes of energetic, interventionist, Europe-oriented government, also had more contemporary relevance than the nostalgic *noblesse oblige* of the more paternalistic Wets. When the Thatcher government got into deep electoral difficulties during the third term, and as the highly sensitive issue of European integration began to divide the party, opposition to Mrs Thatcher's rule ultimately coalesced around Heseltine, who effectively ousted her as Leader in 1990, but proved unable to secure the Leadership for himself.

Moderate Tories, however, had some reason to be pleased about the accession of John Major, whose conciliatory style of leadership was closer to the Tory tradition than the 'conviction-politics' of Margaret Thatcher.[38] Moderates held influential positions in the Major government: Heseltine rejoined the Cabinet as Environment Secretary, Hurd remained at the Foreign Office, and Chris Patten assumed the party chairmanship. Their exertions were critical to the Tories' post-Thatcher revival, both before and during the 1992 election campaign. There was, nevertheless, no question but that a fundamental revolution had taken place within the Conservative party, that had taken power away from its old paternalistic establishment and given it to the new 'middle-class', which Major represents. Conservative moderation survives as a force within the party because the tenets of moderation have remained essential to the party's role in British politics since Disraeli, but the meritocratic moderates of Major's Cabinets did not share the aristocratic background of the old-fashioned moderates. As yet not a single hereditary peer has been appointed to the Cabinet by Major.

The US: moderate Republicanism in the Reagan–Bush era

In the American Republican party the moderates had really lost the battle for the soul of the party well before Ronald Reagan entered the White House. Subsequent to the Goldwater débâcle the Republican right had established their control over the national party, and the move towards a primary system of selecting presidential nominees consolidated their power by virtually excluding from the process old-style party elites – Wall Street and Madison Avenue money, traditional party organizations – that had been decisive in nominating contests in the 1940s. The 'new politics' placed a premium on mobilizing funds and organizations from ideological activists and stridently conservative single-issue groups, a game which the Republican right with their more ideological style was much more suited to play than the old moderate establishment.[39]

The moderates did not leave the field of presidential politics in the GOP entirely without a struggle however. During the 1960s a group of younger 'progressive-Republican' activists in Cambridge, Massachusetts founded the Ripon society, which was intended to be an intellectual counterweight to the new right. As a sounding board for policy innovation Ripon actually succeeded quite well, and their policy proposals such as the volunteer army, welfare reform and revenue-sharing were all eventually adopted by the Nixon administration.[40]

But to defeat the right, Ripon needed to fight them at the grassroots of the party where they had established formidable strength, and in the new politics the right had inherent advantages in their ability to mobilize over the self-described moderates. While moderate support among the general public might appear wide, it was not deep enough to generate a viable activist constituency. The Republican moderates compounded the problem in the 1968 nominating campaign by initially supporting the hopeless candidacy of Michigan Governor George Romney, and only switching to New York Governor Nelson Rockefeller when it was too late to effect the outcome. Rockefeller mounted a spirited campaign funded entirely out of his personal fortune and staffed largely by his own retainers, but like Ripon his strength lay among old-style party elites, and it was Nixon with assiduous courting of the right who emerged with the nomination.[41]

During the Nixon and Ford administrations (1969–77), moderate Republicans adopted a accommodationist strategy, which on the evidence of the administration's actual policy output was rather effective. While making rhetorical gestures to the right on issues such as busing the agenda of the Nixon administration was fairly similar to that of the Ripon society: revenue-sharing was introduced; the draft was ended, the Environmental Protection Agency was established; and school-desegregation was implemented at a rapid pace. On foreign policy Nixon ultimately ended the Vietnam War and pursued *détente* with the Soviet Union and Red China. On economic policy he explicitly declared himself a Keynesian, and introduced a prices and incomes policy in 1971. Moreover, the domestic policy personnel of the administration were almost all drawn from the establishment wing of the Republican party. In truth, despite Nixon's association throughout his political career with the Republican right, his was very much a moderate-Republican administration. The same was generally true of the brief administration of Gerald Ford, although Ford was more economically conservative than Nixon.[42]

By the time that Ford and Ronald Reagan fought for the Republican nomination in 1976, the moderate wing of the Republican party was virtually extinct in presidential-nominating politics; and although the moderates rallied behind Ford, the lack of an effective moderate-Republican presence at the party's grassroots, meant that Ford was driven right wards in order to compete with Reagan. This has been the pattern of Republican presidential nominating politics ever since. The present base of the moderate wing of the party, being confined largely to New England and a few states of the Upper Midwest and Pacific Northwest, is simply not extensive enough to sustain a moderate-Republican presidential campaign. It is also clear that the effects of electoral realignment have worked to the disadvantage of the moderate Republicans, since much of their natural constituency of upper-middle-class WASP professionals has drifted more towards the Democratic party since 1968, as the Republican party has become more southern and western in its cultural/ideological complexion.[43]

Part of this process was the movement of prominent Republican liberals such New York Mayor John Lindsay, and Congressman (later Senator) Donald Riegle into the Democratic party in the early 1970s. If a moderate had serious presidential aspirations (as Lindsay and Riegle did) then it was hard to make an argument for staying in a Republican party which had moved in such a conservative direction at this level. In 1980 moderate Congressman John Anderson ran a spirited campaign for the GOP nomination which won him plaudits from the news media, but not a single primary election – even in normally moderate Republican territory like New England. Concluding from this that he could never be nominated by the Republicans, Anderson launched a quixotic third party campaign for the general election that probably damaged Democrat Jimmy Carter more than it did the Republican, Reagan.[44]

Other moderates adopted a more accommodationist approach. George Bush ridiculed the new right gospel of supply-side economics in his 1980 campaign, and adopted a strong 'pro-choice' position on abortion. After having been easily beaten by Ronald Reagan for the nomination, however, Bush learned that it was impossible to secure the Republican presidential nomination in the face of the outright hostility of the Republican right. Bush's strategy for winning the GOP nomination in the future was to accept Reagan's offer of the vice-presidential nomination in 1980, to repudiate all of his past views which conflicted with those of the party's right wing, and to be unswervingly loyal to Reagan.

The strategy worked brilliantly for Bush on the next occasion that the Republican nomination was open in 1988. He was able to run for the nomination as Reagan's anointed heir and thus effectively neutralized opposition from the right of the party. By contrast, other moderates who adopted a more offensive strategy succeeded in arousing a great deal of enmity from the rank and file conservatives at the party's grassroots, without noticeably strengthening the position of moderates inside the party. Connecticut Senator Lowell Weicker is a case in point. His fulminations against the new right's social agenda on the Senate floor earned plaudits from the news media and liberal circles, but left him more isolated and irrelevant than ever within the Republican party, both in Washington DC and in his own state. A fitting end to the tortured relationship between Connecticut's *enfant terrible* and the Republican party was his defeat by Democrat Joseph Lieberman in 1988, largely due to an extensive anti-Weicker campaign among hard-line Republican Conservatives. Weicker returned to torment the Republicans once again, however, by winning the governorship of the state as an Independent in 1990, but in national politics he is unlikely to become significant at any time in the short-term future.

As with the succession of John Major in Britain, Bush as president gained a reputation for greater moderation than Reagan, largely on the basis of style and rhetoric. On policy terms by far the most significant departure was Bush's decision to raise taxes in the 1990 budget agreement with Congress, which created outrage on some quarters of the party and became the most important 'gripe' of Buchanan in his unsuccessful (but far from negligible) challenge for the Republican nomination in 1992. His success in the Gulf War and the collapse of Soviet power in 1991, strengthened his position considerably, and on most of the sensitive social/cultural issues which matter a great deal to those who participate in GOP primaries, Bush adhered to a conservative position. On domestic policy Bush talked of a 'kinder, gentler nation', and swore to be both the 'environmental' president and the 'education' president, while also paying more attention to the needs of minorities. On none of these matters, however, Bush did alter policy significantly from the Reagan administration, although there was certainly a difference in tone and rhetoric from the Reagan years.

At the presidential level, therefore, moderate Republicanism was extinct by 1980, due to the erosion of the New Deal voting alignments and the advent of the primary system for making presidential nominations. George Bush may have acquired a reputation as a moderate Republican, but he could only have won the presidency by the route that he eventually followed; using the vice-presidency to ingratiate himself with Republican conservatives and secure his position as Reagan's heir apparent. Moderates who adopted an overtly confrontational approach to the new right, like Lowell Weicker, condemned themselves to irrelevance within the Republican party.

On the other hand moderate Republicanism was by no means dead in other sections of the GOP and the 1990s held some promise of a revival. In the US Senate and – to a much lesser extent – the House of Representatives, certain states and districts continued to return moderate Republicans because these were the only kinds of Republicans that could win there. Moderates who have worked within Congress to shape legislation in their direction such as

Senators Arlen Specter, John Danforth, Mark Hatfield, Nancy Kassebaum and Bob Packwood – have been very influential on Capitol Hill where their support has often meant the difference between the success or failure of a presidential initiative. Even in the House, where the moderate Republican contingent is much smaller, the Wednesday Group has continued to play a significant role. In the states the administrative nature of the gubernatorial office has meant that Republican governors tend to come from the moderate side of the party, and a number of Republican moderates were elected in 1990 in states such as California, Ohio, Illinois and Minnesota.

Thus while moderate Republicanism is likely to remain peripheral in presidential politics simply due to the dynamics of the present-day presidential nominating process, it is by no means extinct in other sections of the Republican party.

Conclusion: moderates lost and found

From our analysis of the Conservative and Republican parties during the Thatcher–Reagan decades it is clear that the centre did not disappear in either party but shifted somewhat to the right in accordance with the times. The economic and social breakdown of the post-war Keynesian/interventionist consensus during the 1960s led ultimately to the forging of a new consensus around a more free-market oriented approach to economic policy, by the Thatcher and Reagan administrations.

In addition to the effects of ideological and electoral realignments, however, the positions of moderates in both parties was undermined by changes in the whole structure of partisan politics – growing levels of affluence and education, the rise of the white-collar middle-class, the breakdown of traditional community structures, and the advent of the electronic news media as the principal means of political communication – which have combined to produce a more populistic style of politics. The moderate establishment within both the Conservative and Republican parties, representing traditional social and political elite groups were particularly ill-suited to this new style of politics. In addition, in the new politics the emphasis on ideology – often more in terms of rhetoric and style rather than actual substance – proved to be a very valuable tool in arousing mass activist support. Moderate values such as 'pragmatism' did not possess nearly the same degree of mobilizing capacity.

There has nevertheless been a considerable difference in the degree to which the Conservative and Republican parties have been affected by these developments.

In the US, where the party structures had always been loose and undisciplined in comparison to the UK, the process of party decomposition is much more advanced. The party organizations have been reduced to little more than national, state, and local, fundraising operations, and candidates at all levels are selected in primary elections where the electorate is disproportionately composed of middle-class single-issue and ideological activists. In this situation it is hardly surprising that moderate Republicans have been effectively eliminated from presidential politics since 1968. The dynamics of the contemporary presidential selection process simply work against any self-consciously moderate candidate or campaign, and favours the outsider, the populist and the ideologue.

In Great Britain, however, the party structures have remained intact and formidable. This is largely due to the fact that British government hinges on maintaining a majority in the House of Commons, and is not dispersed among three or four different branches as in the United States. The concentration of governmental power in Britain requires that the political parties who compete to win a Commons majority be centralized and disciplined in a way that the American parties never have been. Thus in Britain despite all the socio-economic changes outlined above, traditional party structures and norms have persisted, and particularly in the Conservative party which has been oriented towards winning political power above all else, rather than any specific ideology. As a consequence moderates in the Conservative party remain a much stronger force than among the Republicans, because pragmatism is built into the very nature and structure of the party.

This also partly explains why the Conservatives have not been so clearly divided into moderate or Conservative 'wings' or 'factions' as their American counterparts.[45] The Conservative party does have consistently right-wing and consistently left-wing 'tendencies', but they account together for only a minority of the party's MPs, most of whom tend to congregate in a somewhat amorphous centre position.[46] The 'great middle' of the Tory party wants to gain power and to hang onto it, and will follow the course necessary to do so. It was the loss of Mrs Thatcher's electoral appeal, and not her ideology, that finally brought her down because the great middle of the Conservative party in parliament feared that she was dragging the party down to electoral defeat. The emergence of ostensibly more moderate leadership in both parties with the accessions of Messrs Major and Bush, is partly due to the apparent exhaustion of the free-market ideologies of the 1970s and 1980s. In each case the new right came up against the limits which popular opinion would accept as far as the dismantling of the welfare state was concerned. Anti-Communism and a militant defence posture also lost much of their appeal with the ending of the Cold War and the disintegration of the Soviet bloc. Finally, the 'social agenda' of the new right (emphasizing family values, religiosity and opposition to abortion and sexual promiscuity), though more significant in the USA than the UK, never won wide popular acceptance in societies where traditional values seemed to be of decreasing relevance to most of the population.

The contrasting outcomes of the 1992 elections for the Conservative and Republican Parties in Britain and America held important implications for the factional balance within the two parties.

John Major's surprising victory in the British general election, seemed to be a vindication of his more pragmatic approach to government. Yet his moderate-dominated Cabinet soon got into deep political trouble as the British economic recession deepened and the government was forced to devalue the pound through withdrawal from the European Monetary System. These setbacks coincided with the submission to the House of Commons of the controversial Maastricht Treaty on European unity, which was bitterly opposed by Baroness Thatcher and a determined group of Conservative MPs. As the Tory ructions over Europe continued to plague the party, Major's only advantage lay in the fact that as in the 1990 leadership contest, all his likely successors were more pro-European and more 'moderate' than himself, and were therefore even more unacceptable to right-wing, nationalist Conservatives.

In the United States the decisive electoral repudiation of George Bush, who had almost made a political career out of accommodating the right wing of the party, appeared to provide a tremendous opportunity for a revival of moderate Republicanism. Republican moderates could also take heart from the success of the relatively moderate Bill Clinton in securing the Democratic nomination, and

the apparent intellectual exhaustion of American conservatism after
the end of the Cold War and a dozen years of conservative Republican control of the presidency. The disarray on the Republican
right might further provide an opening in 1996 for a prominent
moderate like California Governor Pete Wilson or Massachusetts
Governor William Weld to mount a serious challenge for the GOP
nomination. Whether that opportunity can be grasped by the
Republican moderates without a national grassroots base of support to match the resources of the GOP right, is another matter.

Notes

1   See Daniel Bell, *The End of Ideology: on the Exhaustion of Political Ideas in the Fifties* (Cambridge, MA: Harvard University Press, 1988),
esp. pp. 393–447.

2   On the antecedents of moderate Toryism see Ian Gilmour, *Inside
Right: Conservatism, Policies and the People* (London: Quartet Books,
1978); Samuel H. Beer, *Modern British Politics: Parties and Pressure
Groups in the Collectivist Age* (London: Faber & Faber, 1965), pp. 3–32,
245–76; and Philip Norton & Arthur Aughey, *Conservatives and Conservatism* (London: Temple Smith, 1981), pp. 15–89.

3   See Clinton L. Rossiter, *Conservatism in America: the Thankless
Persuasion*, 2d ed (New York: Random House, 1962); and Louis Hartz,
The Liberal Tradition in America (New York: Harcourt, Brace & World,
1955).

4   See Richard A. Hofstadter, *The Age of Reform: from Bryan to
FDR* (New York: Knopf, 1955), pp. 131–72.

5   See Jacob K. Javits, *Order of Battle: a Republican's Call to Reason* (New York: Pocket Books, 1966), pp. 56–108.

6   Nicol C. Rae, *The Decline and Fall of the Liberal Republicans: from 1952 to the Present* (New York: Oxford University Press, 1989),
pp. 10–45.

7   Beer, *Modern British Politics*, pp. 91–102.

8   Rae, *The Decline and Fall of the Liberal Republicans*, pp. 10–45.

9   Beer, *Modern British Politics*, pp. 302–90.

10   Rae, *The Decline and Fall of the Liberal Republicans*, pp. 25–45.

11   See James Q. Wilson, *The Amateur Democrat: Club Politics in
Three Cities* (Chicago: University of Chicago Press, 1962).

12   See Angus Campbell, Philip E. Converse, Warren E. Miller &
Donald E. Stokes, *The American Voter* (New York: John Wiley & Sons,
1960); and David Butler and Donald E. Stokes, *Political Change in
Britain: the Evolution of Electoral Choice* (London: Macmillan, 1969).

13   See Everett Carll Ladd, Jr. with Charles D. Hadley, *Transformations
of the American Party System* (New York: Norton, 1978) and Anthony
Heath, Roger Jowell and John Curtice, *How Britain Votes* (Oxford:
Pergamon, 1985).

14 See Samuel H. Beer, *Britain Against Itself: the Political Contradictions of Collectivism* (New York: Norton, 1982) pp. 107–208; and Norman H. Nie, Sidney Verba & John R. Petrocik, *The Changing American Voter*. enlarged ed (London: Harvard University Press, 1979).

15 Beer, *Britain Against Itself*, pp. 169–80.

16 See Walter Dean Burnham, *Critical Elections and the Mainsprings of American Politics* (New York: Norton, 1970); Ladd & Hadley, *Transformations of the Party System*; and Martin P, Wattenbery, *The Decline of American Political Parties 1952–80* (Cambridge, MA: Harvard, 1984).

17 See Nigel Ashford, 'The European Economic Community' in Zig Layton-Henry (ed.), *Conservative Party Politics* (London: Macmillan, 1980), pp. 95–125.

18 On the 'ratchet effect' see Denis Kavanagh, *Thatcherism and British Politics: the End of Consensus* (Oxford: Oxford University Press, 1987), pp. 116–17.

19 Benjamin Disraeli, *Coningsby, or, The New Generation*, 3 vols (1844), Bk II, ch. 5.

20 On 'Heathism' and 'Powellism' see Norton & Aughey, *Conservatives and Conservatism*, pp. 144–56; and Andrew Gamble, *The Free Economy and the Strong State: the Politics of Thatcherism* (London: Macmillan, 1988), pp. 67–73.

21 Norton & Aughey, ibid., pp. 144–56; and Gamble, ibid., pp. 73–80.

22 On the ousting of Heath and Thatcher's victory see Hugo Young, *One of Us: a Biography of Margaret Thatcher* (London: Pan, 1990), pp. 81–99.

23 See Rae, *The Decline and Fall of the Liberal Republicans*, pp. 46–53; Miles, *The Odyssey of the American Right* (New York: Oxford University Press, 1980); and William Rusher, *The Rise of the Right* (New York: William Morrow, 1984).

24 Rae, ibid., pp. 46–77. On the Goldwater nomination see Robert A. Novak, *The Agony of the GOP 1964* (New York: Macmillan, 1965).

25 Ladd and Hadley, *Transformations of the Party System*, pp. 129–274.

26 Kevin P. Phillips, *The Emerging Republican Majority* (New York: Anchor Books, 1970). See also Gillian Peele, *Revival and Reaction: The Right in Contemporary America* (Oxford: Clarendon Press, 1984).

27 On Thatcher as Opposition Leader see Kavanagh, *Thatcherism and British Politics*, pp. 201–7; and Young, *One of Us*, pp. 100–31.

28 See Peter Riddell, *The Thatcher Government* (London: Basil Blackwell, 1985), pp. 41–56; and Young, ibid., pp. 192–222.

29 Surveys of the Conservative party both in the House of Commons and the country during the 1980s, revealed remarkably limited enthusiasm for 'Thatcherism' as an ideology. See Ivor Crewe & Donald D. Searing, 'Ideological Change in the British Conservative Party', *American Political Science Review*, 82 (1988) 361–84; and Philip Norton, ' "The Lady's Not For Turning": But What About the Rest of the Party? Margaret

Thatcher and the Conservative Party 1979–89', paper presented at the Annual Meeting of the American Political Science Association, Atlanta, GA, August 1989.

30   Young, *One of Us*, pp. 494–95; and Peter Jenkins, *Mrs Thatcher's Revolution: the Ending of the Socialist Era* (London: Pan, 1988), pp. 173–78. Pym's grouping gained 32 members but never became a significant force within the parliamentary party.

31   On Westland see Young, *One of Us*, pp. 427–63; and Jenkins, *Mrs Thatcher's Revolution*, pp. 185–204.

32   On Heseltine's position as the leader of the 'internal opposition' see Bruce Anderson, *John Major: the Making of the Prime Minister* (London: Fourth Estate, 1991), pp. 30–8.

33   Anderson, ibid., pp. 19–29.

34   On the Howe and Lawson resignations, see Anderson, ibid., pp. 38–96.

35   On the Meyer challenge see Anderson, pp. ibid., 71–82.

36   On the first ballot and Thatcher's resignation, see Robert Shepherd, *The Power Brokers: the Tory Party and its Leaders* (London: Hutchinson, 1991), pp. 1–52; and Anderson, ibid., pp. 98–158.

37   Shepherd, ibid., pp. 53–79; and Anderson, ibid., pp. 159–194.

38   On Major's style see Shepherd, *The Power Brokers*, pp. 199–221; and Anderson, *John Major*, pp. 195–306.

39   See Byron E. Shafer, 'The Notion of an Electoral Order: the Structure of electoral Politics at the Accession of George Bush', in *The End of Realignment? Interpreting American Electoral Eras*, edited by Byron E. Shafer, (Madison: University of Wisconsin Press, 1991), pp. 37–84.

40   On Ripon see Rae, *The Decline and Fall of the Liberal Republicans*, pp. 79–86.

41   On the 1968 nominating campaign see Rae, ibid., pp. 88–99; Theodore H. White, *The Making of the President 1968* (London: Jonathan Cape, 1969); and Lewis Chester, Godfrey Hodgson and Bruce Page, *An American Melodrama: the Presidential Campaign of 1968* (London: Andre Deutsch, 1969).

42   See A. James Reichley, *Conservatives in an Age of Change: the Nixon and Ford Administrations* (Washington, DC: Brookings Institution, 1981).

43   See Ladd & Hadley, *Transformations of the Party System*, pp. 232–274.

44   On Anderson, see Rae, *ibid.*, pp. 138–144.

45   On Conservative party 'factions' and 'tendencies' see Richard Rose, 'Parties, Factions and Tendencies in Britain', *Political Studies*, 12 (1964) 33–46; and Patrick Seyd, 'Factionalism in the 1970s', in Zig Layton Henry (ed.), *Conservative Party Politics*, pp. 231–43.

46   Norton's analysis of the parliamentary Conservative party found that 'Thatcherites' accounted for only 19 per cent of Tory MPs and that the Moderates accounted for only 18 per cent. Norton, ' "The Lady's Not For Turning" '.

Anglo-American think tanks under Reagan and Thatcher

Given the radical reputation of both the Reagan Administration and the Thatcher Government the question of how political ideas and policies were generated and formulated is clearly of some significance. One widely identified source of such policy making, in Britain and the United States, has been those policy research units – or think tanks – associated with the political right. It is certainly true that such bodies as the American Enterprise Institute, the Heritage Foundation, the Hoover Institution, the Institute of Economic Affairs, the Centre for Policy Studies and the Adam Smith Institute gained a much more prominent public position during the 1980s and that those bodies generally claim some role in the great 'battle of ideas' that seems to have been so decisively won by the right during that decade. The purpose of this chapter is three-fold. First, to determine what think tanks are, what they do, and to what extent Anglo-American comparisons are legitimate. Second, to examine the work of the major Anglo-American think tanks during the 1980s. Third, to assess what impact these organisations had on specific policy making for both administrations and in the creation of an intellectual justification for Reagan and Thatcher's actions.

To some extent this chapter breaks new ground. Both the academic and journalistic literature on conservative think tanks, especially in Britain, is strikingly modest given their widespread prominence through the 1980s. Cross-national comparisons of think tank activities are virtually non-existent. One possible explanation for this comes in the slippery nature of the term and the difficulty in establishing any specific definition of think tanks. The actual phrase is borrowed from World War II US military jargon, a think tank being a secure room where plans and strategy could be safely discussed. The phrase gained currency in its current context from the early 1950s onwards. A broad definition of a think tank would be a non-profit public policy research institution with substantial organisational autonomy. That explanation hardly reveals much about the character and nature of these entities. Ann Cooper comes closer to that with a three pronged definition stating:

Think tank *n* 1: a nesting place for former high-level government officials waiting for their party to regain the White House 2: a university-style setting where scholars can ruminate free from the burden of lecturing students 3: an aggressively ideological institution whose young analysts synthesize the research of others, producing terse, topical papers designed for mass consumption in Washington.[1]

However, Peter Kelley[2] may be cynically accurate when he describes such bodies as 'an arrangement by which millions of dollars are removed from the accounts of willing corporations, the government, and the eccentric wealthy and given to researchers who spend much of their time competing to get their name in print'. Either way, as will become evident, establishing a precise boundary between think tanks and certain university research institutions or between think tanks and pressure groups is frequently problematic.

Matters barely improve when one attempts to provide a categorisation of think tanks. This is difficult for either Britain or America but finding a division that credibly accommodates the two is profoundly testing. Academic orthodoxy in the United States tends to subdivide think tanks into three categories: universities without students; contract research organisations; and advocacy tanks.

'Universities without students' describes large institutions with a considerable staff – usually drawn fom university faculties – working predominantly on book length projects. Such groups differ from universities in the absence of any teaching requirement and that the subject areas investigated are policy-oriented and designed to appeal to a different audience from conventional academic research. Of the various American think tanks to be considered here, the American Enterprise Institute and the Hoover Institution more closely fit this model and while none of the British conservative groups is large enough to truly match it the Institute of Economic Affairs comes nearest at least in its aspirations and self-perception.

The second category, 'contract research organisations,' are distinguished by a research agenda produced mostly to satisfy the demands of particular government departments and agencies. Major American examples of this group would be think tanks such as the Rand Corporation (operating in defence-related fields) or the Urban Institute (covering liberal domestic policy). None of the Conservative think tanks really fits this category, although the AEI has done work in this field and its less partisan offshoot, the Centre for Strategic and International Studies based at Georgetown University, would fit here. Of the British groups only the Centre for Policy Studies has ever approached this category and that only on an expansive interpretation of its work.

'Advocacy tanks' describes the last and latest grouping of think tanks. These have a high-profile ideological and philosophical agenda and collective ethos. Advocacy tanks are interested in placing their own views into the political arena and of campaigning aggressively on current policy issues. As such they tend to specialise in short-term pamphlets and papers rather than book length exercises. It is this category that is most difficult to distinguish from pressure groups as both are essentially interested in political lobbying. Of the American organisations under consideration the Heritage Foundation very definitely suit this sub-set and in Britain the Centre for Policy Studies and, particularly, the Adam Smith Institute would join it as well.

This division, while having some use and validity for organisational purposes, should not be taken too strongly. The American Enterprise Institute, for example, has at various times undertaken research that would fit all three categories. The Heritage Foundation, while primarily – as they would be the first to admit – an advocacy unit, have also published some massive pieces of research of a flavour akin to the universities without students model. Nevertheless, this division does help to give a taste of what makes these various institutions different and distinct.

Before outlining the major organisations and analysing their activities, style, and putative influence some important differences between think tanks in Britain and the United States have to be mentioned.

The first concerns the sheer size and scale. There are considerably more think tanks in the United States – estimates of the total running as high as a thousand – of which some one hundred could be described as conservative in their political orientation. They cover a much wider field of policy issues than their British counterparts, many specialising in particular aspects of economic, domestic, or foreign policy. There has been a considerable expansion in the field of legal policy which has no real point of comparison with the United Kingdom. Many of the leading groups in the United States are based outside Washington, DC-for example the Hoover Institution and the Institute for Contemporary Studies in California, the Heartland Institute in Chicago, and the Manhattan Institute (which commissioned Charles Murray's highly influential Losing Ground) in New York City. Most of the considerable expansion of US think tanks during the 1980s occurred at the sub-federal level with there now being some sixty conservative, free market, or libertarian organisations based outside the national capital.

In Britain, by contrast, there were only three groups – the Institute of Economic Affairs, the Centre for Policy Studies, and the Adam Smith Institute – that could be labelled as conservative inclined think tanks, although the Social Affairs Unit shadowed certain think tank functions. They all try to cover a very broad range of policy questions with little formal specialisation between them. In order to carry credibility in Britain not only must a think tank be based in London but ideally it should locate its main office in Westminster. Far from the British think tank community expanding into the localities, what expansion there has been has happened in precisely the opposite – supranational – direction with offices opening in Brussels to monitor and lobby the European Commission and Parliament.

In budgetary terms the two nations also produce very different results. The largest of the British groups, the Institute of Economic Affairs, operated on a budget of approximately £750,000 in 1990. The Centre for Policy Studies raised approximately £300,000 and the Adam Smith Institute around £200,000. By contrast, the American Enterprise Institute operated off a budget of over $8,000,000 in the same year, the Hoover Institution about $17,000,000 and the Heritage Foundation some $18,000,000. Indeed, the salary of one individual Heritage employee, the chief fundraiser, virtually equalled the entire estimated annual budget of the Adam Smith Institute. This difference in budget, largely the consequence of a much stronger corporate, foundation and individual philanthropic tradition in the United States, obviously affects both staffing levels and the range of activities the respective think tanks are able to produce. The IEA would rarely have more than eight full-time employees, the American Enterprise Institution has nearly 50 resident scholars and Heritage has a staff of 135. No British think tank could possibly emulate the publications output of their American cousins.

Having noted this it should be pointed out that in order to have political influence think tanks in the United States have to be larger given the huge number of policy-makers in the executive and legislature one would need to influence in order to promote a policy or agenda. Arguably, the different nature of British politics, with a relatively small and easily identified set of political actors, compensates somewhat for the fact that the British groups are smaller and poorer.

Who are the think tanks?

Given the vastly greater numbers of think tanks in the United States any decision to award some of them with greater influence than others is inevitably somewhat subjective. However, both by size and range of activities three groups – the American Enterprise Institute, the Hoover Institution, and the Heritage Foundation – do appear to place themselves at the head of the pack. The history and character of these organisations, especially their evolution during the 1980s will be outlined alongside the record of the three British groups.

The American Enterprise Institute

The American Enterprise Association was founded in 1943 by Lewis H. Brown, the President of the Johns Manville Corporation. Having operated on a distinctly modest scale for the first decade of its history it began to expand rapidly after William J. Baroody was recruited from the US Chamber of Commerce in 1954 to take the position of executive vice president. As the background of these individuals implies the AEA was designed with the views and interests of corporate America in mind, views that became increasingly less well represented in the rest of the think tank world after the Brookings Institution abandoned its anti-New Deal position of the 1930s and began its voyage towards 1960s liberalism.

In 1960, the AEA became the AEI (the original title smacked

too much of a trade association or lobby group) and it began to develop a much acclaimed public relations and media wing to promote its research output. The 1970s saw the AEI come of age. A highly successful fund-raising drive allowed the organisation to recruit former President Gerald Ford as a distinguished Fellow in 1977 and to begin publishing a range of influential periodicals such as as Regulation, Public Opinion, and the AEI Economist. Reagan's victory in 1980 led to the departure of over twenty members of staff to the new Administration. Ironically, this loss of talent presaged a set of difficulties that the AEI faced in the 1980s. Overexpansion, poor management, and a certain tension between the needs of academic integrity and conservative propagandising led to a severe budget crunch with funds falling from $12,000,000 in 1984 to $7,500,000 two years later. This led to the appointment of a new head Christopher DeMuth who, in turn, recruited high profile conservatives such as Robert Bork and Richard Perle in a largely successful attempt to regain the group's right-wing credentials. By 1992, the AEI's standing had been greatly enhanced and the budget back in eight figures.

The Hoover Institution

The Hoover Institution on War, Revolution, and Peace was founded in 1919 through a gift by Herbert Hoover who established a library and archive collection based on the events of World War I. Although Hoover is strictly speaking an independent organisation the nature of their benefaction puts it within Stamford University's orbit of governance. A relationship that has proved far from easy as Hoover moved into a more assertively conservative mode from the 1960s onwards while the Stamford faculty has gravitated towards a chic liberalism of the politically correct kind.

Hoover's role was revolutionised by two events. The first was the arrival as director of W. Glenn Campbell, a brilliant organiser and fundraiser whose energy saw the Institution expand to its current budget of $17,000,000 with an endowment of over $120,000,000. This money was used to build a high-profile research staff and programme of visiting fellows including monetarist guru Milton Friedman and leading black conservative Thomas Sowell. The second development was the Institution's increasingly close relationship with then Governor Ronald Reagan. Reagan became Hoover's third honorary fellow (the others being Solzhenitsyn and Hayek) and considerable numbers of the Hoover faculty followed Reagan to Washington in the 1980s in either a full- or part-time capacity. The most prominent of these being Martin Anderson, Hoover senior fellow, who was Reagan's chief domestic advisor during the 1980 campaign and served as Head of the Office of Policy Development from 1981–82.

Campbell's somewhat involuntary retirement in 1989 not withstanding, the scale of Hoover's resources should ensure it retains a very high profile even after Reagan becomes a distant memory in Washington.

The Heritage Foundation

Without doubt the greatest success story among conservative think tanks on either side of the Atlantic was the incredible boom in the budget and the public prominence of the Heritage Foundation during the 1980s. Established in 1973 by a set of relatively junior and relatively extreme conservative congressional aides and supported by a grant of some $250,000 by the brewing magnate Joseph Coors, its annual budget rose to $2,000,000 by 1977, $10,000,000 by 1983, and $17,500,000 by 1989. Heritage is distinct in two ways. It is the advocacy tank par excellence and, very unusually for a think tank, raises a sizeable proportion of its budget through individual small contributions solicited by direct mail.

In its early years Heritage busied itself with slightly fringe conservative causes. For example it backed moves against homosexual teachers in Florida and left-wing or multi-cultural textbooks in West Virginia. Heritage really came to prominence when it commissioned a massive research project, the 3,000 page conservative policy prescription *Mandate for Leadership*. Shrewdly, a more manageable 1,000-page version was produced for the benefit of the media who utterly lapped it up pronouncing it the gospel of the incoming Reagan Administration giving Heritage undreamed of national exposure and the instant status of academic respectibility.

With AEI on the wane, Heritage followed up this success by creating a highly publicised jobs' bank designed to match conservative activists to the Reagan Administration and began publishing, *The Annual Guide to Public Policy Experts*, a who's who of conservative academics. The second *Mandate for Leadership* followed in 1984 and a third in 1989, establishing Heritage as the premier American advocacy organisation.

The Institute of Economic Affairs

The oldest of the British groups, the Institute of Economic Affairs was first mooted by its primary founder Anthony Fisher in 1955 and established with the support of Arthur Seldon and Ralph Harris two years later. The organisation was devised with two rather different motives in mind. The first was to uphold and promote the ideals of *laissez-faire* capitalism – especially those of Hayek – that had been almost extinguished from British university economics with the rampant triumph of Keynesianism. The second reflected a concern about the political direction of the Conservative Party in the 1950s where the somewhat centrist approach of R. A. Butler and Harold Macmillan appeared to hold sway supported by the activities of Butler's brainchild, the Conservative Research Department. This tension between the academic and political aspects of the IEA's work has frequently and disruptively surfaced.

Although the IEA had some influence over Enoch Powell's wing of the Conservatives in the 1960s and maintained links with prominent Liberals such as Jo Grimmond, its position and budget expanded with Sir Keith Joseph's rising star and Mrs Thatcher's capture of the Conservative leadership in 1975. Internal divisions through the 1980s over how much to compromise the IEA's academic clout and independence by an overly close relationship with the Conservative party led to the departure of its director, Graham Mather, in 1992 and a possibly permanent wound to its effectiveness.

The Centre for Policy Studies

The Centre for Policy Studies was founded predominantly by Sir Keith Joseph, but supported by Margaret Thatcher, in the wake of the Conservatives' defeat in the election of October 1974. Initially touted by Joseph as an academic institution designed to investigate relative economic performance – on which basis Edward Heath grudgingly decided to give it official sanction – the CPS became much more than that once Mrs Thatcher ousted Heath from the Conservative leadership.

Under its talented, if unpredictable, director Alfred Sherman, author or co-author of many of Sir Keith Joseph's born-again capitalist tracts of 1974, the CPS became the primary publishing vehicle of both Joseph and Thatcher plus a host of other conservative analysts. It swiftly became an explicit rival to the Conservative Research Department whose output and director (Chris Patten) were regarded with deep suspicion if not hostility by many of Mrs Thatcher's entourage. In terms of influencing the party leader the CPS appear to have outpointed the Research Department during this period.

As will become evident, it proved impossible to maintain quite such a harmonious relationship between the CPS and the leadership once the Tories actually gained office in 1979. The CPS appeared to drift, suffering from a crisis of purpose during the early and middle 1980s until a new director, David Willetts, provided a fresh intellectual cutting edge to the organisation.

The Adam Smith Institute

The youngest, most aggressively ideological, and self-confessed *enfant terrible* of the British think tanks, the Adam Smith Institute was conceived by Dr Madsen Pirie, an engaging capitalist intellectual, in 1977 and offices opened in 1978. The Adam Smith Institute resembles the IEA is its promotion of free market ideology but tends to offer more practical free market solutions to political problems, rather than engaging in the rather dry and didactic style of that organisation. The ASI aimed to be different from the CPS with fewer institutional ties to the Conservative Party organisation. However, as the ASI's enthusiasm for the Thatcher regime blossomed maintaining such strict independence became more challenging.

In many ways the ASI can be seen as a small-scale Heritage Foundation. It too specialises in relatively short and issue-oriented publications. It followed Heritage's *Mandate for Leadership* with its own OMEGA Project of the early 1980s to provide a free market blueprint for wide-ranging and radical political reform. It also copies American conservative bodies by providing political ratings of MPs against free market criteria. Its primary constraint is money. Without the tradition of big giving from conservative families and foundations and with little history of major political direct mail marketing in the UK, the Adam Smith Institute has to get by on a budget that would seem pretty tiny to its American counterparts.

Think tank influence in the 1980s

Conservative think tanks entered the 1980s against a starkly different history and background both on the role of outside policy innovators in the political system generally, and on the interaction between the Conservative/Republican Party establishments and such innovators in particular.

The nature of the American political system has always been more conducive to outside 'experts' than the Westminster model and the Republican party has been at least as enthusiastic towards conservative thinkers as the Democrats have been towards liberal intellectuals. Herbert Hoover not only founded his own think tank in 1919 but was a noted supporter of relatively experimental social science methodology while in the White House. Even before the depression he commissioned (but got the Rockefeller Foundation to fund) an enormous survey of national trends by various outside experts. Their final 1,500-page report was published too late to help Hoover (January 1933) many of its themes were taken up by the incoming President, Franklin D. Roosevelt and the 'Brains Trust' team he brought with him.

The Republican Party supported the creation of a set of new bodies after World War II – the Council of Economic Advisers, the National Security Council, and the Central Intelligence Agency – all of which had the effect of further advancing the cause of policy entrepreneurs in government. Congress itself, from 1947 onwards, expanded existing bodies such as the Congressional Research Service and the policy research wing of the General Accounting Office, and added new creations such as the Congressional Budget Office. Once again the net impact was to heighten the standing of outside specialists.[3]

When the Republicans returned to the White House after a twenty-year absence Eisenhower continued, albeit in a more formal and structured manner than FDR, to promote and rely on such outside knowledge. Towards the end of his presidency he, like Hoover, turned to the men of ideas forming a National Commission to assess national performance and outline goals for the coming decade. The next Republican incumbent, Richard Nixon, continued this approach with his appointment of Harvard professors Daniel Moyniban and Henry Kissinger as his chief advisers on domestic and foreign policy respectively.

Thus when Ronald Reagan succeeded to the presidency it was with a long standing trend for political recruitment and idea formulation by outside policy groups firmly established.

That was certainly not true for the United Kingdom. The seeming ascendance of conservative inclined think tanks in British politics needs to be understood against a perspective provided by their having previously spent many years in what one observer aptly described as 'a kind of intellectual Siberia'[4].

A certain deep mistrust of ideology and of intellectuals has been embodied in repeated references to the virtues of 'pragmatism' and the reluctance of successive leaders of the Conservative Party to contemplate too much debate over the nature and meaning of conservatism. Whilst defeat in 1945 forced the Tories to take policy more seriously than it had done previously, most serious enquiry into the social sciences of the kind undertaken in think tanks had been dominated by the politically engaged socialist academics who were associated with groups such as the Fabian Society, Political and Economic Planning and the London School of Economics.

Conservative leaders may have tended to avoid promoting too much independently-minded research under party auspices for philosophical reasons but it was also for straightforward tactical considerations. In particular, the belief associated with Churchill, that it was invariable imprudent to provide the opposition with 'hostages to fortune' before an election. In an atmosphere more conducive to independent inquiry (such as that more often found within the extra-parliamentary Labour Party) different agendas and different 'factions' tended to undermine the sense of party unity which was deemed crucial to electoral success. The notion that polity innovation won elections had few friends.

This attitude might best be outlined in the traditional role of the Conservative conference. This existed to approve (not initiate or even seriously debate) policy and improve morale. The extra-parliamentary Conservative party neither expected, nor was it granted, any truly significant role in policy-making and the same attitude froze out the think tanks.

Conservative tradition professed to combine a healthy suspicion of ideology and of intellectuals with a tactical reluctance to allow extra-parliamentary actors to concern themselves with questions of policy. These were properly the concern of ministers and the

Party Leader. Thus, although Churchill displayed little enthusiasm for domestic policy after 1945, his deputy Rab Butler retained tight control over policy, chiefly by virtue of his leadership of a reinvigorated Conservative Research Department. Deliberations tended to be left to small *ad hoc* groups; drawn from within the Parliamentary party but overseen by confidants of the party leader. Conservative policy-making thus depended upon informal, frequently secret, arrangements in which the balance of opinion was ultimately determined by patronage bestowed from the leadership. Without such patronage groups such as the Institute of Economic Affairs would have no prospect of genuinely influencing the Conservatives either in office or opposition. The IEA never had such sponsorship and therefore had precious little influence.

Given such a background – even with Mrs Thatcher as a much more sympathetic leader – British conservative think tanks were well advised to approach the Conservative Party with some caution. Throughout the 1980s there persisted what one participant described as a 'non-aggression pact' between the think tank community and the political body to whom they were attempting to sell policy.[5]

During the Reagan–Thatcher decade some fairly powerful claims were made on behalf of conservative think tanks. In the United States, Martin Anderson would argue:[6]

The intellectual world of the United States consists of the Universities, think tanks, publishing houses, and the media. This is where almost all new policy ideas come from. And it is these ideas, strategies, and plans that represent real power in policymaking. In the final analysis it is intellectuals who really dominate the policy agenda of the United States.

Anderson also noted with some satisfaction the influence that one major Hoover Institution publication – *The United States in the 1980s* – had on Mikhail Gorbachev. Gorbachev raised the contents of the book, which he claimed proved US ill-will towards the USSR, in meetings with House Speaker Tip O'Neill, and with Ronald Reagan at the Geneva summit of 1985. Perhaps equally significant though is that, as Anderson admits, O'Neill had never heard of the publication and according to Reagan's long-standing biographer, Lou Cannon,[7] neither had the President despite the fact that he was an honorary fellow of Hoover.

Claims for the power of British conservative think tanks have been more modest but nonetheless exist. It was unusual during much of the 1980s for any newspaper report of these group's activities not to be presaged by the word influential. Furthermore, when a leftish equivalent of the CPS/ASI – the Institute for Public Policy Research – was established, that body claimed to want to reproduce the success of the right-wing organisations.

Yet, as this analysis will show, if influence means providing specific examples of public policy that can solely or even predominantly be shown as the responsibility of the think tanks, then wild claims for think tank influence should be muted. The primary source of think tank strength has been on media perceptions of the credibility of conservative ideas.

Even during the period in opposition for both Reagan and Thatcher the think tanks were one of a number of sources for political ideas. Although Martin Anderson created a campaign advisory team some 450 strong for Reagan's 1980 campaign, many of the names were there to give Reagan's candidacy intellectual clout rather than because they were engaged in a hands-on policy creating effort. As Anderson himself admitted:[8] '. . . It's a myth that Reagan had these research institutes. . . . No institute is big enough to provide all the advice a candidate needs'. Even Reagan's economic programme cannot be claimed for any individual think tank. As Anderson again concedes Reagan's economic policies came directly out of the heart of the Republican economic establishment. Many members of that establishment, such as Milton Friedman, were associated with individual think tanks but they had established their names and ideas before arriving at those bodies and were signed up by them to give those think tanks greater status.

The heart of Reagan's new economic ideas – the massive tax cuts outlined in the Kemp-Roth proposals – were adopted in that form basically, as David Stockman outlines,[9] to keep Kemp out of the 1980 presidential contest and to get Kemp and his supporters on board the Reagan campaign. As for the candidate himself, in his memoirs[10] Reagan denies that his enthusiasm for tax cutting came from supply-side economic theory instead citing his experience as a top income tax bracket movie star in the 1940s and an obscure Muslim philosopher called Ibn Khaldoon.

In Britain, the ideological shift in the conservative leadership did not correspond to, nor reflect, a great sea-change in the upper eschelons of the parliamentary party itself. Despite the obvious implications in the shift from Heath to Thatcher and the considerable powers of patronage which are conferred upon the leader of the Conservative Party, Mrs Thatcher remained subject to constraints which ensured that, despite the change in style and rhetoric, there remained a marked reluctance to commit the Shadow Cabinet on substantive matters of policy, as many of her *ad hoc* advisers from the think tanks now sought. Such reluctance derived from a mix of political calculation and uncertainty as to what the future would hold.

Contrary to accusations at the time, the IEA and CPS had not worked out any total, complete, policy agenda by 1975. Neither were they able to do so by 1979 when problems such as the vexed question of trade union reform seemed, if anything, even more insurmountable than had previously been supposed. The 'Monetarists' were agreed on the priority of reducing inflation but disagreements existed within them about the precise combination of policy instruments to be used. More fundamentally, many members of Mrs Thatcher's team were privately sceptical about the ideas being produced by Sir Keith Joseph and his allies at the CPS.

It is curious that the party leadership should display such an unconservative interest in the work of intellectuals and matters of ideology while retaining a conventional reluctance to discuss policy in detail prior to the election. Documents issued by the party between 1975 and 1979 provide remarkably few pointers as to the direction of policy under some future Conservative government. The leadership was partly reacting against the political style of Edward Heath, who had insisted on policy being prepared in great detail during the 1966–70 period much of which he had been oblige to amend or abandon in office. Ill-defined debates over Conservative policy also enabled Mrs Thatcher to unite the parliamentary party behind her leadership by avoiding any seismic rift over party ideology. Very few 'hostages to fortune' were available to either Labour opponents or potential critics within the Shadow Cabinet.

In the final analysis few observers could deny that the role of think tanks in the policy construction of both Reagan and Thatcher was modest and that the electoral triumphs of 1979 and 1980 were primarily the consequence of the collapse of social democracy under Callaghan and Carter.

The vast number of political appointments within the federal bureaucracy inevitably made it easier for think tank activists to enter the Reagan Administration than was the case in Britain. This permeability of administrative elites saw many senior members of the American Enterprise Institute and the Hoover Institution come into government. Probably the most prominent of these was Martin Anderson who moved from Hoover to lead Reagan's Office of Policy Development. The vast majority of the senior appointees came from the policy celebrities hired by the think tanks in the 1970s. It is unclear to what extent such individuals took with them the agenda of their home think tank or whether, instead, they took their own particular views and expertise on the individual area they were appointed in.

The experience for the individuals concerned and their former think tanks was not always a happy one. Martin Anderson, for example, was back at the Hoover Institution within two years of his appointment in the White House. The relative decline of the AEI can be traced to the fact that so many of its leading lights emigrated to the Reagan Administration which was not a problem that its emerging rival, the Heritage Foundation, suffered.

Heritage did mount the most coherent effort to influence the Administration by staff placement. Heritage opened an office of executive branch liaison after the 1980 elections. This boasted a much publicised 'job bank' housing the resumés of approved conservative activists. However, both the numbers of people actually placed (some estimates were as low as thirty nine) and whether they were appointed purely because of the Heritage connection have been a matter of dispute. After the 1988 elections Heritage sent out some 2,500 resumés to the incoming Bush Administration but there is little evidence of any substantial success.

When Mrs Thatcher assumed office in 1979, experienced colleagues believed that her reformist zeal would soon be tempered by the burdens of power. Those associated with the think tanks were equally fearful that the Government and Prime Minister would come to favour traditional techniques of compromise in the face of the many challenges they anticipated. In the event, both sides were forced to submit more qualified verdicts on 'Thatcherism'. Conservative sceptics had underestimated both Mrs Thatcher's own determination and the extent to which the party would permit her to engage in a restrained form of presidential government once her position had been consolidated. Mrs Thatcher's own instinctive

conviction had been reinforced by a sense of intellectual commitment in part derived from her association with think tanks in
opposition.

Nonetheless, relations between the Conservative leadership and
the think tanks were strained during Mrs Thatcher's first term of
government. The daunting resources of Whitehall and the daily
demands of government made the party leadership less accessible
to members of the think tanks than had hitherto been the case. A
major bone of contention was that against the advice of some of
her closest supporters, Mrs Thatcher was willing to rely upon
career civil servants for policy advice in government.

Matters were particularly tense between the new regime and
the Centre for Policy Studies. The CPS director Alfred Sherman
organised a group of businessmen and CPS sympathisers – the
'Argonauts' – in an attempt to have influence over Thatcher.
Little came of that venture and with his sway over even Sir Keith
Joseph waning, Sherman quit in 1983. A Sherman protégé, John
Hoskins, moved into Downing Street to head the Policy Unit but
his drive to turn that body into a vehicle for radical agenda setting
was swamped by all the other short-term problems the new government faced. He too did not stay long. The disappointment felt
by the think tanks was summed up in the title of a set of essays
published by the IEA in 1982 entitled 'Could Do Better'. Only
much later in the Thatcher period, in the run-up to the 1987
election when Mrs Thatcher was consciously casting around for
new policy ventures were warm relations fully restored.

Neither was there much in the way of placing think tank
sympathisers in government. Given the British system of government the best way this could be done was through the Special
Adviser scheme, the small network of essentially political individuals
seconded into the Civil Service for as long as the individual Minister
held office. In Mrs Thatcher's third term the Adam Smith Institute
discovered the virtues of this approach after one associate, Michael
Simmonds, landed the post at the Department of Trade and Industry working for Nicholas Ridley. Unfortunately for the ASI the
overwhelming majority of Special Advisers are appointed either
from Conservative Central Office or are personal associates of
Ministers. Further, the politicians most likely to appoint ASI
employees to such positions are almost certainly those like Ridley
who are most sympathetic to the ASI outlook already.

There was no necessary or automatic coincidence between the interests and agendas of the think tanks and that of Reagan and Thatcher. The priorities of conservative think tanks on either side of the Atlantic were formulated in a rather *ad hoc* manner. For most groups the main sources of ideas came from the interests of their staff, from associated academics, from financial sponsors, from the work of their rivals on both the left and the right, and from assessments of probable media interest. These factors combined could produce a set of campaigns and publications of minimal interest to the governments concerned. Of the six think tanks examined here only the AEI (very occasionally) and the CPS (under David Willetts in the later Thatcher years) would actually approach Cabinet members and ask them what areas they would like to see research conducted on. The Adam Smith Institute would take on projects that people literally brought in off the streets and under Mrs Thatcher would rarely make contact with politicians while deciding their interests.

This characterisation is least true of the Heritage Foundation which specialises in producing short policy papers for easy political consumption. Event at Heritage most contacts are with congressional aides rather than practising politicians and certain parts of Heritage's programme are distinctly esoteric.

All of this may explain why the number of public policies and laws that can be placed at the door of think tanks is so small. There is virtually no example of any legislation on either side of the Atlantic that was entirely and uniquely due to one individual think tank. In the United States the conservative think tanks can claim to have had some influence over arms control policy, regulatory relaxation, and elements of the Tax Reform Act of 1986. Divided party control of the White House and Congress should of course be recognised as a mitigating factor restricting success. The Heritage Foundation claimed in 1982 that 62 per cent of its proposals in *Mandate for Leadership* had been enacted but as James Rosenthal pointed out[11] closer examination of Heritage's claims questions the validity of that estimate and there is little proof of any causal relationship between Heritage endorsing a proposal and the Reagan Administration supporting it. It might also be significant that 1982 was the last time Heritage publicly offered such a measure of its success.

In Britain, the IEA is entitled to claim some credit for the initial popularity of monetarism in the Government, the CPS has some claim to have kept privatisation at the front of the political agenda, the ASI put a lot of thought and energy into the mechanics of individual privatisations. The think tanks have also had some impact in those relatively few areas of public policy where the Government committed itself to the principle of reform without having much idea of the details it desired – local government finance reform, the National Health Service review of 1988/89, and (under John Major) the Citizen's Charter would all fall in this area. Indeed, the ASI's claim to have fathered the extremely unpopular community charge or poll tax may be the closest example in either Britain or America of an individual think tank nearly authoring a piece of major legislation.

One possible explanation for this lack of specific policy success is that both Reagan and Thatcher managed to develop forms of in-house think tanks of their own.

During Ronald Reagan's highly productive opening term policy-making came to be made in a set of Cabinet Councils, essentially cabinet sub-committees, set up by Edwin Meese, Counsellor to the President. They achieved such a role because they proved to be the only means to deal effectively with issues that cut across government departments. Martin Anderson, as Head of Policy Development, soon found that he and his officials abandoned any notion of dealing with new policy initiatives in favour of serving as a policy implementation unit. Anderson created a special staffing organisation out of his office to service these Cabinet Councils. Each of these *de facto* secretariats were headed by an executive secretary, all of whom were chosen by Anderson. Once policy was generated in this manner it went to the Legislative Strategy Group headed by Jim Baker, White House Chief of Staff, that proved brilliantly effective in pushing such proposals through Congress. This system broke down during Reagan's second term and arguably so did the Reagan Administration.

Mrs Thatcher also became an enthusiast for Cabinet committees although in her case this may have been motivated as much by a need to outwit her Cabinet opponents as to promote inter-departmental efficiency. Her period also saw the blooming of the Downing Street Policy Unit into something of a mini think tank.[12] Mrs Thatcher had inherited both the Central Policy Review Staff, created by Edward Heath, that technically served as a think tank

to the whole Cabinet and the Downing Street Policy Unit chiefly
built up under Wilson and Callaghan. An institutional conservative, Mrs Thatcher started off with an initial suspicion of both
bodies but came to have a distinct preference for the Policy Unit
which served only the Premier. In 1983, the CPRS, which had
proved increasingly vulnerable to producing highly controversial
propositions that then were placed in the hands of the press by
Cabinet opponents, was scrapped and the Downing Street Policy
Unit rose in stature to become the main non-ministerial source
of political ideas to her. Furthermore, civil service resentment at
the supposed policy role of the Unit and of external think tanks represented a powerful incentive for a certain policy dynamism within
the civil service itself which might not otherwise have been so
forthcoming during the Thatcher era. Similar arguments could be
made for the career bureaucracy in the United States.

One important conclusion on the work of think tanks in the
1980s is that perhaps the most critical factor in determining a
think tank's prestige and influence is its ability to sway the media,
especially the quality press. The chief means by which conservative think tanks get their ideas and arguments into the public
domain is through newspaper and television coverage of their
various reports and proposals. This is by far the most successful
way of bringing such ideas to the attention of the policy-making
community.

The advocacy think tanks feed off the press more than any
other category. For groups such as the Heritage Foundation and
the Adam Smith Institute the amount of media interest a pamphlet
manages to attract (which is not always predictable) virtually
determines its place among the policy priorities of the group. As
James Allen Smith has argued: '. . . it has sometimes seemed that
the new "war of ideas" amounts to little more than the aggressive
application of the techniques of public relations, marketing, and
survey research to the discussion of public issues . . .'[13] In a sense
then the think tanks are important because the media believes they
are important and the media believes in this importance because
the think tanks tell them they are.

However, one should not be too cynical. There is no doubt that
senior members of the Reagan Administration and, in Britain, Mrs
Thatcher herself, would regularly read the output of think tanks.
Although this might not necessarily lead automatically to political

action it must have had some influence over the climate of ideas within these governments. The fact that Mrs Thatcher was known to read think tank pamphlets late at night gave them a certain kudos even if she was initially alerted to them by the press.

Although it is difficult to quantify, conservative think tanks have also made a significant impact on politics in Britain and the United States precisely because of this media profile. Until the middle of the 1970s the conservative movement had virtually no presence in the media and appeared intellectually feeble. The phrase 'conservative intellectual' was virtually a contradiction in terms. The rising public status of such right-wing groupings has been to give a certain legitimacy to both the Reagan and Thatcher Administrations and their policies – admittedly some of it *ex post facto* – and to turn sets of individual policy decisions into part of what has seemed, to much of the political elite in both countries, a great movement of ideas. This belief in the importance of ideas and policy is an absolutely integral part of what has made the Reagan Administration seem more important than President Eisenhower's and the Thatcher years more significant that the thirteen years of Tory rule between 1951 and 1964.

One should perhaps conclude by arguing that although the relatively small list of their policies adopted by Reagan and Thatcher mitigates against some of the wilder arguments over think tank power, it does not render think tanks irrelevant. Many political prescriptions that would have been previously deemed too radical for mainstream political discussion did gain that exposure in the 1980s, and to a large extent this was because of the friendly interaction between conservative think tanks and these particular leaders. Whether this interaction of ideas will have a longer run impact on public policy is impossible to predict. It is reasonably clear that the release of these theories into the public domain via the media has had a dramatic effect on what constitutes the politically imaginable.

Conservative think tanks after Reagan and Thatcher

The leadership transition from Reagan to Bush and from Thatcher to Major was not an entirely comfortable experience for either set of think tanks. Neither of the new leadership teams seemed to share the same interest or zeal for policy innovation that their predecessors so obviously enjoyed and this requires think tanks who want political influence to change their approach somewhat.

In the United States this has had a considerable impact on think tanks. The centre-right outlook of the Bush Administration and its east coast establishment tendencies theoretically offered an opportunity for the American Enterprise Institute to extend its influence. However, the AEI's capacity to court Bush openly was limited by its own slow recovery from the financial nadir of the 1983–87 period. The AEI was thus faced with a dilemma. In order to raise more money it needed to move its public posture to the right – as the recruitment of Bork and Perle showed – but to maximise its prospects with Bush it needed to gravitate to the centre. This was not an easy puzzle to solve.

The Hoover Institution, like other conservative groups, reacted to the seeming indifference of the Bush Administration by retreating back into its academic shell and by taking a renewed interest in the affairs of California. An accelerated trend towards think tank development at the state and local level was a marked by-product of George Bush's occupation of the White House.

The Heritage Foundation was probably more traumatised by Reagan's retirement than the others. As an explicitly advocacy body it operates best in a political atmosphere conducive to radical political change. George Bush's centrist instincts coupled with continued, indeed enhanced, divided party control of government was hardly to Heritage's advantage. The Foundation was unsure over whether to co-operate with Bush on certain specific areas of agreement or whether to abandon his Administration altogether and enter a form of internal opposition. As Burton Y. Pines, senior vice president and director of research at Heritage, put it: 'I think you could say conservatives are confused right now'.[14] The conservative community would argue that it was precisely the Bush Administration's distaste for political ideas that led to its policy drift and ultimate electoral demise.

The loss of Margaret Thatcher has also provoked considerable soul-searching among the British think tank regime. The basic issue has been the same one of whether to compromise ideological integrity for continued political influence.

The most public example of this angst has been seen at the Institute of Economic Affairs. Here, Graham Mather, director-general from 1987, decided that a modest amount of adjustment to adapt to the new political order was needed. IEA papers on the Citizen's Charter and European policy were commissioned that offered views clearly compatible with the Major Government. Mather's tactics were supported by the businessmen and corporations that bankrolled the IEA. They were not popular with the IEA's founding fathers Lord Harris and Arthur Seldon and with some of the academics who had regularly contributed to the IEA's output. The dispute went public when Seldon resigned in 1991 after failing to oust Mather. A distinctly frosty truce held between the two factions until Mather resigned to form his own think tank, the European Policy Forum, which had a high-profile launch attended by the Prime Minister in the spring of 1992. As Mather managed to take with him both his deputy and a number of the IEA's financial backers he may well come out of this dispute better than the organisation that forced him out.

The Centre for Policy Studies has also had to undergo some change. It has always been rather unclear – given the quasi-official status the group acquired from having had Mrs Thatcher as one of its founders – whether the first loyalty of the CPS was to her personally, to the party leader regardless of personality, or to itself. This uncertainty has restricted the CPS research agenda in the sense that any work strikingly critical of the government would have been especially embarrassing for Mrs Thatcher. Although the then director, David Willetts, handled the transition skilfully and John Major smoothed matters by agreeing to become a patron of the CPS, what exact function the CPS sees for itself in the 1990s is not absolutely obvious.

Ironically, given its reputation as the most radically Thatcherite of the conservative think tanks, the Adam Smith Institute has thus far made the smoothest move from the Thatcher to the Major era. The ASI had spotted John Major's rising star much earlier than most and had courted him well before he became such an overt leadership hopeful. The ASI has put a great deal of effort into fleshing out Major's Citizen's Charter and as a result Dr Madsen Pirie was appointed to the committee advising the Prime Minister on implementing the Charter. John Major repeated the compliment by using the fifteenth anniversary dinner of the group in June 1992 to make a radical and highly publicised speech on education policy. How long Pirie and his director, Eamonn Butler, can continue this curious relationship without damaging their own credibility or without some other issue such as Europe driving a wedge between the ASI and the Government cannot be predicted. While it lasts the ASI/Major link remains the most interesting of the post-Thatcher era.

Despite these divisions over tactics, conservative think tanks are more likely to expand than contract over the 1990s. They have become an established part of the political process and the policy-making community on both sides of the Atlantic now expect there to be think tanks churning out ideas for consideration. So, crucially, does the media. In the United States the trend towards more specialist and more sub-federal groups will continue unless a conservative Republican President comes to power. In Britain, although money is a major constraint, the possibility of a greater number of more specialist think tanks is very real. Think tanks – and conservative intellectualism – will be part of Anglo-American politics without Ronald Reagan and Margaret Thatcher's benefaction. This does not mean that coming to terms with their departure will become much easier but inevitably it will happen.

Notes

1   Anne Cooper, 'Tanked Up', National Journal, 30 November 1985.

2   R. Kent Weaver, 'The Changing World of Think Tanks', P. S., September 1989.

3   James Allen Smith, *The Idea Brokers* (New York, Free Press, 1991).

4   Hugh Stephenson, *Mrs Thatcher's First Year* (London, Jill Norman, 1980).

5   Interview with Graham Mather by Tim Hames, June 1992.

6   Martin Anderson, *Revolution* (San Diego, Jovanovich, 1988).

7   Lou Cannon, *Reagan* (New York, Simon & Schuster, 1991).

8   Martin Anderson, *Revolution* (San Diego, Jovanovich, 1988).

9   David Stockman, *The Triumph of Politics* (New York, Coronet, 1986).

10   Ronald Reagan, *An American Life* (New York, Hutchinson, 1990).

11   James Rosenthal, 'Heritage Hype', *The New Republic*, 2 September 1985.

12   See David Willetts, 'The Role of the Prime Minister's Policy Unit', *Public Administration*, vol. 65.

13   James Allen Smith, *The Idea Brokers* (New York, Free Press, 1991).

14   James Barnes, 'Still Missing Reagan', *National Journal*, 2 March 1991.

11 *Andrew Adonis and Tim Hames*

Conclusion

No single theme emerges from this attempt to analyse the Reagan and Thatcher regimes in tandem. Some chapters have indicated dramatic policy changes and considerable success in altering the political landscape. Others have shown greater elements of continuity and relative failure in redesigning politics. Similarly, the chapters have varied significantly in their assessment of the ease with which comparisons between the two administrations can be made. In some cases the adjustments required to make comparison possible have stressed the differences between parliamentary and presidential government (although quasi-presidential might be a more appropriate description), others have stressed the different nature of – and social bases for – conservatism as a philosophy, others still have stressed differing national interests, culture, immediate political history, and short-term policies and events.

Such is the nature of comparative politics. It does, though, beg two obvious questions which this concluding chapter will try and address. Is there enough in common between the two regimes that is significantly different from other periods where conservative administrations have coincided across the Atlantic? Has there, in other words, been an Anglo-American 'Conservative Revolution'? And if there has not what, if anything, did happen worthy of note and discussion?

In considering these two questions it is helpful to look afresh at certain critical aspects of the Reagan and Thatcher era, notably being the changing nature of Anglo-American electoral politics, the evolution of political debate in both countries in the 1980s, and the importance of leadership style in understanding Reagan and Thatcher. We shall proceed to look at how George Bush and John Major have handled the job of succeeding these two dynamic leaders. Some – inevitably tentative – answers can then be offered to the questions posed.

The electoral legacy

Ronald Reagan and Margaret Thatcher were supremely successful electoral politicians. The Conservative and Republican parties held office for twelve years simultaneously. The closest parallel this century is the dual conservative dominance of the 1950s, but that decade saw three British prime ministers serving alongside President Eisenhower. Excluding the National Government period alongside Franklin Roosevelt (which also saw three UK premiers), the longest simultaneous Labour/Democrat stretch is the six years between 1945 and 1951. Truman and Attlee's periods in office is the left's only stint remotely comparable to the eight years that Ronald Reagan and Margaret Thatcher overlapped.

There is a certain tempting symmetry in this. Attlee provided Britain with its own New Deal, with World War II serving as a catalyst for social and electoral change in Britain comparable to the depression in the United States. Eisenhower and the three Tory premiers of the 1950s presided over conservative adjustment to this new Keynesian/social democratic order. Reagan and Thatcher initiated the rejection of that order first in their own parties and then in the wider political system. That is to simplify, of course, but the existence of a certain symmetry is undeniable. The initial mutual dominance of the (relatively) left wing parties (1945–53 in the US, 1945–51 UK), a period of centrist conservative leadership (1952–1960 US, 1951–64 UK), a patchy period of left, right, then left again, (1961–69 Democratic; 1969–77 Republican; 1977–1981 Democratic; 1964–70 Labour; 1970–74 Tory; 1974–79 Labour) before the Reagan–Thatcher era of radical right-wing predominance. Indeed, one would only have to switch the states of Illinois and Texas in 1960 (as opponents of electoral fraud might) to give an unnerving fit to the pattern of Anglo-American elections between 1945 and the defeat of George Bush in 1992.

In the new electoral coalitions of the 1980s more patterns can be found. Conservative and Republican success at the ballot box was founded on a changing regional and class distribution of the conservative vote. This success came despite received wisdom in the 1970s that 'fundamentalist' leadership was a liability. Mrs Thatcher was supposed to be too right-wing and too upper middle-class, Ronald Reagan too right-wing and too quirky; the voters had other ideas.

For the two parties, change in the regional composition of their vote has been striking ('vote' referring only to the presidential level in the United States). In Britain, as Andrew Adonis's chapter in this volume highlights, the Conservatives consolidated support, particularly in conurbations, across an area – southern England – in which they were strong already, their progress assisted by population changes that increased the electoral importance of their target region. In the United States, the GOP expanded into an arena where its previous presidential impact had been minimal – the states of the old confederacy – with such success that the South now represents the natural Republican electoral college base.

On both sides of the Atlantic this regional change reflects an altering class/income base to the right-wing vote. The key to Conservative success lies in the creation of a new Tory working-class or lower middle-class in the south and middle of England that had previously inclined to Labour. The vital element in Reagan's triumph was the new votes of blue-collar men historically attached to the Democrats. Economic considerations loomed large in both re-orientations but there were also comparable elements of social conservatism and foreign policy nationalism added as well. Even the psephological slang is similar, Britain's 'Essex Man' and 'C2' finding parallels with the 'Bubbas', 'Joe Sixpacks' and 'Reagan Democrats' of 1980s American electoral fame. In the Anglo-American elections of 1992, the post-Reagan and post-Thatcher question of whether the support of these groups could be retained was central to most analysis of the electoral outcome. In Britain, John Major courted these groups and clung on to them; George Bush's defeat was due to the partial shift of the new southern voter and the wider defection of northern 'Reagan Democrats'.

In Britain and America there were also losses. Conservative support slipped sharply among the UK minorities of Scotland and Wales just as Republican prospects among the racial minorities of blacks and hispanics eroded. The two also saw defections from highly educated, usually public-sector employed, sections of the middle classes.

The degree of compatability should not be pushed too far. Religion provides a striking difference between the two nations, as Gillian Peele has noted here in a different context. The wholesale transfer of evangelical protestants into the Reagan camp has no parallel in the United Kingdom. Yet, all things taken into account, it does seem substantially easier to construct a joint analysis for the dual electoral hegemony of Reagan and Thatcher than of, say, Eisenhower and Macmillan, Coolidge and Baldwin, let alone McKinley and Salisbury. It also seems reasonable to assume that Reagan (at the presidential level) and Thatcher bequeathed an electoral legacy more problematic for their opponents than any of these other combinations.

The policy and political legacy
Politics, we are constantly informed, is the art of the possible. This bland and to some extent tautologous statement hides the real issue of interest: to what extent can the possible be changed? The most powerful claim to advance the significance of Reagan or Thatcher is that they altered perceptions of the politically possible in a substantial and long-lasting manner. Did they? Equally important from our perspective, if they did, was it to comparable effect.

Of the two, Mrs Thatcher undoubtedly had a more transformative impact – partly because her radicalism proved to have greater dynamism in office, and partly because of her greater legislative power. Reagan never enjoyed a Republican House of Representatives and only briefly, in 1981–82, *a de facto* conservative majority.

Essays in this volume have shown certain areas where a radical redefinition of the possible was tried but, on balance, failed. The attempt to create an Anglo-American economic order escaping the post-war constraints on their respective economies must ultimately be placed in this category. Both administrations revived interest in many micro aspects of economic life and had some achievements to their name in those fields. But neither Milton Friedman (as applied and amended by Mrs Thatcher) nor Arthur Laffer (as practised by Mr Reagan) proved the basis for a new and durable economic order.

In the 1985–88 period Britain and America looked as if they might be on the edge of a virtuous circle of low inflation, falling unemployment, and high economic growth. In retrospect these

gains, evident though they were at the time, were largely purchased by disadvantageous external balances and disturbingly high
levels of personal, corporate and (in the US) governmental debt.
Real enthusiasts for Reaganomics and Thatcherism blame the re-
cessions of the 1990s on their successors, Bush for implementing
tax increases in October 1990 and Major for forcing Britain into
the Exchange Rate Mechanism at virtually the same time. It would,
however, be an extremely charitable observer who held there to be
a real Anglo-American economic revolution in the 1980s destroyed
by later apostasy.

In other areas the status quo triumphed in parallel. Reagan and
Thatcher's periodic attempts to use their governments as catalysts
for change in public morals or social values appear to have achieved
little. More prominently, both had designs on the 'Beveridge' part
of the Keynesian–Beveridge consensus, a transparent distaste for
the operation of the welfare state in their respective countries.
Ventures into this area, whether they be Reagan's musings on
entitlement programmes and social security or Mrs Thatcher's itch
to tackle the welfare nexus, met with few victories and many
political wounds. Apart from certain cutbacks in funding little
changed in this part of the political arena.

Finally, and more cautiously, one might argue that Reagan and
Thatcher aimed to change the assumptions on which the respective foreign policy of their two countries was based. After an
initial departure from the 'establishment consensus' on foreign
policy Reagan rapidly returned to it. As Tim Hames's chapter
argues here, Mrs Thatcher had an evident enthusiasm for altering
the balance of British foreign policy but very little changed in
practice.

However, there are other areas where, to varying extents, the
nature of the politically possible was substantially changed. Two
important aspects of political life in the 1970s – the 'ungovernability syndrome' and the widespread national gloom and self-
doubt – were largely eradicated in the 1980s, though more
completely in Britain than in the US. British politics was dominated
in the 1970s by notions of ungovernability. As a consequence of
Margaret Thatcher, the notion that Governments lack the will
or tools to govern now looks somewhat improbable. A similar
if milder affliction was present in America. There, President Reagan,
regardless of what one thinks of his policy prescriptions, did

show that presidents could genuinely affect and alter public policy outcomes.

Similarly, although assessing such matters is highly problematic, British politics and society seemed to have shaken off much of the deterministic despondency about its character so manifest fifteen years before. That is less true of the United States where the Reagan-hyped self-confidence of 1984 gave way to another bout of national soul-searching in the 1990s.

The primary comparative success of Reagan and Thatcher in altering perceptions of the possible must lie in their achievement in changing perceptions of the role of markets and the role of the state in the economy. Here the relative values of low unemployment and low inflation have been dramatically altered (more so in the Britain) – and the politically possible in terms of government electability and unemployment have spectacularly changed. The legitimacy of higher taxation levels to fund socially desired programmes has again been transformed. Arguably, President Reagan was further ahead on this issue thanks to his radical reforms of 1981 and 1986, but the British electoral contest of 1992 had strong shades of Bush versus Dukakis on the tax question. Finally, the relative strength of management and organised labour and the extent of government ownership of industry have been dramatically reappraised. In each case the impact has been greater in Britain, largely because unions were more powerful and nationalisation more widespread in the first place. Some of the non-legislative reasons behind union decline and innovations in the state's role are very similar in each country.

Once again, Reagan and Thatcher seem to have more in common, allowing for considerable differences in emphasis, then do other Anglo-American conservative administrations holding office contemporaneously. Although the legacy of agenda change is somewhat varied, its substance is unquestioned.

Leadership style

Although leadership style is an amorphous concept, it is not an irrelevant one. In the case of Margaret Thatcher and Ronald Reagan it is integral to understanding why they saw each other as soulmates and vital to any examination of how they ran their governments. It is also absolutely critical to appreciating their electoral appeal. In his analysis of the British electorate after the 1987 election,

Ivor Crewe[1] demonstrated the across a whole range of issues and values the voters had not been Thatcherised. Indeed, in a gamut of important matters there was ample evidence of public opinion shifting to the left during the Thatcher years. Nevertheless, on issues relating to statecraft Mrs Thatcher scored significantly. This led him to conclude that: 'Cohesion, purpose and success take precedence over policy and ideology in voters' eyes; that is the lesson of Mrs Thatcher's and Thatcherism's astonishing success.' Comments similar to these have been made by many American observers, for example Martin Wattenberg,[2] in trying to solve the paradox of Ronald Reagan's personal popularity when so many of the specific positions he supported were often rejected by electors.

Both leaders believed in the supreme importance of political leadership. Each believed that conviction politics necessitated conviction leadership. They shared a strong faith in the possibility of national revival. Lou Cannon[3] has centred much of his explanation of Reagan and his appeal in terms of the man's almost mystical faith in American self-mythology and in this book Peter Riddell highlights similar traits in Mrs Thatcher.

That style manifested itself in three distinct ways. First, a willingness to take stark positions, at considerable risk to their political reputations, on issues which other politicians might have played down or avoided. This was invariably followed by an appeal to the public to support the clarity of this stance. For Reagan, issues such as the air traffic controllers strike of 1981, the invasion of Grenada and the bombing of Libya, plus a willingness to sanction various audacious anti-terrorist actions all fit this trend. Similarly, Mrs Thatcher's handling of the British miners' strike, the Falkland's War and many European Council meetings demonstrated a willingness to distinguish herself very bluntly from politics and politicians as usual.

Secondly, there was a public, almost theatrically public, aversion to political compromise and deal-making. Ronald Reagan and Margaret Thatcher spoke of consensus in terms of contempt and conventional diplomacy with similar distaste. This was particularly pronounced in their economic goals. In reality each had to swallow their fair share of compromises (Reagan on terrorism and Thatcher on Europe for instance) but much preferred to deny it and rarely advertised it. This would lead both of them – but particularly Mrs Thatcher – to take stances knowing full well their political unpopularity. Ronald Reagan demonstrated that on matters such as South African sanctions, the Contra rebels in Nicaragua, and his pursuit of the Strategic Defence Initiative. Margaret Thatcher did likewise on various measures of privatisation, on National Health Service reform and (fatally) the community charge/ poll tax. Each seemed to have enjoyed putting a certain machismo in their political style and this may be one explanation for the changing gender composition of their parties' respective electorates in the 1980s.

Thirdly, their mutual leadership style was notable for the role it gave to ideas and ideology in their public pronouncements and policy priorities. As Lou Cannon rightly points out[4]: 'What George Bush dismissed as the "vision thing" was for Reagan the central purpose of the presidency.' Bush, quoting Woody Allen, once quipped that 90 per cent of life was just showing up. It is difficult to imagine Ronald Reagan agreeing with such sentiments. Virtually all accounts of Mrs Thatcher as Prime Minister stress the same notion. Politics was about ideas and the implementation of those ideas or it was not worth very much.

One should be careful not to exaggerate the pattern, as there were important differences between the two leaders. As many observers have noted, it is improbable that Mrs Thatcher would have ever appointed anyone like Ronald Reagan to one of her cabinets. If he had been appointed he would not have lasted. Whereas Reagan was a semi-detached member of an activist administration directing it along broad lines of conservative principle but delegating heavily, Margaret Thatcher was a hyperactive member of an activist administation. Over-delegation to subordinates rarely figures in observations of the Thatcher years. There were also important differences in how they saw their own office. Ronald Reagan had a powerful impression of himself as a citizen politician. Mrs Thatcher saw herself as a professional politician in every sense.

Although the Reagan–Thatcher style was an essential element in their appeal it was not universally appreciated even within their own governments and parties. A style some found as inspirational others perceived as divisive and needlessly polarising. It was, however, distinctive, and in matters of leadership style just as in their electoral coalitions and policy legacies a comparison can be made between the two political figures that one would not easily make between any other pair of Anglo-American conservative figures this century. This leadership style was also an important part in the overall inheritence of George Bush in January 1989 and John Major in November 1990.

Policy evolution under Bush and Major
It would be facile to claim that the change from Reagan to Bush and Thatcher to Reagan has made no difference to public policy in Britain and America. It surely has. But the differences, especially the evident commonality of approach between Bush and Major in dealing with their mixed legacies, says a great deal about the distinctive aspects of Reagan and Thatcher. It also implies a great deal for what will survive and what will come to be seen as transient and purely personal about their periods in office.

The first advantage that Bush and Major gained on reaching their new positions was significant popularity and a reasonable head of goodwill. Bush gained his in large part because of Reagan's popularity ratings, Major in large part because of Thatcher's unpopularity ratings at the time of her fall, although subsequently re-evaluated by opinion poll assessments of her whole tenure taken after that demise. Bush and Major were both identified, not least by the media, as representing a sense of continuity with their predecessors' approach and policies and had benefited from their political patronage. This clearly irritated both men who from the outset tried to distinguish themselves from their erstwhile leaders.

Although there were real changes in policy substance, the most deliberate changes came in the style of political leadership. The initial dilemma for both incoming leaders lay in staffing their governments – specifically, how to balance holdovers from the old regime with new people solely associated with themselves. For George Bush, having received an electoral mandate of his own before taking office, matters were obviously easier. They were made more comfortable still by Reagan's order in late 1988 for all members of his administration to submit their resignations. In the event only four members of Reagan's last cabinet – Attorney-General Richard Thornburgh, Treasury Secretary Nicholas Brady, CIA chief William Webster, and Education Secretary Lauro Cavazos – remained in office (James Baker missed just five months of the entire 1981–92 stretch). All of these had been appointed in the last two years of Reagan's regime. Only Brady was still in office by 1992.

For John Major reshaping his team was more difficult. Prominent Thatcher supporters Cecil Parkinson and David Waddington voluntarily relinquished office. Major cleared out Professor Brian Griffiths, head of the Downing Street Policy Unit, Bernard Ingham, Mrs Thatcher's controversial press secretary and Charles Powell, a high-profile civil servant. But he had to wait until after his election victory in April 1992 to create a cabinet in his own image – and then, with the constraints of the British parliamentary system, he was obliged to use virtually the same material as would have been available to Thatcher had she remained. That said, there were just four members – Lord Mackay (Lord Chancellor), Douglas Hurd (Foreign Secretary) John Gummer (Agriculture) and David Hunt (Wales) – occupying the same jobs that they had held on the day Mrs Thatcher resigned, two of whom have sinced moved on.

Bush and Major substantially altered the leadership style of their predecessors. Bush's call for a 'kinder, gentler nation' is clearly complemented by Major's desire for a nation 'at ease with itself'. Both men abandoned the distictive features of the Reagan–Thatcher style. The quest for policy clarity was downplayed, the distaste for compromise and consensus significantly recast, and the role of ideas and ideology muted. Although the two came from very different generations and personal backgrounds, both sought a lighter, less strident, and more managerial style of government. This led to criticism from Reagan–Thatcher backers that the two men stood for nothing distinctive.

There were identifiable policy changes. George Bush stressed education, the environment (at least until 1992), and ethics in government in a way Reagan had not. He negotiated with Congress over Nicaragua and moved his stance on South Africa closer to the political centre. Most significantly he entered a dialogue with Congress over the budget deficit that led him to abandon his 'no new taxes' pledge of 1988. John Major restored the indexation of child benefit, made conciliatory moves towards the homeless and other disadvantaged groups. He stressed the need for high-quality public services (which any genuine Thatcherite would regard as a contradiction in terms). Public spending has thus far been protected in this recession unlike the 1981/82 experience. Most dramatically he abandoned the Poll Tax and made much more friendly noises towards the European Community.

Nonetheless, it could be argued that these changes flowed from the switch in leadership style outlined above. Most of the fundamentals have kept their place. In terms of electoral strategy that is certainly the case. John Major's electoral themes in March/ April 1992 – low taxation, sound money, anti-unions, anti-devolution, anti-proportional representation, criticism of Labour for being overly interested in European union – all of these would have rested quite comfortably with Mrs Thatcher. John Major wanted to revive Mrs Thatcher's electoral constituency; there is no evidence of him searching for a new one. The American elections of 1992 saw Bush emphasise very similar themes to Reagan's of 1980 and 1984 and Bush's own, largely Reagan inspired, campaign of 1988. Apart from a vague desire to increase the proportion of blacks voting Republican, he seemed quite comfortable chasing Reagan's coalition rather than attempting to shape a new one. Despite this, he could not resurrect Reagan's coalition.

It is therefore leadership style rather than the electoral and political legacies of the Reagan–Thatcher era which appears to have been changed in the 1990s. This may have policy consequences, but British and American politics for the remainder of this decade will be shaped in a mould chiefly cast by Reagan and Thatcher.

A Conservative Revolution?

At the outset two questions were asked. Is there enough in common between the Reagan Administration and the Thatcher Government that is sufficiently unique to merit special attention? Is it legitimate to describe this phenomena as a 'Conservative Revolution', and if it is not how should we evaluate it?

Although successive essays in this collection have stressed the differences and distinctions between Reagan and Thatcher, they have noted common themes aplenty. As this chapter has argued, across the broad spectrum of issues and events there is much more that is compatible between Ronald Reagan and Margaret Thatcher than a comparison of any other pair of conservative leaders this century would provide. It is also fairly implausible to think that more would be learned about politics in the 1980s by comparing either Reagan or Thatcher with other prominent political figures of the 1980s – Kohl, Mitterrand, Hawke, or Mulroney, say, rather than with each other. With all the caution and caveats that comparative politics always requires, this study concludes that there is sufficient in common across the Reagan Administration and the Thatcher Government to justify their being considered and studied in tandem.

The extent to which all of this justifies the label 'Conservative Revolution' is much more problematic. Some, particularly their internal party opponents, would be reluctant to call Reagan and Thatcher conservatives – arguing that their emphasis on free markets makes them old-style liberals rather than true conservatives. Without wading into these – largely semantic – waters, this argument appear to us misplaced. Although Margaret Thatcher and Ronald Reagan quite dramatically altered the emphasis of the various strands that constitute the traditions of their parties, they emphatically did not invent new ones. They drew on traditions of limited government and market capitalism which dated back a century and more on both sides of the Atlantic.

However, are the policies they practised uniquely conservative? That is less straightforward. A number of governments from the political left – in France, Spain, Australia, and New Zealand – have also enacted key elements of the Reagan–Thatcher agenda such as privatisation and substantial tax reductions and reform. That said, in most of these cases the policies were commonly adopted as a matter of political and economic necessity rather than with any native enthusiasm. For the most part they were publicly dubbed 'Thatcherite' or 'Reaganite'. It is also true that party activists of the right are generally more comfortable with these policy stands than those of the left – witness the fate of Roger Douglas in New Zealand.

Has there been a Conservative revolution in Britain? Many perfectly cautious observers, such as Peter Jenkins,[5] have used the term 'revolution' in their analysis of British politics in the 1980s. A great deal of the underlying assumptions and structure of British political life have seen a very dramatic shift. The policy agenda, the notion of the economically and politically possible, and electoral prospects have been severely shaken. The opposition Labour and Liberal Democrat parties have been forced substantially to recast their own philosophies and programmes in response to the impact of Thatcherism. There is also the paradox that while the vast majority of political thinkers in Britain are still on the left of the ideological spectrum, it is the right who are seen (even on the left) as leading the market of political ideas. Thatcherism very nearly created a conservative revolution in Britain. We say nearly because on a range of policy matters its effect was much less powerful, and on the primary task it set for itself – long-term economic renewal – its impact was only partially transformative.

In the United States, although Reaganites like to speak of a revolution, and some serious commentators such as Martin Anderson have used the word,[6] one feels more comfortable arguing against it. There have been important changes in the policy agenda, the notion of the politically and economically possible, and electoral prospects. There has also been an impact on the Democratic party and a similar paradox in intellectual debate. In no respect have they been as dramatic as Britain. As has been stressed throughout, this difference resulted from the stronger position of the United States at the beginning of the 1980s and Reagan's lack of a majority in the House of Representatives. Furthermore, the biggest single agent for the changes outlined here was the massive budget deficit, which was an accidental by-product rather than the core of the Reagan Administration.

What happened to Anglo-American politics in the 1980s? Ronald Reagan and Mrs Thatcher were at the cutting edge in a global reassessment of government economic management and the role of the state in public life. That reassessment began in the 1970s and both Reagan and Thatcher have a special importance because they led the debate, and were foremost in implementing policies issuing from it. They gave policy flesh to the market-liberal skeleton. They are also particularly valuable administrations to study because they are a microcosm of the impact of this global change. They bring into stark relief the strengths and weaknesses, the successes and limitations, of this approach. The market returned in triumph to the economic domain in the 1980s, its moral and intellectual victory sealed by the collapse of communism in central/eastern Europe and the former Soviet Union. The Thatcher–Reagan duo expressed the points of the decade. It is important to recognise the extent to which market principles are not a cure-all and the caution of politicians and public opinion about the extention of those principles into other areas of post-war policy and public life. This is again demonstrated by reference to the Reagan–Thatcher period in office.

Whether or not John Major can keep, or the Republicans can restore, the diverse and often fractious conservative coalition, and whether conservatives can build on the strengths of their political legacy and eliminate some of its limitations are issues that will dominate much of Anglo-American politics in the 1990s. The inheritance with which they grapple may not amount to a conservative revolution. It does constitute a very plausible *coup d'état*.

Notes

1 Ivor Crewe in Robert Skidelsky (ed.), *Thatcherism* (London, Chatto & Windus, 1988), p. 49.
2 Martin Wattenberg in Anthony King (ed.), *The New American Political System*, 2nd edn (Washington, D. C., American Enterprise Institute, 1990). See also Byron Shafer in Shafer (ed.), *The End of Realignment?* (Madison, Wisc, University of Wisconsin, 1991).
3 Lou Cannon, *Reagan* (New York, Simon & Schuster, 1991).
4 Ibid., p. 793.
5 Peter Jenkins, *Mrs Thatcher's Revolution* (London, Pan, 1987).
6 Martin Anderson, *Revolution* (San Diego, Jovanovich, 1988).

Index